C++ Fundamentals

Hit the ground running with C++, the language that supports tech giants globally

Antonio Mallia and Francesco Zoffoli

C++ Fundamentals

Author: Antonio Mallia and Francesco Zoffoli

Technical Reviewer: Rajesh Mani

Managing Editor: Vishal Kamal Mewada

Acquisitions Editor: Koushik Sen

Production Editor: Nitesh Thakur

Editorial Board: David Barnes, Ewan Buckingham, Shivangi Chatterji, Simon Cox, Manasa Kumar, Alex Mazonowicz, Douglas Paterson, Dominic Pereira, Shiny Poojary, Saman Siddiqui, Erol Staveley, Ankita Thakur, and Mohita Vyas

First Published: March 2019

Production Reference: 1080319

ISBN: 978-1-78980-149-1

Published by Packt Publishing Ltd.

Livery Place, 35 Livery Street

Birmingham B3 2PB, UK

Table of Contents

Classes   83

Standard Library Containers and Algorithms   181

Preface

About the Book

C++ Fundamentals begins by introducing you to the C++ compilation model and syntax. You will then study data types, variable declaration, scope and control flow statements. With the help of this book, you'll be able to compile fully working C++ code and understand how variables, references, and pointers can be used to manipulate the state of the program. Next, you will explore functions and classes – the features that C++ offers to organize a program – and use them to solve more complex problems. You will also understand common pitfalls and modern best practices, especially the ones that diverge from the C++98 guidelines.

As you advance through the chapters, you'll study the advantages of generic programming and write your own templates to make generic algorithms that work with any type. This C++ book will guide you in fully exploiting standard containers and algorithms, understanding how to pick the appropriate one for each problem.

By the end of this book, you will not only be able to write efficient code, but also be equipped to improve the readability, performance, and maintainability of your programs.

About the Authors

Francesco Zoffoli is a professional software engineer currently working for Bloomberg LP in London.

He became enthusiast about modern C++ when joining the financial industry after a master degree in Computer Science and Engineering at Politecnico di Milano.

He is passionate about programming languages, maintainable software and large distributed systems.

He uses C++ for his personal projects as well as his day-to-day job to deliver scalable, efficient and resilient systems.

Antonio Mallia is a C++ enthusiast with half a decade of experience in the industry as a software engineer and is currently pursuing a PhD in computer science at NYU Tandon School of Engineering in New York City.

His research interest is mainly related to information retrieval, with a strong focus on improving the efficiency of large-scale systems. For this reason, C++ plays an important role in most of his projects and contributes to their success.

Objectives

- C++ compilation model
- Apply best practices for writing functions and classes
- Write safe, generic, and efficient code with templates
- Explore the containers that the C++ standard offers
- Discover the new features introduced with C++11, C++14, and C++17
- Get to grips with the core language features of C++
- Solve complex problems using object-oriented programming in C++

Audience

If you're a developer looking to learn a new powerful language, or are familiar with C++ but want to update your knowledge with the modern paradigms of C++11, C++14, and C++17, this book is for you. To easily understand the concepts in the book, you must be familiar with the basics of programming.

Approach

C++ *Fundamentals* perfectly balances theory and exercises. Each module is designed to build on the previous module. The book contains multiple activities that use real-life business scenarios for you to practice and apply your new skills in a highly relevant context.

Minimum Hardware Requirements

For the optimal student experience, we recommend the following hardware configuration:

- Processor: Intel Core i3 or equivalent
- Memory: 4 GB RAM
- Storage: 10 GB available space

Software Requirements

You'll also need the following software installed in advance:

- **OS**: Any desktop Linux version or macOS, or Windows 7, 8.1, or 10

- **For Windows 10 systems**: Windows subsystem for Linux (this is only available in the latest versions)

- **Browser**: Use one of the latest browsers, such as Firefox, Chrome, Safari, Edge, or IE11

- Modern C++ compiler

Additional Resources

The code bundle for this book is also hosted on GitHub at https://github.com/TrainingByPackt/Cpp-Fundamentals.

We also have other code bundles from our rich catalog of books and videos available at https://github.com/PacktPublishing/. Check them out!

Conventions

Code words in text, database table names, folder names, filenames, file extensions, pathnames, dummy URLs, user input, and Twitter handles are shown as follows: "Create a file named **HelloUniverse.cpp** and save it."

A block of code is set as follows:

```
#include <iostream>
int main() {
  std::cout << "Hello Universe" << std::endl;
  return 0;
}
```

New terms and important words are shown in bold. Words that you see on the screen, for example, in menus or dialog boxes, appear in the text like this: "Select **System** info from the **Administration** panel."

Getting Started

Lesson Objectives

By the end of this chapter, you will be able:

- Explain the C++ compilation model
- Execute the **main()** function
- Illustrate the declaration and definition of variables
- Determine built-in arithmetic types, references, and pointers
- Explain the scope of a variable
- Use control flow statements
- Define and utilize arrays

In this chapter, you will learn about the usage of variables and control flow statements to create more robust programs.

Introduction

C++ has been a major player in the software development industry for more than 30 years, supporting some of the most successful companies in the world.

In recent years, interest in the language has been growing more than ever, and it is an extremely popular choice for large-scale systems, with many big companies sponsoring its advancement.

C++ remains a complex language, which puts a lot of power in the hands of the developer. However, this also comes with a lot of opportunities to make mistakes. It is a unique language as it has the ability to enable programmers to write high-level abstractions while retaining full control of hardware, performance, and maintainability.

The C++ Compilation Model

It is fundamental to know how C++ compilation works to understand how programs are compiled and executed. Compiling C++ source code into machine-readable code consists of the following four processes:

1. Preprocessing the source code.

2. Compiling the source code.

3. Assembling the compiled file.

4. Linking the object code file to create an executable file.

Let's start with a simple C++ program to understand how compilation happens.

Create a file named **HelloUniverse.cpp** and save it on the **Desktop** after copy-pasting the following code:

```cpp
#include <iostream>
int main(){
    // This is a single line comment
    /* This is a multi-line
        comment */
    std::cout << "Hello Universe" << std::endl;
    return 0;
}
```

Now, using the **cd** command on the Terminal, navigate to the location where our file is saved and execute the following command if you are on UNIX:

```
> g++ -o HelloUniverse HelloUniverse.cpp
> ./HelloUniverse
```

If you are on a Windows system, a different compiler must be used. The command to compile the code with the Visual Studio compiler is as follows:

```
> cl /EHsc HelloUniverse.cpp
> HelloUniverse.exe
```

This program, once executed, will print **Hello Universe** on the Terminal.

Let's demystify the C++ compilation process using the following diagram:

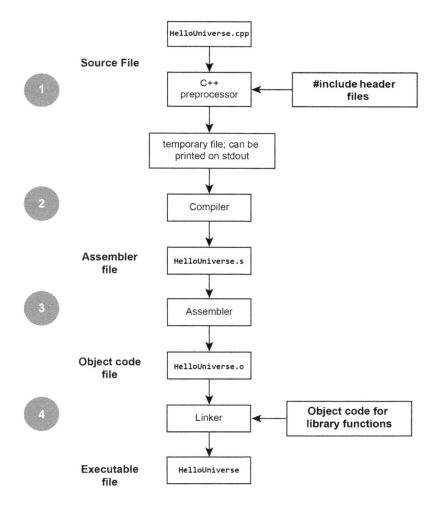

Figure 1.1: C++ compilation of the HelloUniverse file

1. When the C++ preprocessor encounters the **#include <file>** directive, it replaces it with the content of the file creating an expanded source code file.

2. Then, this expanded source code file is compiled into an assembly language for the platform.

3. The assembler converts the file that's generated by the compiler into the object code file.

4. This object code file is linked together with the object code files for any library functions to produce an executable file.

Difference Between Header and Source Files

Source files contain the actual implementation code. Source files typically have the extension **.cpp**, although other extensions such as **.cc**, **.ccx**, or **.c++** are also quite common.

On the other hand, header files contain code that describes the functionalities that are available. These functionalities can be referred to and used by the executable code in the source files, allowing source files to know what functionality is defined in other source files. The *most* common extensions for header files are **.hpp**, **.hxx**, and **.h**.

To create an executable file from the header and the source files, the compiler starts by preprocessing the directives (preceded by a **#** sign and generally at the top of the files) that are contained in them. In the preceding **HelloUniverse** program, the directive would be **#include**. It is preprocessed by the compiler before actual compilation and replaced with the content of the **iostream** header, which describes standard functionality for reading and writing from streams.

The second step is to process each source file and produce an object file that contains the machine code relative to that source file. Finally, the compilers link all the object files into a single executable program.

We saw that the preprocessor converts the content of the directives into the source files. Headers can also include other headers, which will be expanded, creating a chain of expansions.

For example, let's assume that the content of the **logger.hpp** header is as follows:

```
// implementation of logger
```

Let's also assume that the content of the **calculator.hpp** header is as follows:

```
#include <logger.hpp>
// implementation of calculator
```

In the **main.cpp** file, we include both directives, as shown in the following code snippet:

```
#include <logger.hpp>
#include <calculator.hpp>


int main() {
  // use both the logger and the calculator
}
```

The result of the expansion will be as follows:

```
// implementation of logger
// implementation of logger
// implementation of calculator
int main() {
  // use both the logger and the calculator
}
```

As we can see, the logger has been added in the resulting file twice:

- It was added the first time because we included **logger.hpp** in the **main.cpp** file

- It was added the second time because we included **calculator.hpp**, which then includes **logger.hpp**

Included files that are not directly specified in a **#include** directive in the file we are compiling, but are instead included by some other included file, are called **transitive included files**.

Often, including the same header file multiple times creates a problem with multiple definitions, as we will see in *Lesson 2*, *Functions*, and *the Lesson 03*, *Classes*.

Including the same file multiple times is very likely because of the transitive included files we explained before, and will often result in a compilation error. In C++, there is a convention to prevent problems that originate from including a header file multiple times: **include guards**.

An include guard is a specific pattern of instructing the preprocessor to ignore the content of the header if it has been included before.

It consists of writing all the header code inside the following structure:

```
#ifndef <unique_name>
#define <unique_name>
// all the header code should go here
#endif /* <unique_name> */
```

Here, **<unique_name>** is a name unique throughout the C++ project; it typically consists of the header file name, such as **LOGGER_HPP** for the **logger.hpp** header.

The preceding code checks whether a special preprocessor variable, **<unique_name>**, exists. If it does not exist, it defines it and it proceeds to read the content of the header. If it exists, it will skip all the code until the **#endif** part.

Since initially the special variable does not exist, the first time the preprocessor includes a header, it creates the variable and proceeds to read the file. The subsequent times, the variable is already defined, so the preprocessor jumps to the **#endif** directive, skipping all the content of the header file.

Compilation is a process that ensures that a program is syntactically correct, but it does not perform any checks regarding its logical correctness. This means that a program that compiles correctly might still produce undesired results:

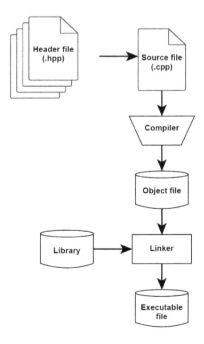

Figure 1.2: Compilation and linking processes for an executable file

Every C++ program needs to define a starting point, that is, the part of the code the execution should start from. The convention is to have a uniquely named main function in the source code, which will be the first thing to be executed. This function is called by the operating system, so it needs to return a value that indicates the status of the program; for this reason, it is also referred to as the **exit status code**.

Let's see how we can compile a program.

Together with C, C++ is the language with the most supported hardware and platforms. This means that there are many C++ compilers, produced by many different vendors. Each compiler can accept parameters in a different way, and it's important to consult the manual of the compiler you are using when developing in C++ to understand the available options and their meaning.

We'll now see how to compile a program with two of the most common compilers: the Microsoft Visual Studio compiler and GCC.

Compiling a File into an Object File

To compile the **myfile.cpp** file in to an object file named **myfile.obj**, we can run the following commands:

MSVC	GCC
cl /EHsc /s myfile.cpp	g++ -c -o myfile.obj myfile.cpp

Figure 1.3: Compiling the CPP file

When we compile, it is common to include some headers.

We can include the headers defined in the C++ standard without performing any action, but in case we want to include user-defined headers, we need to tell the compiler in which folders to look up the header files.

For MSVC, you need to pass the parameter as **/I path**, where **path** is the path to the directory to look in for the header.

For GCC, you need to pass the parameter as **-I path**, where **path** has the same meaning as in MSVC.

If **myfile.cpp** is including a header in the **include** directory, we would compile the file with the following commands:

MSVC	GCC
`cl /EHsc /s /I include myfile.cpp`	`g++ -c -I include -o myfile.obj myfile.cpp`

Figure 1.4: Compiling the CPP file with the include directory

We can compile several files in their respective object files, and then link them all together to create the final application.

Linking Object Files

To link together two object files called **main.obj** and **mylib.obj** into an executable, we can run the following commands:

MSVC	GCC
`link main.obj mylib.obj /out:main.exe`	`g++ main.obj mylib.obj -o main`

Figure 1.5: Compiling two object files

With MSVC, we will create an executable named **main.exe**, while with **g++**, the executable will be named **main**.

For convenience, MSVC and GCC offer a way to compile several files into an executable, without the need to create an object file for each file, and then link the files together.

Even in this case, if the files are including any user-defined header, you need to specify the header location with the **/I** or **-I** flags.

To compile the **main.cpp** and **mylib.cpp** files together, which uses some headers from the **include** folder, you can use the following commands:

MSVC	GCC
`cl /EHsc /I include main.cpp mylib.cpp /Fe:main.exe`	`g++ -I include main.cpp mylib.cpp -o main`

Figure 1.6: Compiling files with include folder

Working with the main Function

In the next chapter, we will discuss functions in more depth; for now, we can define the **main** function, which does nothing, apart from returning a successful status code in the following way:

```
int main()
{
    return 0;
}
```

The first line contains the definition of the function, constituted by the return type **int**, the name of the **main** function, and the list of arguments, which in this case is an empty list. Then, we have the body of the function, delimited by curly braces. Finally, the body is composed of a single instruction that will return a successful status code.

> **Note**
>
> As opposed to C, in a C++ program, the return statement is optional. The compiler automatically adds **return 0** if you don't explicitly return a value.

We will discuss these topics in more detail later; what is important to know is that this is a valid C++ program that can be compiled and executed.

> **Note**
>
> Most C compilers can compile C or C++ by determining the language based on the file extension.

Exercise 1: Compiling and Executing the main Function

In this exercise, we will create a source file named **main.cpp** containing the code. Compile the file and run the program. We will be using it to explore the C++ environment:

1. Using your favorite text editor (Sublime Text, Visual Studio Code, Atom, or Notepad++ if you use Windows), create a new file and name it **main.cpp**.

2. Write the following code in the **main.cpp** file and save it:

    ```cpp
    int main()
    {
      return 0;
    }
    ```

3. Compile the **main.cpp** file using the following command:

    ```
    //On UNIX:
    > g++ main.cpp

    //On Windows:
    > cl /EHsc main.cpp
    ```

4. The compilation process will produce an executable file, which will be named **main.exe** on a Windows system and **main.out** on a UNIX one.

Built-in Data Types

In most programming languages, data is stored in variables, which are labels that refer to the part of memory defined by the programmer. Each variable has an associated type. The type defines what kind of values the variable can hold.

The built-in data types of C++ are divided into two categories:

- **Primitive data types**: Can be used directly by the user to declare variables

- **Abstract or user defined data types**: Are defined by the user, for example, to define a class in C++ or a structure

Primitive Data Types

Primitive data types consist of the following types:

- **Integer**: The `int` type stores a whole number value ranging from **-2147483648** to **2147483647**. This data type usually takes up **4** bytes of memory space.

- **Character**: The `char` type stores character data. It is guaranteed to be big enough to represent any UTF-8 single byte code unit; for UTF-16 and UTF-32, `char16_t` and `char32_t` are used, respectively. `char` typically takes 1 byte of memory space.

- **Boolean**: The `bool` data type is capable of holding one of two values: `true` or `false`.

- **Floating-point**: The `float` type is used for storing single precision floating point values. This data type usually takes up 4 bytes of memory space.

- **Double floating point**: The `double` type is used for storing double precision floating point values. This data type usually takes up 8 bytes of memory space.

- **Void**: The `void` type is a valueless data type that is used for functions that do not return a value.

- **Wide character**: The `wchar_t` type is also used to represent character sets, but allows for greater size. While char supports characters between 8 and 32 bits, a wide character is 2 to 4 bytes long.

The character types `char` and `wchar_t` hold numeric values corresponding to the characters in the machine's character set.

Datatype Modifiers

The numeric types offered by the C++ programming language fall into three categories:

- Signed
- Unsigned
- Floating point

The signed and unsigned types come with different sizes, which means each of them can represent a smaller or larger range of values.

Integer types can be signed or unsigned, where signed types can be used to distinguish between negative or positive numbers, while unsigned can only represent numbers greater than or equal to zero.

The signed keyword is optional; the programmer only needs to specify it if the type is unsigned. Thus, `signed int` and `int` are the same types, but they are different from `unsigned int`, or just `unsigned` for brevity. Indeed, if it is not specified, an unsigned type always defaults to `int`.

Integers, as previously mentioned, can come in different sizes:

- `int`
- `short int`
- `long int`
- `long long int`

The `short int` type, or just `short`, is guaranteed to be at least 16 bits according to the standard. This means it can hold values in the range of `-32768` to `32767`. If it was also `unsigned`, so `unsigned short int` or just `unsigned int`, this range would be `0` to `65535`.

> ### Note
>
> The effective size in memory of types can change based on the platform for which the code is compiled. C++ is present in many platforms, from supercomputers in data centers to small embedded chips in industrial settings. To be able to support all these different types of machines, the standard only sets the minimum requirements on built-in types.

Variable Definition

A variable is named storage that refers to a location in memory that can be used to hold a value. C++ is a strongly-typed language and it requires every variable to be declared with its type before its first use.

The type of the variable is used by the compiler to determine the memory that needs to be reserved and the way to interpret its value.

The following syntax is used to declare a new variable:

```
type variable_name;
```

Variable names in C++ can contain letters from the alphabet, both upper and lower case, digits and underscores (_). While digits are allowed, they cannot be the first character of a variable name. Multiple variables of the same type can all be declared in the same statement by listing their variable names, separated by commas:

```
type variable_name1, variable_name2, …;
```

This is equivalent to the following:

```
type variable_name1;
type variable_name2;
type ...;
```

When declaring a variable, its value is left undetermined until an assignment is performed. It is also possible to declare a variable with a given value; this operation is also referred to as **variable initialization**.

One way – and probably the most common one – to initialize a variable, also referred to as **C-like initialization**, uses the following syntax:

```
type variable_name = value;
```

Another solution is constructor initialization, which we will see in detail in *Lesson 3, Classes*. Constructor initialization looks like this:

```
type variable_name (value);
```

Uniform initialization or list initialization introduces brace initialization, which allows for the initialization of variables and objects of different types:

```
type variable_name {value};
```

Demystifying Variable Initialization

When a variable is initialized, the compiler can figure out the type needed to store the value provided, which means that it is not necessary to specify the type of the variable. The compiler is indeed able to deduct the type of the variable, so this feature is also referred to as **type deduction**. For this reason, the **auto** keyword has been introduced to replace the type name during initialization. The initialization syntax becomes this:

```
auto vvariable_name = value;
```

Another way to avoid directly providing a type is to use the **decltype** specifier. It is used to deduce a type of a given entity and is written with the following syntax:

```
type variable_name1;

decltype(variable_name1) variable_name2;
```

Here, **variable_name2** is declared according to the type deducted from **variable_name1**.

> ### Note
>
> Type deduction using the **auto** and **decltype** keywords has been introduced by the C++11 standard to simplify and facilitate variable declaration when the type cannot be obtained. But at the same time, their extended use when not really needed can reduce code readability and robustness. We will see this in more detail in *Lesson 4, Generic Programming and Templates*.

In the following code, we will check a valid statement for variables by creating a new source file named **main.cpp** and analyzing the code one line at a time.

Which one of the following is a valid statement?

```
int foo;

auto foo2;

int bar = 10;

sum = 0;

float price = 5.3 , cost = 10.1;

auto val = 5.6;

auto val = 5.6f;

auto var = val;

int   a = 0, b = {1} , c(0);
```

Pointers and References

In the previous section, variables have been defined as portions of memory that can be accessed by their name. In this way, the programmer does not need to remember the memory location and size that's reserved, but can conveniently refer to the variable name.

In C++, the way to retrieve the actual memory address of a variable is done by preceding the variable name with an ampersand sign (**&**), also known as the **address-of operator**.

The syntax to use the concept of the address-of operator is as follows:

```
&variable_name
```

Using this in code will return the physical memory address of the variable.

Pointers

A data structure that's capable of storing a memory address in C++ is known as a **pointer**. A pointer always points to an object of a specific type, and because of that we need to specify the type of the object that's pointed to when declaring the pointer.

The syntax to declare a pointer is as follows:

```
type * pointer_name;
```

Multiple declarations in the same statement are also possible when it comes to a pointer, but it is important to remember that an asterisk (*****) is needed for each pointer declaration. An example of multiple pointer declaration is as follows:

```
type * pointer_name1, * pointer_name2, *...;
```

When the asterisk is specified only for the first declaration, the two variables will have different types. For example, in the following declaration, only the former is a pointer:

```
type * pointer_name, pointer_name;
```

> **Note**
>
> Independently of the pointed variable type, a pointer will always occupy the same size in memory. This derives from the fact that the memory space needed by the pointer is not related to a value stored by the variable, but to a memory address that is platform-dependent.

Intuitively, a pointer assignment has the same syntax as any other variable:

```
pointer_name = &variable_name;
```

The previous syntax will copy the memory address of the **variable_name** variable into the pointer named **pointer_name**.

The following code snippet will first initialize **pointer_name1** with the memory address of **variable_name**, and then it initializes **pointer_name2** with the value stored in **pointer_name1**, which is the memory address of **variable_name**. As a result, **pointer_name2** will end up pointing to the **variable_name** variable:

```
type * pointer_name1 = &variable_name;

type * pointer_name2 = pointer_name1;
```

The following implementation is invalid:

```
type * pointer_name1 = &variable_name;

type * pointer_name2 = &pointer_name1;
```

This time, **pointer_name2** would be initialized with the memory address of **pointer_name1**, resulting in a pointer that points to another pointer. The way to point a pointer to another pointer is to use the following code:

```
type ** pointer_name;
```

Two asterisks (*****) indicate the **type** that's pointed is now a pointer. In general, the syntax simply requires an asterisk (*****) for each level of indirection in the declaration of the pointer.

To access the actual content at a given memory address, it is possible to use the dereference operator (*****), followed by the memory address or a pointer:

```
type variable_name1 = value;

type * pointer_name = &variable_name1;

type variable_name2 = *pointer_name;
```

The value contained by **variable_name2** is the same as the one contained by **variable_name1**. The same applies when it comes to assignment:

```
type variable_name1 = value1;

type * pointer_name = &variable_name1;

*pointer_name = value2;
```

References

Unlike a pointer, a reference is just an alias for an object, which is essentially a way to give another name to an existing variable. The way to define a reference is as follows:

```
type variable_name = value;

type &reference_name = variable_name;
```

Let's examine the following example:

```cpp
#include <iostream>

int main()
{
   int first_variable = 10;
   int &ref_name = first_variable;
   std::cout << "Value of first_variable: " << first_variable << std::endl;
   std::cout << "Value of ref_name: " << ref_name << std::endl;
}
//Output
Value of first_variable: 10
Value of ref_name: 10
```

We can identify three main differences with pointers:

- Once initialized, a reference remains bound to its initial object. So, it is not possible to reassign a reference to another object. Any operations performed on a reference are actually operations on the object that has been referred.

- Since there is not the possibility to rebind a reference, it is necessary to initialize it.

- References are always associated with a variable that's stored in memory, but the variable might not be valid, in which case the reference should not be used. We will see more on this in the *Lesson 6, Object-Oriented Programming*.

It is possible to define multiple references to the same object. Since the reference is not an object, it is not possible to have a reference to another reference.

In the following code, given that **a** is an integer, **b** is a float, and **p** is a pointer to an integer, verify which of the variable initialization is valid and invalid:

```
int &c = a;

float &c = &b;

int &c;

int *c;

int *c = p;

int *c = &p;

int *c = a;

int *c = &b;

int *c = *p;
```

The const Qualifier

In C++, it is possible to define a variable whose value will not be modified once initialized. The way to inform the compiler of this situation is through the **const** keyword. The syntax to declare and initialize a **const** variable is as follows:

```
const type variable_name = value;
```

There are several reasons to enforce immutability in a C++ program, the most important ones being correctness and performance. Ensuring that a variable is constant will prevent the compilation of code that accidentally tries to change that variable, preventing possible bugs.

The other reason is that informing the compiler about the immutability of the variable allows for optimizing the code and logic behind the implementation of the code.

> **Note**
>
> After creating an object, if its state remains unchanged, then this characteristic is known as immutability.

An example of immutability is as follows:

```
#include <iostream>
int main()
{
  const int imm = 10;
  std::cout << imm << std::endl;
  //Output: 10
  int imm_change = 11;
  std::cout << imm_change << std::endl;
  //Output: 11
  imm = imm_change;
  std::cout << imm << std::endl;
  //Error: We cannot change the value of imm
}
```

An object is immutable if its state doesn't change once the object has been created. Consequently, a class is immutable if its instances are immutable. We will learn more about classes in *Lesson 3, Classes*.

Modern C++ supports another notion of immutability, which is expressed with the **constexpr** keyword. In particular, it is used when it is necessary for the compiler to evaluate the constant at compile time. Also, every variable declared as **constexpr** is implicitly **const**.

The previous topic introduced pointers and references; it turns out that even those can be declared as **const**. The following is pretty straightforward to understand, and its syntax is as follows:

```
const type variable_name;
const type &reference_name = variable_name;
```

This syntax shows how we can declare a reference to an object that has a **const** type; such a reference is colloquially called a **const reference**.

References to **const** cannot be used to change the object they refer to. Note that it is possible to bind a **const** reference to a non-**const** type, which is typically used to express that the object that's been referenced will be used as an immutable one:

```
type variable_name;

const type &reference_name = variable_name;
```

However, the opposite is not allowed. If an object is **const**, then it can only be referenced by a **const** reference:

```
const type variable_name = value;

type &reference_name = variable_name;

// Wrong
```

An example of this is as follows:

```
#include <iostream>

int main()

{

    const int const_v = 10;

    int &const_ref = const_v;

    //Error

    std::cout << const_v << std::endl;

    //Output: 10

}
```

Just like for references, pointers can point to the **const** object, and the syntax is also similar and intuitive:

```
const type *pointer_name = &variable_name;
```

An example of this is as follows:

```
#include <iostream>

int main()

{

    int v = 10;
```

```
    const int *const_v_pointer  = &v;
    std::cout << v << std::endl;
    //Output: 10
    std::cout << const_v_pointer << std::endl;
    //Output: Memory location of v
}
```

const object addresses can only be stored in a pointer to **const**, but the opposite is not true. We could have a pointer to **const** point to a non-**const** object and, in this case, like for a reference to **const**, we are not guaranteed that the object itself will not change, but only that the pointer cannot be used to modify it.

With pointers, since they are also objects, we have an additional case, which is the **const** pointer. While for references saying **const** reference is just a short version of reference to **const**, this is not the case for the pointer and has a totally different meaning.

Indeed, a **const** pointer is a pointer that is itself constant. Here, the pointer does not indicate anything about the pointed object; it might be either **const** or non-**const**, but what we cannot change instead is the address pointed to by the pointer once it has been initialized. The syntax is as follows:

```
type *const pointer_name = &variable_name;
```

As you can see, the **const** keyword is placed after the * symbol. The easiest way to keep this rule in mind is to read from right to left, so **pointer-name > const > * > type** can be read as follows: **pointer-name** is a **const** pointer to an object of type **type**. An example of this is as follows:

```
#include <iostream>
int main()
{
    int v = 10;
    int *const v_const_pointer = &v;
    std::cout << v << std::endl;
```

```
    //Output: 10
    std::cout << v_const_pointer << std::endl;
    //Output: Memory location of v
}
```

> **Note**
>
> Pointer to const and const to pointer are independent and can be expressed in the same statement:
>
> **const type *const pointer_name = &variable_name;**
>
> The preceding line indicates that both the pointed object and the pointer are **const**.

The Scope of Variables

As we have already seen, variable names refer to a specific entity of a program. The live area of the program where this name has a particular meaning is also called a **scope** of a name. Scopes in C++ are delimited with curly braces, and this area is also called a **block**. An entity that's declared outside of any block has a **global scope** and is valid anywhere in the code:

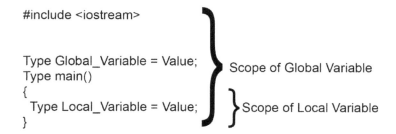

Figure 1.7: Scope of a variable

The same name can be declared in two scopes and refers to different entities. Also, a name is visible once it is declared until the end of the block in which it is declared.

Let's understand the scope of global and local variables with the following example:

```
#include <iostream>
int global_var = 100;
//Global variable initialized

int print(){
  std::cout << global_var << std::endl;
  //Output: 100
  std::cout << local_var << std::endl;
  //Output: Error: Out of scope
}
int main()
{
  int local_var = 10;
  std::cout << local_var << std::endl;
  //Output: 10
  std::cout << global_var << std::endl;
  //Output: 100
  print();
  //Output:100
  //Output: Error: Out of scope
}
```

Scopes can be nested, and we call the containing and contained scope the outer and inner scope, respectively. Names declared in the outer scope can be used in the inner one. Re-declaration of a name that was initially declared in the outer scope is possible. The result will be that the new variable will hide the one that was declared in the outer scope.

Let's examine the following code:

```
#include <iostream>
int global_var = 1000;

int main()
```

```
{
  int global_var = 100;
  std::cout << "Global: "<< ::global_var << std::endl;
  std::cout << "Local: " << global_var << std::endl;
}
Output:
Global: 1000
Local: 100
```

In the next chapter, we will explore how to use local and global variables with functions.

In the following code, we will find the values of all the variables without executing the program.

The following program shows how variable initialization works:

```
#include <iostream>
int main()
{
  int a = 10;
  {
    int b = a;
  }
  const int c = 11;
  int d = c;
  c = a;
}
```

Control Flow Statements

In a program, it is rare to provide useful functionality by just executing a linear sequence of operations. Commonly, a program must be able to react in different ways in response to different situations or execute the same operation multiple times in different contexts.

We will now see the control flow statements C++ offers to the programmer to control the sequence of operations to be executed.

Selection Statement – if-else

C++ provides conditional execution support, where the **if** keyword indicates whether or not to execute the following statement or block, depending on the fulfillment of the condition provided:

```
if (condition) statement
```

If the expression named **condition** evaluates to **true**, then the statement is executed; otherwise, it will be ignored and the program will continue with the subsequent code.

The conditionally executed code can be a single statement or an entire block containing multiple ones. These statements needs to be enclosed in braces (**{}**) to form a block:

```
if (condition) {
    statement_1;
    statement_2;
    statement_N;
}
```

> **Note**
>
> It is common to forget the brace brackets and write the control statement in the following manner:
>
> **if (condition)**
>
> **statement1**
>
> **statement2**
>
> In such a case, the compiler will not warn you, and it will execute **statement1** depending on the condition, but always execute **statement2**. To avoid such a situation, it can be a good practice to always add the braces.

It is possible to specify what to execute instead when the condition evaluates to **false**. This is done through the **else** keyword, which is followed by a statement or a block.

The following syntax is used to indicate that **statement1** should be executed if the **case** condition evaluates to **true**, and otherwise **statement2** is executed:

```
if (condition) statement1 else statement2
```

Finally, we can concatenate on multiple if-else statements to produce a more complex branching logic. Let's examine the following example:

```
if (condition1) {

  statement1

} else if (condition2) {

  statement2

} else {

  statement3

}
```

With this generic structure, it is possible to check the unlimited number of conditions and execute only the corresponding statement or the final one contained in the **else** branch.

It is important to be aware that once one of the conditions is met, all of the ones that follow are discarded, for example:

```
if (x > 0) {

  // When x is greater than 0, statement1 is executed.

  // If that is not the case, the control jumps to the else block.

  statement1

} else if (x > 100) {

  statement2

}
```

The previous code will always execute **statement1** for any positive **x**, regardless of whether it is greater than 100 or not.

An alternative way is to sequence several **if** keywords, as follows:

```
if (condition1)
  // If condition1 is true, statement1 is executed
  statement1
if (condition2)
  // if condition2 is true then statement2 is executed
  statement2
  /* independently whether condition1 and condition2 is true or not, the
  statement3 will be executed */
statement3
```

Let's demystify the previous logic with the following example:

```cpp
#include <iostream>
int main()
{
  int x = 10;
  if  (x > 0){
    std::cout << x << std::endl;
  }
  if (x > 11 ){
    std::cout << x << std::endl;
  }
  else{
    std::cout << x-1 << std::endl;
  }
}


Output:
10
9
```

In this way, all the conditions are evaluated independently and more than one statement can potentially be executed.

> **Note**
>
> As the **else** statement has no condition defined, after evaluating the **if** statement, the control comes to the **else** block to execute the statement.

Selection Statement – switch

Another selection statement, with similarities to the **if-else** concatenation construction, is the **switch** statement. It is limited to constant expressions and is mainly used to check for a value among a number of possible expressions:

```
switch (expression)
{
  case constant1:
    group-of-statements-1;
  break;

  case constant2:
    group-of-statements-2;
  break;
...
  default:
    default-group-of-statements;
  break;
}
```

The **expression** present in the parentheses following the **switch** keyword is evaluated against multiple cases, searching for the first equality between the expression and the constants. If none of the cases match, the default one (if it exists, since it is optional) is executed.

It is important to keep in mind that the order of evaluation is sequential, and as soon as one of the constants matches, the corresponding group of statements are executed. The **break** keyword prevents them from further execution. If the **break** keyword is not included, all statements following the case, including the ones under different labels, are also executed.

We will explore the break keyword more in the *Jump statements – break and continue* section.

Iteration Statement – for loop

The **for** loop is a construct that's used to repeat a statement a certain number of times. The syntax of the **for** loop is as follows:

```
for (initialization; condition; increase){
    statement1;
    statement2;
    ...
    statementN;
}
```

The **for** loop consists of two parts: the **header** and the **body**. The former controls how many times the latter is repeated. The header is the part enclosed by parentheses and it is formed by **initialization**, **condition**, and **increase** statements. The body can be a single statement or a block of multiple ones.

The initialization statement is typically (but not necessarily) used to declare a new variable, usually a counter, and to initialize it to a certain value. The initialization statement is executed only once, at the beginning of the loop.

Secondly, the condition statement is checked. This is similar to the condition that's checked for an **if** statement. If the condition is **true**, the body of the loop is executed, otherwise the program continues its execution with the instruction after the body of the **for** loop.

After the body executes, the **increase** statement is executed. This usually changes the counter of the initialization statement. The condition is then checked again and, if **true**, the steps are repeated. The loop ends when the condition evaluates to **false**.

The fields in the header of a **for** loop are optional and can be left blank, but the **semicolons** cannot be omitted. When the condition is omitted, it always evaluates to **true**. For example, the following corresponds to an infinite loop where the statement is executed unconditionally:

```
for ( ; ; ) statement;
```

Another variant of the **for** loop is called a range-based for loop, the syntax for which is as follows:

```
for ( declaration : range ) statement;
```

A range is a sequence of elements, like arrays, which are explained in the next section. This range-based **for** loop is used to iterate over all elements of these sequences. The **range** is the name of the sequence, and in the **for** declaration, the name is a temporary variable that's declared for every iteration of the loop. This is used to store the current element. The declaration needs to be the same type as the elements contained in the range.

> **Note**
>
> A range-based **for** loop is a good example where **type** deduction and the use of the **auto** keyword for the declaration makes the code more readable and helps the programmer find the right type to use.

A loop placed inside a loop is known as a **<u>nested loop</u>**. Let's look at the following diagram to understand what a nested for loop is:

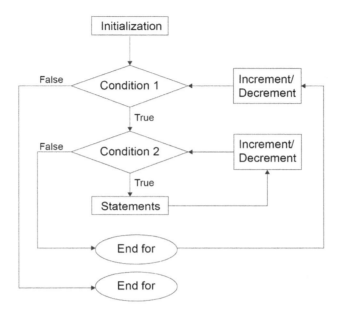

Figure 1.8: Nested for loop

Using the following example, let's explore how a nested for loop works and print a reverse half-triangle on the console:

```cpp
#include <iostream>
int main()
{
  for (int x = 0; x < 5; x++){
    for (int y = 5; y > x; y--){
      std::cout << "*";
    }
    std::cout <<"\n" ;
  }
}
Output:
*****
****
```

```
***
**
*
```

Iteration Statement – while loop

Another iteration statement is the **while** loop. It is simpler than the **for** loop. The syntax for it is as follows:

```
while (condition) statement;
```

It repeats the statement until the condition is met. When the condition is not **true** anymore, the loop ends and the program continues its execution right after the loop:

> **Note**
>
> A **while** loop can always be expressed using a **for** loop.
>
> Here is an example: **for (; condition ;) statement;**

Iteration Statement – do-while loop

A similar loop is the **do-while** loop, where the condition is checked after the execution of the statement, instead of before. It uses the following syntax:

```
do statement while (condition);
```

It guarantees at least one execution of the statement, even though the condition never evaluates to **true**.

Jump Statements – break and continue

The **break** keyword is used to end a loop independently, regardless of whether it fulfils its condition. In the following program, when **condition2** becomes **true**, the break statement will immediately terminate the **while** loop:

```
while (condition1){
    statement1;
    if (condition2)
        break;
}
```

Alternatively, the **continue** statement is used to skip the rest of the body's loop in the current iteration. In the following example, when **condition2** evaluates to **true**, **continue** is called, causing the program to reach the end of the loop, skipping **statement2** and continuing with the next iteration:

```
while (condition1){
    statement1;
    if (condition2)
        continue;
    statement2;
}
```

> **Note**
> The **break** and continue statements can be used in both **for** and **while** loops.

The try-catch block

During the execution of a program, an anomaly may occur. We refer to these runtime problems as **exceptions**, and they represent the response to an exceptional circumstance that arises outside of the normal functioning of a program. Designing code that's resilient to errors is one of the hardest things a programmer has to deal with.

Exceptions are generally thrown using the **throw** keyword when something that cannot be handled is encountered by the program. This is also referred to as **raising an exception**.

The **try** keyword is followed by a block containing statements that might throw one or more exceptions. These exceptions can be caught by one or more **catch** clauses, which are sequentially listed after the **try** block. The syntax for this is as follows:

```
try {
    statement1;
} catch (exception-declaration1) {
    statement2;
} catch (exception-declaration2) {
    statement3;
}
...
```

A **catch** block consists of the **catch** keyword, the exception declaration, and a block. Based on the exception thrown inside the **try** block, one **catch** clause is selected and the corresponding block is executed. Once the **catch** block has terminated, the program continues its execution with the statement following the last **catch** clause.

Let's examine the following example to understand how try-catch conditional statements handle exceptions:

```cpp
#include <iostream>
int main()
{
  int x = 10;
  try {
    std::cout << "Inside try block" << std::endl;
    if (x > 0) // True
    {
      throw x;// Following statement will be skipped
      std::cout << "After throw keyword" << std::endl;
    }
  }
  catch (int x ) {
    std::cout << "Inside catch block: Exception found" << std::endl;
  }
  std::cout << "Outside try-catch block" << std::endl;
}
Output:
Inside try block
Inside catch block: Exception found
Outside try-catch block
```

Exercise 2: Counting the Number of Times a Specific Number Appears in a Given List

In this exercise, we will discuss using the **if** statement and a **for** loop to count our magic number. Here, we will be trying to find all numbers that are divisible by 3, ranging from 1 to 30.

> **Hint**
>
> To find out if a number is divisible by another, use the modulo (%) operator.

Now, let's perform the following steps:

1. Import all the required header files:

   ```
   #include <iostream>
   ```

2. We need to store the number of times a number is divisible by 3 in a counter. For this reason, we define and initialize the **count** variable to **0**:

   ```
   unsigned count = 0;
   ```

3. Now, we will use a **for** loop that produces values from 1 to 30 so that we can check whether they are divisible by 3 or not:

   ```
   for(unsigned x = 1; x <= 30; x++){
   }
   ```

4. Finally, we will check in the body of the **for** loop by using an **if** statement and the expression **x%3 == 0**, which evaluates to **true** if the division has a remainder equal to **0**:

   ```
   if (x%3 == 0) {
      count++;
   }
   ```

5. If the previous condition returns to **true**, then the **x** variable is divisible by **3** and we can increment the counter.

6. Finally, we can print **count**:

   ```
   std::cout << count << std::endl;
   ```

Bonus exercises:

- Find how many numbers are divisible by 11 within the range of 1 to 100

- Print all the numbers that are not divisible by 3 within the range of 1 to 30

Activity 1: Finding the Factors of 7 between 1 and 100 Using a while Loop

In the following activity, we will use a `while` loop and implement the previous concept from the earlier exercise to print the numbers between 1 and 100 that are divisible by 7.

Now, let's rewrite the previous code using a `while` loop in the following way:

1. Create a variable of the `unsigned` type.

2. Now, write the logic to print the numbers that are divisible by **7** using the `while` loop.

3. Then, we have to increase the value of **i** after each iteration. Use the following code:

    ```
    i++;
    ```

    The solution for this activity can be found on page 282.

Arrays

An **array** is a data structure containing a series of elements of the same type that have been placed in contiguous memory locations that can be individually accessed by their position.

Arrays have fixed sizes and cannot be extended; this contributes to their runtime performance, with a cost in terms of limited flexibility.

Array Declaration

Like any other variable, arrays need to be declared before they can be used. An array declaration has the following form:

```
type name [elements];
```

Here, **type** is the type of the contained elements, **name** is the identifier of the **array** variable, and elements is the length of the array, so it signifies the number of elements contained within.

The term **elements** needs to be a constant expressions that is known at compile time, since that is the time when the array size is evaluated to determine the dimension of the block of static memory to allocate.

When an array is declared, its content is left undetermined, which means that the elements are not set to any specific value. This is often confusing for programmers as you might expect that the elements are initialized to the default value for the array type.

Array Initialization

Array elements can be specifically initialized at declaration time by enclosing these initial values in braces:

```
int foo [5] = { 1, 2, 11, 15, 1989 };
```

When we initialize a list array, we can also omit its length as it will be determined by the number of values provided. The following declaration is equivalent to the previous one:

```
int foo [] = { 1, 2, 11, 15, 1989 };
```

If the number of elements is provided, but the array is initialized with fewer elements, then the remaining value will be *zero-initialized*, for example:

```
int foo [5] = { 1, 2, 11 };
```

The previous code is equivalent to the following:

```
int foo [5] = { 1, 2, 11, 0, 0 };
```

Accessing the Values of an Array

The values of an array can be accessed in the same way as any other values of the same type. The following is the syntax to access an array:

```
name[index]
```

An element of an array can be accessed to store a new element or to read its value.

For example, the following statement updates the value at position 4 of the previously declared array named **foo**:

```
foo [4] = 15
```

The following is used to copy the content of the element at position 2 into a new variable:

```
int x = foo [2]
```

It is important to notice that the elements at positions **4** and **2** refer to the fifth and third elements, respectively. This is due to the fact that indexing starts from **0**. The following diagram illustrates how index entries work in arrays:

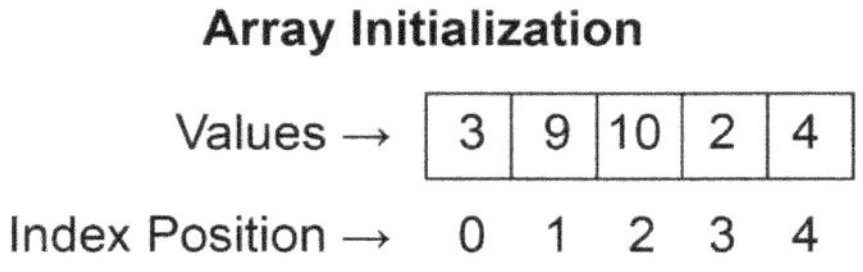

Array Initialization

Values → | 3 | 9 | 10 | 2 | 4 |

Index Position →   0   1   2   3   4

Figure 1.9: Initializing a one-dimensional array

Exceeding the valid range of indices for an array is syntactically correct, so the compiler will not produce any errors. Accessing an array out of bounds in C++ is considered an undefined behavior, which means that the code's behavior is not prescribed by the language specification. This can result in runtime errors such as bugs caused by access to an unallocated location in memory or program termination (segmentation fault) due to an attempt to access memory not owned by the program.

Multidimensional Arrays

Multidimensional arrays are commonly described as *arrays of arrays*, where an array's elements are other arrays.

The following syntax illustrates a bi-dimensional array:

```
type name [n][m];
int bi_array [3][4]
```

Here, **n** is the dimension of the array and **m** is the dimension of its elements.

Typically, in a bi-dimensional array like the previous one, the first dimension is referred to as the **row** and the second one is referred to as the **column**.

Multidimensional arrays are not limited to two dimensions; they can have as many dimensions as needed, but keep in mind that the memory that's used increases exponentially with each dimension. Similar to one-dimensional arrays, multidimensional arrays can be initialized by specifying a list of initializers, one for each row. Let's examine the following code:

```
#include <iostream>
int main()
{
```

```
   int foo [3][5] = {{ 1, 2, 11, 15, 1989 }, { 0, 7, 1, 5, 19 }, { 9, 6, 131,
1, 2 }};
   for (int x = 0; x < 3; x++)
   {
     for (int y = 0; y < 5; y++)
     {
       std::cout <<"Array element at [" << x << "]" << "[" << y << "]: "<<
foo[x][y] << std::endl;
     }
   }
}
Output:
Array element at [0][0]: 1
Array element at [0][1]: 2
Array element at [0][2]: 11
Array element at [0][3]: 15
Array element at [0][4]: 1989
Array element at [1][0]: 0
Array element at [1][1]: 7
Array element at [1][2]: 1
Array element at [1][3]: 5
Array element at [1][4]: 19
Array element at [2][0]: 9
Array element at [2][1]: 6
Array element at [2][2]: 131
Array element at [2][3]: 1
Array element at [2][4]: 2
```

Alternatively, since the compiler can infer the length of the internal arrays from the definition, the nested braces are optional and provided only for readability:

```
int foo [3][5] = {1, 2, 11, 15, 1989, 0, 7, 1, 5, 19, 9, 6, 131, 1, 2};
```

Activity 2: Defining a Bi-Dimensional Array and Initializing Its Elements

In this section, we will define a bi-dimensional array (**3x3**) of type integer and write a program to assign each element the addition of their corresponding index entries in the array:

1. Define an array of integers of size **3x3**.

2. Iterate over each element of the array using a nested **for** loop and assign the product values **x** and **y** to the index.

> **Note:**
>
> The solution for this activity can be found on page 282.

Summary

In this chapter, we saw the basic structure and syntax of the language. We started with an overview of the compilation model, the process of transforming C++ source code into an executable program. We wrote, compiled, and ran our first program, a simple **main** function that successfully returns an exit/return code.

We described the built-in arithmetic types that the language offers.

We learned how to declare and define variable names, and what the difference is between references and pointers. We also saw the use of the **const** qualifier and its advantages.

Furthermore, we talked about control flow statements and how to exploit them to perform more complex actions.

Finally, we presented arrays and multidimensional arrays, and the operation to perform to initialize them and access their values. In the next chapter, we will learn what functions in C++ are, and how and why we should use them in our code.

2

Functions

Lesson Objectives

By the end of this chapter, you will be able to:

- Explain what functions are and how to declare them
- Utilize local and global variables
- Pass arguments to functions and return values from functions
- Create overloaded functions and call them appropriately
- Apply the concept of namespaces in organizing functions

In this chapter, we are going to look at functions in C++, how to use them, and why we would want to use them.

Introduction

Functions are a core tool in a programmer's toolkit for writing maintainable code. The concept of a function is common in almost every programming language. Functions have different names in various languages: procedures, routines, and many more, but they all have two main characteristics in common:

- They represent a sequence of instructions grouped together.

- The sequence of instructions is identified by a name, which can be used to refer to the function.

The programmer can call, or invoke a function when the functionalities provided by the function are needed.

When the function is called, the sequence of instructions is executed. The caller can also provide some data to the function to be used in operations within the program. The following are the main advantages of using functions:

- **Reduces repetition**: It often occurs that a program needs to repeat the same operations in different parts of the codebase. Functions allow us to write a single implementation that is carefully tested, documented, and of high quality. This code can be called from different places in the codebase, which enables code reusability. This, in turn, increases the productivity of the programmer and the quality of the software.

- **Boosts code readability and modification**: Often, we need several operations to implement a functionality in our program. In these cases, grouping the operations together in a function and giving a descriptive name to the function helps to express what we want to do instead of how we do it.

  Using functions greatly increases the readability of our code because it's now composed of descriptive names of what we are trying to achieve, without the noise of how the result is achieved.

  In fact, it is easier to test and debug as you may only need to modify a function without having to revisit the structure of the program.

- **Higher level of abstraction**: We can give a meaningful name to the function to represent what it should achieve. This way, the calling code can be concerned with what the function is supposed to do, and it does not need to know how the operations are performed.

> **Note**
>
> Abstraction is the process of extracting all relevant properties from a class and exposing them, while hiding details that are not important for a specific usage.
>
> Let's take a tree as an example. If we were to use it in the context of an orchard, we could abstract the tree to be a "machine" that takes a determined amount of space and, given sunlight, water, and fertilizers, produces a certain number of fruits per year. The property we are interested in is the tree's fruit production ability, so we want to expose it and hide all the other details that are not relevant to our case.
>
> In computer science, we want to apply the same concept: capture the key fundamental properties of a class without showing the algorithm that implements it.

A prime example of this is the **sort** function, which is present in many languages. We know what the function expects and what it is going to do, but rarely are we aware of the algorithm that is used to do it, and it might also change between different implementations of the language.

In the following sections, we will demystify how function declaration and definition works.

Function Declaration and Definition

A `function` declaration has the role of telling the compiler the name, the parameters, and the return type of a function. After a function has been declared, it can be used in the rest of the program.

The definition of the function specifies what operations a function performs.

A declaration is composed of the type of the returned value, followed by the name of the function and by a list of parameters inside a pair of parentheses. These last two components form the signature of the function. The syntax of a function declaration is as follows:

```
// Declaration: function without body
return_type function_name( parameter list );
```

If a function returns nothing, then the type **void** can be used, and if a function is not expecting any parameters the list can be empty.

Let's look at an example of a function declaration:

```
void doNothingForNow();
```

Here, we declared a function named **doNothingForNow()**, which takes no arguments and returns nothing. After this declaration, we can call the **doNothingForNow()** function in our program.

To call a function that does not have any parameters, write the name of the function followed by a pair of parentheses.

When a function is called, the execution flow goes from the body of the function currently being executed to the body of the called function.

In the following example, the execution flow starts at the beginning of the body of **main** function and starts executing its operations in order. The first operation it encounters is the call to **doNothingForNow()**. At that point, the execution flow goes into the body of **doNothingForNow()**.

When all the operations inside a function are executed, or the function instructs them to go back to the caller, the execution flow resumes from the operation after the function call.

In our example, the operation after the function call prints **Done** on the console:

```
#include <iostream>


void doNothingForNow();


int main() {
  doNothingForNow ();
  std::cout << "Done";
}
```

If we were to compile this program, the compilation would succeed, but linking would *fail*.

In this program, we instructed the compiler that a function called **doNothingForNow()** exists and then we invoked it. The compiler generates an output that calls **doNothingForNow()**.

The linker then tries to create an executable from the compiler output, but since we did not define **doNothingForNow()**, it cannot find the function's definition, so it fails.

To successfully compile the program, we need to define **doNothingForNow()**. In the next section, we will explore how to define a function using the same example.

Defining a Function

To define a function, we need to write the same information that we used for the declaration: the return type, the name of the function, and the parameter list, followed by the function body. The function body delimits a new scope and is composed of a sequence of statements delimited by curly braces.

When the function is executed, the statements are executed in order:

```
// Definition: function with body

return_type function_name( parameter_list ) {

   statement1;

   statement2;


   ...

   last statement;

}
```

Let's fix the program by adding the body for **doNothingForNow()**:

```
void doNothingForNow() {

   // Do nothing

}
```

Here, we defined **doNothingForNow()** with an empty body. This means that as soon as the function execution starts, the control flow returns to the function that called it.

> **Note**
>
> When we define a function, we need to make sure that the signature (the return value, the name, and the parameters) are the same as the declaration.
>
> The definition counts as a declaration as well. We can skip the declaration if we define the function before calling it.

Let's revisit our program now since we have added the definition for our function:

```cpp
#include <iostream>

void doNothingForNow() {
  // do nothing
}

int main() {
  doNothingForNow();
  std::cout << "Done";
}
```

If we compile and run the program, it will succeed and show **Done** on the output console.

In a program, there can be multiple declarations of the same function, as long as the declarations are the same. On the other hand, only a single definition of the function can exist, as mandated by the **One Definition Rule** (**ODR**).

> **Note**
>
> Several definitions of the same function may exist if compiled in different files, but they need to be identical. If they are not, then the program might do unpredictable things.
>
> The compiler is not going to warn you!

The solution is to have the declaration in a **header** file, and the definition in an **implementation** file.

A header file is included in many different implementation files, and the code in these files can call the function.

An implementation file is compiled only once, so we can guarantee that the definition is seen only once by the compiler.

Then, the linker puts all of the outputs of the compiler together, finds a definition of the function, and produces a valid executable.

Exercise 3: Calling a Function from main()

In our application, we want to log errors. To do so, we have to specify a function called `log()`, which prints **Error!** to the standard output when called.

Let's create a function that can be called from several files, and put it in a different header file that can be included:

1. Create a file named **log.h** and declare a function called **log()** with no parameters and that returns nothing:

   ```
   void log();
   ```

2. Now, let's create a new file, **log.cpp**, where we define the **log()** function to print to the standard output:

```
#include <iostream>
// This is where std::cout and std::endl are defined

void log() {
  std::cout << "Error!" << std::endl;
}
```

3. Change the **main.cpp** file to include **log.h** and call **log()** in the **main()** function:

```
#include <log.h>

int main() {
  log();
}
```

4. Compile the two files and run the executable. You will see that the message **Error!** is printed when we execute it.

Local and Global Variables

The body of a function is a code block that can contain valid statements, one of which is a **variable definition**. As we learned in *Lesson 1*, *Getting Started*, when such a statement appears, the function declares a **local variable**.

This is in contrast to global variables, which are the variables that are declared outside of functions (and classes, which we will look at in *Lesson 3*, *Classes*).

The difference between a local and a global variable is in the *scope* in which it is declared, and thus, in who can access it.

> **Note**
>
> Local variables are in the function scope and can only be accessed by the function. On the contrary, global variables can be accessed by any function that can see them.

It is desirable to use local variables over global variables because they enable **encapsulation**: only the code inside the function body can access and modify the variable, making the variable invisible to the rest of the program. This makes it easy to understand how a variable is used by a function since its usage is restricted to the function body and we are guaranteed that no other code is accessing it.

Encapsulation is usually used for three separate reasons, which we will explore in more detail in *Lesson 3, Classes*:

- To restrict the access to data used by a functionality

- To bundle together the data and the functionality that operates on it

- Encapsulation is a key concept that allows you to create abstractions

On the other hand, global variables can be accessed by *any* function.

This makes it hard to be sure of the function's value when interacting with them, unless we know not only what our function does, but also what all the other code in the program that interacts with the global variable does.

Additionally, code that we add later to the program, might start modifying the global variable in a way that we did not expect in our function, breaking the functionality of our function without ever modifying the function itself. This makes it extremely difficult to modify, maintain, and evolve programs.

The solution to this problem is to use the **const** qualifier so that no code can change the variable, and we can treat it as a value that never changes.

> **Note**
> Always use the **const** qualifier with global variables whenever possible.
>
> Try to avoid using mutable global variables.
>
> It is a good practice to use global **const** variables instead of using values directly in the code. They allow you to give a name and a meaning to the value, without any of the risks that come with mutable global variables.

Working with Variable Objects

It is important to understand the relationship between variables, objects, and the lifetime of objects in C++ to write programs correctly.

> **Note**
>
> An object is a piece of data in the program's memory.
>
> A variable is a name we give to an object.

There is a distinction in C++ between the scope of a variable and the lifetime of the object it refers to. The scope of a variable is the part of the program where the variable can be used.

The lifetime of an object, on the contrary, is the time during execution wherein the object is valid to access.

Let's examine the following program to understand the lifetime of an object:

```cpp
#include <iostream>
/* 1 */ const int globalVar = 10;
int* foo(const int* other) {
    /* 5 */ int fooLocal = 0;
     std::cout << "foo's local: " << fooLocal << std::endl;
    std::cout << "main's local: " << *other << std::endl;
    /* 6 */ return &fooLocal;
}
int main()
{
    /* 2 */ int mainLocal = 15;
    /* 3 */ int* fooPointer = foo(&mainLocal);
    std::cout << "main's local: " << mainLocal << std::endl;
```

```
      std::cout << "We should not access the content of fooPointer! It's not
valid." << std::endl;

      /* 4 */ return 0;

}
```

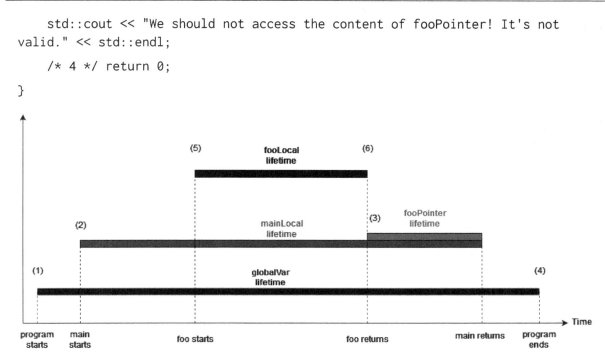

Figure 2.1: Lifetime of an object

The lifetime of a variable starts when it is initialized and ends when the containing block ends. Even if we have a pointer or reference to a variable, we should access it only if it's still valid. **fooPointer** is pointing to a variable which is no longer valid, so it should not be used!

When we declare a local variable in the scope of a function, the compiler automatically creates an object when the function execution reaches the variable declaration; the variable refers to that object.

When we declare a global variable instead, we are declaring it in a scope that does not have a clear duration – it is valid for the complete duration of the program. Because of this, the compiler creates the object when the program starts before any function is executed – even the **main()** function.

The compiler also takes care of terminating the object's lifetime when the execution exits from the scope in which the variable has been declared, or when the program terminates in the case of a global variable. The termination of the lifetime of an object is usually called **destruction**.

Variables declared in a scope block, either local or global, are called **automatic variables**, because the compiler takes care of initializing and terminating the lifetime of the object associated with the variables.

Let's look at an example of a local variable:

```
void foo() {
    int a;
}
```

In this case, the variable **a** is a local variable of type `int`. The compiler automatically initializes the object it refers to with what is called its **default initialization** when the execution reaches that statement, and the object will be destroyed at the end of the function, again, automatically.

> **Note**
>
> The default initialization of basic types, such as integers, is doing nothing for us. This means that the variable **a** will have an unspecified value.

If multiple local variables are defined, the initialization of the objects happens in the order of declaration:

```
void foo() {
    int a;
    int b;
}
```

Variable **a** is initialized before **b**. Since variable **b** was initialized after **a**, its object is destroyed before the one **a** refers to.

If the execution never reaches the declaration, the variable is not initialized. If the variable is not initialized, it is also not destroyed:

```
void foo() {
    if (false) {
        int a;
    }
    int b;
}
```

Here, the variable **a** is never default initialized, and thus never destroyed. This is similar for global variables:

```
const int a = 1;


void main() {
  std::cout << "a=" << a << std::endl;
}
```

Variable **a** is initialized before the `main()` function is called and is destroyed after we return the value from the `main()` function.

Exercise 4: Using Local and Global Variables in a Fibonacci Sequence

We want to write a function that returns the 10th number in a Fibonacci sequence.

> **Note**
>
> The *nth* Fibonacci number is defined as the sum of the *n-1th* and the *n-2th*, with the first number in the sequence being 0 and the second being 1.
>
> Example:
>
> 10th Fibonacci number = 8th Fibonacci number + 9th Fibonacci number

We want to use the best practice of giving a name and a meaning to values, so instead of using 10 in the code, we are going to define a **const** global variable, named **POSITION**.

We will also use two local variables in the function to remember the **n-1th** and the **n-2th** number:

1. Write the program and include the following constant global variable after the header file:

```
#include <iostream>

const int POSITION = 10;
const int ALREADY_COMPUTED = 3;
```

2. Now, create a function named **print_tenth_fibonacci()** with the return type as **void**:

```
void print_tenth_fibonacci()
```

3. Within the function, include three local variables, named **n_1**, **n_2**, and **current** of type **int**, as shown here:

```
int n_1 = 1;
int n_2 = 0;
int current = n_1 + n_2;
```

4. Let's create a **for** loop to generate the remaining Fibonacci numbers until we reach the 10th, using the global variables we defined previously as starting and ending indices:

```
for(int i = ALREADY_COMPUTED; i < POSITION; ++i){
        n_2 = n_1;
        n_1 = current;
        current = n_1 + n_2;
}
```

5. Now, after the previous **for** loop, add the following print statement to print the last value stored in the **current** variable:

```
std::cout << current << std::endl;
```

6. In the **main()** function, call **print_tenth_fibonacci()** and print the value of the 10th element of the Fibonacci sequence:

```
int main() {
    std::cout << "Computing the 10th Fibonacci number" << std::endl;
    print_tenth_fibonacci();
}
```

Let's understand the variable data flow of this exercise. First, the **n_1** variable is initialized, then **n_2** is initialized, and right after that, **current** is initialized. And then, **current** is destroyed, **n_2** is destroyed, and finally, **n_1** is destroyed.

i is also an automatic variable in the scope that's created by the **for** loop, so it is destroyed at the end of the **for** loop scope.

For each combination of **cond1** and **cond2**, identify when initialization and destruction occurs in the following program:

```
void foo()
  if(cond1) {
    int a;
  }
  if (cond2) {
    int b;
  }
}
```

Passing Arguments and Returning Values

In the *Introduction* section, we mentioned that the caller can provide some data to the function. This is done by passing arguments to the parameters of the function.

The parameters that a function accept are part of its signature, so we need to specify them in every declaration.

The list of parameters a function can accept is contained in the parentheses after the function name. The parameters in the function parentheses are comma-separated, composed by a type, and optionally an identifier.

For example, a function taking two integer numbers would be declared as follows:

```
void two_ints(int, int);
```

If we wanted to give a name to these parameters, **a** and **b** respectively, we would write the following:

```
void two_ints(int a, int b);
```

Inside its body, the function can access the identifiers defined in the function signature as if they were declared variables. The values of the function parameters are decided when the function is called.

To call a function that takes a parameter, you need to write the name of the function, followed by a list of expressions inside a pair of parentheses:

```
two_ints(1,2);
```

Here, we called the **two_ints** function with two arguments: **1** and **2**.

The arguments used to call the function initialize the parameters that the function is expecting. Inside the **two_ints** function, variable **a** will be equal to **1**, and **b** will be equal to **2**.

Each time the function is called, a new set of parameters is initialized from the arguments that were used to call the function.

> **Note**
>
> **Parameter**: This is a variable that was defined by a function, and can be used to provide data as per the code.
>
> **Argument**: The value the caller wants to bind to the parameters of the function.

In the following example, we used two values, but we can also use arbitrary expressions as arguments:

```
two_ints(1+2, 2+3);
```

> **Note**
>
> The order in which the expression is evaluated is not specified!

This means that when calling **two_ints(1+2, 2+3);**, the compiler might first execute **1+2** and then **2+3**, or **2+3** and then **1+2**. This is usually not a problem if the expression does not change any state in the program, but it can create bugs that are hard to detect when it does. For example, given **int i = 0;**, if we call **two_ints(i++, i++)**, we don't know whether the function is going to be called with **two_ints(0, 1)** or **two_ints(1, 0)**.

In general, it's better to declare expressions that change the state of the program in their own statements, and call functions with expressions that do not modify the program's state.

The function parameters can be of any type. As we already saw, a type in C++ could be a value, a reference, or a pointer. This gives the programmer a few options on how to accept parameters from the callers, based on the behavior it wants.

In the following subsections, we will explore the working mechanism of *Pass by value* and *Pass by reference* in more detail.

Pass by Value

When the parameter type of a function is a value type, we say that the function is taking an argument by value or the argument is passed by value.

When a parameter is a value type, a new local object is created each time the function is called.

As we saw with automatic variables, the lifetime of the object lasts until the execution does not reach the end of the function's scope.

When the parameter is initialized, a new copy is made from the argument provided when invoking the function.

Note

If you want to modify a parameter but do not want or do not care about the calling code seeing the modification, use *pass by value*.

Exercise 5: Calculating Age using Pass by Value Arguments

James wants to write a C++ program to calculate what the age of a person will be after five years by providing their current age as an input.

To implement such a program, he is going to write a function that takes a person's age by value and computes how old they will be in 5 years, and then prints it on the screen:

1. Create a function named **byvalue_age_in_5_years**, as illustrated here. Make sure that the value in the calling code does not change:

    ```
    void byvalue_age_in_5_years(int age) {
      age += 5;
      std::cout << "Age in 5 years: " << age << std::endl;
      // Prints 100
    }
    ```

2. Now, in **main()**, call the function we created in the previous step by passing the variable **age** as a value:

```
int main() {
  int age = 95;
  byvalue_age_in_5_years(age);
  std::cout << "Current age: " << age;
  // Prints 95
}
```

> **Note**
>
> Pass by value should be the default way of accepting arguments: always use it unless you have a specific reason not to.

> The reason for this is that it makes the separation between the calling code and the called function stricter: the calling code cannot see the changes that the called function makes on the parameters.

Passing parameters by value creates a clear boundary between the calling function and the called function, because the parameters are copied:

1. As the calling function, we know that the variables we passed to the functions will not be modified by it.

2. As the called function, we know that even if we modify the provided parameters, there will be no impact on the called function.

This makes it easy to understand the code, because the changes we make to the parameters have no impact outside of the function.

Pass by value can be the faster option when taking an argument, especially if the memory size of the argument is small (for example, integers, characters, float, or small structures).

We need to remember though that passing by value performs a copy of the argument. Sometimes, this can be an expensive operation both in terms of memory and processing time, like when copying a container with many elements.

There are some cases where this limitation can be overcome with the `move` semantic that was added in C++11. We will see more of it in *Lesson 3, Classes*.

Let's look at an alternative to pass by value that has a different set of properties.

Pass by Reference

When the parameter type of the function is a reference type, we say that the function is taking an argument by reference or the argument is passed by reference.

We saw earlier that a reference type does not create a new object – it is simply a new variable, or name that refers to an object that already exists.

When the function that accepts the argument by reference is called, the reference is bound to the object used in the argument: the parameter will refer to the given object. This means that the function has access to the object the calling code provided and can modify it.

This is convenient if the goal of the function is to modify an object, but it can be more difficult to understand the interaction between the caller and the called function in such situations.

> **Note**
>
> Unless the function must modify the variable, always use **const** references, as we will see later.

Exercise 6: Calculating Incrementation of Age using Pass by Reference

James would like to write a C++ program which, given anyone's age as input, prints **Congratulations!** if their age will be 18 or older in the next 5 years.

Let's write a function that accepts its parameters by reference:

1. Create a function named **byreference_age_in_5_years()** of type **void**, as illustrated here:

```
void byreference_age_in_5_years(int& age) {
  age += 5;
}
```

2. Now, in **main()**, call the function we created in the previous step by passing the variable **age** as a reference:

```
int main() {
  int age = 13;
  byreference_age_in_5_years(age);
  if (age >= 18) {
    std::cout << "Congratulations! " << std::endl;
  }
}
```

Contrary to passing by value the speed when passing by reference does not change when the memory size of the object passed.

This makes pass by reference the preferred method when copying an object, since providing pass by value to the function is expensive, especially if we cannot use the **move** semantic that was added in C++11.

> **Note**
>
> If you want to use pass by reference, but you are not modifying the provided object, make sure to use **const**.

With C++, we can use **std::cin** to read input from the console executing the program.

When writing **std::cin >> variable;**, the program will block waiting for some user input, and then it will populate **variable** with the value read from the input as long as it is a valid value and the program knows how to read it. By default, we can assign all the built-in data types and some types defined in the standard library, such as **string**.

Activity 3: Checking Voting Eligibility

James is creating a program to print a message on the console screen: "*Congratulations! You are eligible to vote in your country*" or "*No worries, just <value> more years to go.*" after the user provides their current age as input.

1. Create a function named **byreference_age_in_5_years(int& age)** and add the following code:

```
#include <iostream>

void byreference_age_in_5_years(int& age) {
  if (age >= 18) {
    std::cout << "Congratulations! You are eligible to vote for your
nation." << std::endl;
    return;
```

2. In the **else** block, add the code to calculate the years remaining until they can vote:

```
  } else{
    int reqAge = 18;
  }
}
```

3. In **main()**, add the input stream, as illustrated, to accept the input from the user. Pass the value as a reference in the previous function:

```
int main() {
    int age;
    std::cout << "Please enter your age:";
    std::cin >> age;
```

The solution for this activity can be found on page 284.

Working with const References or r-value References

A temporary object cannot be passed as an argument for a reference parameter. To accept temporary parameters, we need to use **const** references or *r-value* references. The r-value references are references that are identified by two ampersands, **&&**, and can only refer to temporary values. We will look at them in more detail in *Lesson 4, Generic Programming and Templates*.

We need to remember that a pointer is a value that represents the location of an object.

Being a value, it means that when we are accepting a parameter as a pointer, the pointer itself is passed as a value.

This means that the modification of the pointer inside the function is not going to be visible to the caller.

But if we are modifying the object the pointer points to, then the original object is going to be modified:

```cpp
void modify_pointer(int* pointer) {
    *pointer = 1;
    pointer = 0;
}
int main() {
    int a = 0;
    int* ptr = &a;
    modify_pointer(ptr);
    std::cout << "Value: " << *ptr << std::endl;
    std::cout << "Did the pointer change? " << std::boolalpha <<  (ptr == &a);
}
```

Most of the time, we can think of passing a pointer as passing a reference, with the caveat that you need to be aware that the pointer might be null.

Accepting a parameter as a pointer is mainly used for three reasons:

- Traversing the elements of an array, by providing the start pointer and either the end pointer or the size of the array.

- Optionally modifying a value. This means that the function modifies a value if it is provided.

- Returning more than a single value. This is often done to set the value of a pointer passed as an argument and then return an error code to signal whether the operation was performed.

We will see in *Lesson 4*, *Generic Programming and Templates*, how features introduced in C++11 and C++17 allow us to avoid using pointers for some of these use cases, eliminating the possibility of some common classes of errors, such as dereferencing invalid pointers or accessing unallocated memory.

The options of passing by value or passing by reference are applicable to every single parameter the function expects, independently.

This means that a function can take some arguments by value and some by reference.

Returning Values from Functions

Up until now, we have seen how to provide values to a function. In this section, we will see how a function can provide value back to the caller.

We said earlier that the first part of a function declaration is the type returned by the function: this is often referred to as the function's return type.

All the previous examples used **void** to signal that they were returning nothing. Now, it is time to look at an example of a function returning a value:

```
int sum(int, int);
```

The previous function accepts two integers by value as parameters and returns an integer.

The invocation of the function in the caller code is an expression evaluating to an integer. This means that we can use it anywhere that an expression is allowed:

```
int a = sum(1, 2);
```

A function can return a value by using the **return** keyword, followed by the value it wants to return.

The function can use the **return** keyword several times inside its body, and each time the execution reaches the **return** keyword, the program will stop executing the function and go back to the caller, with the value returned by the function, if any. Let's look at the following code:

```
void rideRollercoasterWithChecks(int heightInCm) {
  if (heightInCm < 100) {
    std::cout << "Too short";
    return;
  }
  if (heightInCm > 210) {
    std::cout << "Too tall";
    return;
  }
  rideRollercoaster();
```

```
    // implicit return at the end of the function
}
```

A function also returns to the caller if it reaches the end of its body.

This is what we did in the earlier examples since we did not use the **return** keyword.

Not explicitly returning can be okay if a function has a **void** return type. However, it will give unexpected results if the function is expected to return a value: the returned type will have an unspecified value and the program will not be correct.

Be sure to enable the warning, as it will save you a lot of debugging time.

> **Note**
>
> It is surprising, but every major compiler allows the compiling of functions, which declare a return type other than void, but don't return a value.
>
> This is easy to spot in simple functions, but it is much harder in complex ones with lots of branches.
>
> Every compiler supports options to warn you if a function returns without providing a value.

Let's look at an example of a function returning an integer:

```
int sum(int a, int b) {
    return a + b;
}
```

As we said earlier, a function can use the **return** statement several times inside its body, as shown in the following example:

```
int max(int a, int b) {
    if(a > b) {
        return a;
    } else {
        return b;
    }
}
```

We always return a value that's independent of the values of the arguments.

> **Note**
>
> It is a good practice to return as early as possible in an **algorithm**.

> The reason for this is that as you follow the logic of the code, especially when there are many conditionals, a **return** statement tells you when that execution path is finished, allowing you to ignore what happens in the remaining part of the function.

> If you only return at the end of the function, you always have to look at the full code of the function.

Since a function can be declared to return any type, we have to decide whether to return a value or a reference.

Returning by Value

A function whose return type is a value type is said to return by value.

When a function that returns by value reaches a **return** statement, the program creates a new object, which is initialized from the value of the expression in the return statement.

In the previous function, **sum**, when the code reaches the stage of returning **a + b**, a new integer is created, with the value equal to the sum of **a** and **b**, and is returned.

On the side of the caller, **int a = sum(1,2);**, a new temporary automatic object is created and is initialized from the value returned by the function (the integer that was created from the sum of **a** and **b**).

This object is called **temporary** because its lifetime is valid only while the full-expression in which it is created is executed. We will see in the *Returning by Reference* section, what this means and why this is important.

The calling code can then use the returned temporary value in another expression or assign it to a value.

Add the end of the full expression, since the lifetime of the temporary object is over, it is destroyed.

In this explanation, we mentioned that objects are initialized several times while returning a value. This is not a performance concern as C++ allows compilers to optimize all these initializations, and often initialization happens only once.

> **Note**
>
> It is preferable to return by value as it's often easier to understand, easier to use, and as fast as returning by reference.

> How can returning by value be so fast? C++11 introduced the **move** semantic, which allows moving instead of copying the return types when they support the **move** operation. We'll see how in *Lesson 3*, *Classes*. Even before C++11, all mainstream compilers implemented **return value optimization** (**RVO**) and **named return value optimization** (**NRVO**), where the return value of a function is constructed directly in the variable into which they would have been copied to when returned. In C++17, this optimization, also called **copy elision**, became mandatory.

Returning by Reference

A function whose return type is a reference is said to return by reference.

When a function returning a reference reaches a `return` statement, a new reference is initialized from the expression that's used in the `return` statement.

In the caller, the function call expression is **substituted** by the returned reference.

However, in this situation, we need to also be aware of the lifetime of the object the reference is referring to. Let's look at an example:

```
const int& max(const int& a, const int& b) {
  if (a > b) {
    return a;
  } else {
    return b;
  }
}
```

First, we need to note that this function already has a caveat. The **max** function is returning by value, and it did not make a difference if we returned **a** or **b** when they were equal.

In this function, instead, when **a == b** we are returning **b**, this means that the code calling this function needs to be aware of this distinction. In the case where a function returns a non-**const** reference it might modify the object referred to by the returned reference, and whether **a** or **b** is returned might make a difference.

We are already seeing how references can make our code harder to understand.

Let's look at the function we used:

```
int main() {
    const int& a = max(1,2);
    std::cout << a;
}
```

This program has an error! The reason is that **1** and **2** are temporary values, and as we explained before, a temporary value is alive until the end of the full expression containing it.

To better understand what is meant by "*the end of the full expression containing it*", let's look at the code we have in the preceding code block: **int& a = max(1,2);**. There are four expressions in this piece of code:

- **1** is an integer literal, which still counts as an expression
- **2** is an integer literal, similar to **1**
- **max(expression1, expression2)** is a function call expression
- **a = expression3** is an assignment expression

All of this happens in the declaration statement of variable **a**.

The third point covers the function call expression, while containing the full expression is covered in the following point.

This means that lifetimes **1** and **2** will stop at the end of the assignment. But we got a reference to one of them! And we are using it!

Accessing an object whose lifetime is terminated is prohibited by C++, and this will result in an invalid program.

In a more complex example, such as `int a = max(1,2) + max(3,4);`, the temporary objects returned by the `max` functions will be valid until the end of the assignment, but no longer.

Here, we are using the two references to `sum` them, and then we assign the result as a value. If we assigned the result to a reference, as in the following example, `int& a = max(1,2) + max(3,4);`, instead, the program would have been wrong.

This sounds confusing, but it is important to understand as it can be a source of hard-to-debug problems if we use a temporary object after the full expression in which it's created has finished executing.

Let's look at another common mistake in functions returning references:

```
int& sum(int a, int b) {
  int c = a + b;
  return c;
}
```

We created a local, automatic object in the function body and then we returned a reference to it.

In the previous section, we saw that local objects' lifetimes end at the end of the function. This means that we are returning a reference to an object whose lifetime will always be terminated.

Earlier, we mentioned the similarities between passing arguments by reference and passing arguments by pointers.

This similarity persists when returning pointers: the object pointed to by a pointer needs to be alive when the pointer is later **dereferenced**.

So far, we have covered examples of mistakes while returning by reference. How can references be used correctly as return types to functions?

The important part of using references correctly as return values is to make sure that the object outlives the reference: the object must always be alive – at least until there is a reference to it.

A common example is accessing a part of an object, for example, using an **std::array**, which is a safe option compared to the built-in array:

```cpp
int& getMaxIndex(std::array<int, 3>& array, int index1, int index2) {
    /* This function requires that index1 and index2 must be smaller than 3!
    */
    int maxIndex = max(index1, index2);
    return array[maxIndex];
```

The calling code would look as follows:

```cpp
int main() {
    std:array<int, 3> array = {1,2,3};
    int& elem = getMaxIndex(array, 0, 2);
    elem = 0;
    std::cout << array[2];
    // Prints 0
}
```

In this example, we are returning a reference to an element inside an array, and the array remains alive longer than the reference.

The following are guidelines for using return by reference correctly:

- Never return a reference to a local variable (or a part of it)
- Never return a reference to a parameter accepted by value (or a part of it)

When returning a reference that was received as a parameter, the argument passed to the function must live longer than the returned reference.

Apply the previous rule, even when you are returning a reference to a part of the object (for example, an element of an array).

Activity 4: Using Pass by Reference and Pass by Value

In this activity, we are going to see the different trade-offs that can be made when writing a function, depending on the parameters the function accepts:

1. Write a function that takes two numbers and returns the sum. Should it take the arguments by value or reference? Should it return by value or by reference?

2. After that, write a function that takes two `std::arrays` of ten integers and an index (guaranteed to be less than 10) and returns the greater of the two elements to the given index in the two arrays.

3. The calling function should then modify the element. Should it take the arguments by value or reference? Should it return by value or by reference? What happens if the values are the same?

Take the arrays by reference and return by reference because we are saying that the calling function is supposed to modify the element. Take the index by value since there is no reason to use references.

If the values are the same, the element from the first array is returned.

> **Note**
> The solution to this activity can be found at page 285.

Const Parameters and Default Arguments

In the previous chapter, we saw how and when to use references in function parameters and return types. C++ has an additional qualifier, the **const** qualifier, which can be used independently from the *ref-ness* (whether the type is a reference or not) of the type.

Let's see how **const** is used in the various scenarios we investigated when looking at how functions can accept parameters.

Passing by const Value

In pass by value, the function parameter is a value type: when invoked, the argument is copied into the parameter.

This means that regardless of whether **const** is used in the parameter or not, the calling code cannot see the difference.

The only reason to use **const** in the function signature is to document to the implementation that it cannot modify such a value.

This is not commonly done, as the biggest value of a function signature is for the caller to understand the contract of calling the function. Because of this, it is rare to see **int max(const int, const int)**, even if the function does not modify the parameters.

There is an exception, though: when the function accepts a **pointer**.

In such cases, the function wants to make sure that it is not assigning a new value to the pointer. The pointer acts similar to a reference here, since it cannot be bound to a new object, but provides nullability.

An example could be **setValue(int * const)**, a function that takes a **const** pointer to an **int**.

The integer is not **const**, so it can be changed, but the pointer is **const** and the implementation cannot change it during implementation.

Passing by const Reference

Const is extremely important in pass by reference, and any time you use a reference in the parameters of a function, you should also add **const** to it (if the function is not designed to modify it).

The reason for this is that a reference allows you to modify the provided object freely.

It is error-prone, since the function might modify an object the caller does not expect to be modified by mistake, and it is hard to understand as there is no clear boundary between the caller and the function, again, because the function can modify the state of the caller.

const instead fixes the problem, since a function cannot modify an object through a **const** reference.

This allows the function to use reference parameters without some of the drawbacks of using references.

The function should remove the **const** from a reference, but only if it is intended to modify the provided object, otherwise every reference should be **const**.

Another advantage of **const** reference parameters is that temporary objects can be used as arguments for them.

Returning by const Value

There is no widespread reason to return by **const** value since the calling code often assigns the value to a variable, in which case the **const**-ness of the variables is going to be the deciding factor, or passes the value to a next expression, and it is rare for an expression to expect a **const** value.

Returning by **const** value also inhibits the **move** semantic of C++11, thus reducing performance.

Returning by const Reference

A function should always return by **const** reference when the returned reference is meant to only be read and not be modified by the calling code.

The same concept we applied to object lifetimes when returning references to them also apply to **const**:

- When returning a reference accepted as a parameter, if the parameter is a **const** reference, the returned reference must be **const** as well

- When returning a reference to a part of an object accepted as the **const** reference parameter, the returned reference must be **const** as well

A parameter accepted as a reference should be returned as a **const** reference if the caller is not expected to modify it.

Sometimes, the compilation fails, stating that the code is trying to modify an object that is a **const** reference. Unless the function is meant to modify the object, the solution is not to remove **const** from the reference in the parameter. Instead, look for why the operation that you are trying to perform does not work with **const**, and what the possible alternatives are.

const is not about the implementation, it is about the meaning of the function.

When you write the function signature, you should decide whether to use **const**, as the implementation will have to find a way to respect that.

For example:

```
void setTheThirdItem(std::array<int, 10>& array, int item)
```

This should clearly take a reference to the array since its purpose is to modify the array.

On the other hand, we can use the following:

```
int findFirstGreaterThan(const std::array<int, 10>&  array, int threshold)
```

This tells us that we are only looking into the array – we are not changing it, so we should use **const**.

> **Note**
>
> It is a best practice to use **const** as much as possible, as it allows the compiler to make sure that we are not modifying objects that we do not want to modify.
>
> This can help to prevent bugs.
>
> It also helps to keep another best practice in mind: never use the same variable to represent different concepts. Since the variable cannot be changed, it is less natural to reuse it instead of creating a new one.

Default Arguments

Another feature C++ provides to make life easier for the caller when it comes to calling functions are default arguments.

Default arguments are added to a function declaration. The syntax is to add an **=** sign and supply the value of the default argument after the identifier of the parameter of the function. An example of this would be:

```
int multiply(int multiplied, int multiplier = 1);
```

The caller of the function can call **multiply** either with **1** or **2** arguments:

```
multiply(10); // Returns 10
```

```
multiply(10, 2); // Returns 20
```

When an argument with a default value is omitted, the function uses the default value instead. This is extremely convenient if there are functions with sensible defaults that callers mostly do not want to modify, except in specific cases.

Imagine a function that returns the first word of a string:

char const * firstWord(char const * string, char separator = ' ').

Most of the time, a word is separated by a whitespace character, but a function can decide whether or not it should use a different separator. The fact that a function offers the possibility to provide a separator is not forcing most callers, which simply want to use the space, to specify it.

It is a best practice to set the default arguments in the function signature declaration, and not declare them in the definition.

Namespaces

One of the goals of functions is to better organize our code. To do so, it is important to give meaningful names to them.

For example, in package management software, there might be a function called **sort** for sorting packages. As you can see, the name is the same as the function that would sort a list of numbers.

C++ has a feature that allows you to avoid these kinds of problems and groups names together: **namespaces**.

A namespace starts a scope in which all the names declared inside are part of the namespace.

To create a namespace, we use the **namespace** keyword, followed by the identifier and then the code block:

```
namespace example_namespace {
  // code goes here
}
```

To access an identifier inside a namespace, we prepend the name of the namespace to the name of the function.

Namespaces can be nested as well. Simply use the same declaration as before inside the namespace:

```
namespace parent {
  namespace child {
    // code goes here
  }
}
```

To access an identifier inside a namespace, you prepend the name of the identifier with the name of the namespace in which it is declared, followed by ::.

You might have noticed that, before we were using **std::cout**. This is because the C++ standard library defines the **std** namespace and we were accessing the variable named **cout**.

To access an identifier inside multiple namespaces, you can prepend the list of all the namespaces separated by :: – `parent::child::some_identifier`. We can access names in the global scope by prepending :: to the name–`::name_in_global_scope`.

If we were to only use `cout`, the compiler would have told us that the name does not exist in the current scope.

This is because the compiler searches only in the current namespace and the parent namespaces to find an identifier by default, so unless we specify the `std` namespace, the compiler will not search in it.

C++ helps make this more ergonomic with the help of the **using** declaration.

The **using** declaration is defined by the **using** keyword, followed by an identifier specified with its namespaces.

For example, `using std::cout;` is a **using** declaration that declares that we want to use `cout`. When we want to use all the declarations from a namespace, we can write **using namespace namespace_name**;. For example, if we want to use every name defined in the `std` namespace, we would write: `using namespace std;`.

When a name is declared inside the **using** declaration, the compiler also looks for that name when looking for an identifier.

This means that, in our code, we can use `cout` and the compiler will find `std::cout`.

A **using** declaration is valid as long as we are in the scope in which it is declared.

> **Note**
>
> To better organize your code and avoid naming conflicts, you should always put your code inside a namespace that's specific to either your application or library.
>
> Namespaces can also be used to specify that some code is used only by the current code.

Let's imagine you have a file called **a.cpp** that contains `int default_name = 0;` and another file called **b.cpp** with `int default_name = 1;`. When you compile the two files and link them together, we get an invalid program: the same variable has been declared with two different values, and this violates the **One Definition Rule** (**ODR**).

But you never meant for those to be the same variable. To you, they were some variables that you just wanted to use inside your **.cpp** file.

To tell that to the compiler, you can use anonymous namespaces: a namespace with no identifier.

All the identifiers created inside it will be private to the *current translation unit* (normally the **.cpp** file).

How can you access an identifier inside an anonymous namespace? You can access the identifier directly, without the need to use the namespace name, which does not exist, or the **using** declaration.

> **Note**
>
> You should only use anonymous namespaces in **.cpp** files.

Activity 5: Organizing Functions in Namespaces

Write a function to read the name of a car for a lottery in a namespace based on numerical input. If the user inputs **1**, they win a Lamborghini, and if the user inputs **2**, they win a Porsche:

1. Define the first namespace as **LamborghiniCar** with an **output()** function that will print "**Congratulations! You deserve the Lamborghini.**" when called.

2. Define the second namespace as **PorscheCar** with an **output()** function that will print "**Congratulations! You deserve the Porsche.**" when called.

3. Write a **main** function to read the input of numbers **1** and **2** into a variable called **magicNumber**.

4. Create an **if-else** loop with the **if** condition calling the first namespace with **LamborghiniCar::output()** if the input is **1**. Otherwise, the second namespace is called similarly when the input is **2**.

5. If neither of these conditions are met, we print a message asking them to enter a number between **1** and **2**.

> **Note**
>
> The solution for this activity can be found on page 285.

Function Overloading

We saw how C++ allows us to write a function that takes parameters either by value or by reference, using **const**, and organizes them in namespaces.

There is an additional powerful feature of C++ that allows us to give the same name to functions that perform the same conceptual operation on different types: **function overloading**.

Function overloading is the ability to declare several functions with the same name – that is, if the set of parameters they accept is different.

An example of this is the **multiply** function. We can imagine this function being defined for integers and floats, or even for vectors and matrices.

If the concept represented by the function is the same, we can provide several functions that accept different kinds of parameters.

When a function is invoked, the compiler looks at all the functions with that name, called the **overload set**, and picks the function that is the best match for the arguments provided.

The precise rule on how the function is selected is complex, but the behavior is often intuitive: the compiler looks for the better match between the arguments and the expected parameters of the function. If we have two functions, **int increment(int)** and **float increment(float)**, and we call them with **increment(1)**, the integer overload is selected because an integer is a better match to an integer than a float, even if an integer can be converted into a float. An example of this would be:

```
bool isSafeHeightForRollercoaster(int heightInCm) {
  return heightInCm > 100 && heightInCm < 210;
}


bool isSafeHeightForRollercoaster(float heightInM) {
  return heightInM > 1.0f && heightInM < 2.1f;
}


// Calls the int overload
isSafeHeightForRollercoaster(187);


// Class the float overload
isSafeHeightForRollercoaster(1.67f);
```

Thanks to this feature, the calling code does not need to worry about which overload of the function the compiler is going to select, and the code can be more expressive thanks to using the same function to express the same meaning.

Activity 6: Writing a Math Library for a 3D Game

Johnny wants to implement a *math* library for the video game he is making. It will be a 3D game, so he will need to operate on points representing the three coordinates: x, y, and z.

The points are represented as **std::array<float, 3>**. A library will be used throughout the game, so Johnny needs to be sure it can work when included multiple times (by creating a header file and declaring the functions there).

The library needs to support the following steps:

1. Finding the distance between 2 floats, 2 integers, or 2 points.

2. If only one of the 2 points is provided, the other one is assumed to be the origin (the point at location **(0,0,0)**).

3. Additionally, Johnny often needs to compute the circumference of a circle from its radius (defined as **2*pi*r**) to understand how far enemies can see. **pi** is constant for the duration of the program (which can be declared globally in the **.cpp** file).

4. When an enemy moves, it visits several points. Johnny needs to compute the total distance that it would take to walk along those points.

5. For simplicity, we will limit the number of points to **10**, but Johnny might need up to 100. The function would take **std::array<std::array<float, 3>, 10>** and compute the distance between consecutive points.

    For example (with a list of 5 points): for the array **{{0,0,0}, {1,0,0}, {1,1,0}, {0,1,0}, {0,1,1}}**, the total distance is 5, because going from **{0,0,0}** to **{1,0,0}** is a distance of **1**, then going from **{1,0,0}** to **{1,1,0}** is a distance of **1** again, and so on for the remaining 3 points.

    > **Note**
    >
    > The solution for this activity can be found on page 286.

Make sure that the functions are well-organized by grouping them together.

Remember that the distance between two points is computed as the square root of `(x2-x1)^2 + (y2-y1)^2 + (z2-z1)^2`.

C++ offers the `std::pow` function for the **power function**, which takes the base and the exponent, and the `std::sqrt` function, which takes the number to square. Both are in the `cmath` header.

Summary

In this chapter, we saw the powerful features C++ offers to implement functions.

We started by discussing why functions are useful and what they can be used for, and then we dove into how to declare and define them.

We analyzed different ways of accepting parameters and returning values, how to make use of local variables, and then explored how to improve the safety and convenience of calling them with `const` and default arguments.

Finally, we saw how functions can be organized in namespaces and the ability to give the same name to different functions that implement the same concept, making the calling code not have to think about which version to call.

In the next chapter, we will look at how to create classes and how they are used in C++ to make building complex programs easy and safe.

3

Classes

Lesson Objectives

By the end of this chapter, you will be able to:

- Declare and define a class

- Access the members of a class using objects

- Apply access modifiers to encapsulate data

- Use the static modifier on data members and member functions

- Implement a nested class

- Utilize the friend specifier to access private and protected members

- Use constructors, copy constructors, assignment operators, and destructors

- Overload operators

- Implement functors

In this chapter, we will be learning about classes and objects in C++.

Introduction

In the previous chapter, we saw how we can use functions to combine basic operations into units with a clear meaning. Additionally, in the first chapter, we saw how, in C++, we can store data in basic types, such as integers, chars, and floats.

In this chapter, we will be covering how to define and declare classes and how to access member functions of a class. We will explore what `member` and `friend` functions are and how to use each in a program. Later in the chapter, we will look at how constructors and destructors work. At the end of the chapter, we will explore functors and how you can use them in your programs.

Declaring and Defining a Class

A **class** is a way to combine data and operations together to create new types that can be used to represent complex concepts.

Basic types can be composed to create more meaningful abstractions. For example, *location data* is composed of latitude and longitude coordinates, which are represented as `float` values. With such a representation, when our code needs to operate on a location, we would have to provide both the latitude and longitude as separate variables. This is error-prone, as we might forget to pass one of the two variables, or we could provide them in the wrong order.

Additionally, computing the distance between two coordinates is a complex task and we don't want to write the same code again and again. It becomes even more difficult when we use more complex objects.

Continuing our example on Coordinates, instead of using operations on two `float` types, we can define a type, which stores the location and provides the necessary operations to interact with it.

The Advantages of Using Classes

Classes provide several benefits, such as abstraction, information hiding, and encapsulation. Let's explore each of these in depth:

- **Abstraction**: This allows us to represent a high-level concept. In our previous example with GPS coordinates, we can see that, without classes we need to use two `float` variables, but this does not represent the concept that we want to use. The programmer needs to remember that the two variables have a different meaning and should be used together. Classes allow us to explicitly define a concept, composed by data and operations on that data, and assign a *name* to it.

In our example, we can create a class to represent GPS coordinates. The data will be the two **float** variables to describe **latitude** and **longitude**.

Examples of operations could be ways to compute distances between coordinates, or to check whether a coordinate is inside a specific state. The programmer will directly operate on the class and will not have to interact with the two **float** variables that are used to represent it.

- **Information hiding**: The process of exposing a set of functionalities to the user of the class while hiding the details of how they are implemented in the class.

This approach reduces the complexity of interacting with the class and makes it easier to update the class implementation in the future:

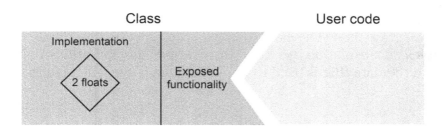

Figure 2.1: The class exposes functionality that the user code uses directly, hiding the fact that it is implemented with two floats

We discussed the fact that we can represent GPS coordinates as latitude and longitude. Later, we might decide to represent a coordinate as the distance from the **North Pole**. Thanks to information hiding, we can change how a class is implemented and the users of the class will not be impacted, since we do not change the functionality offered by the class:

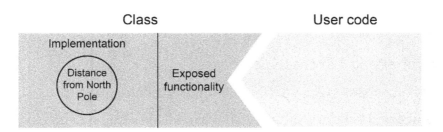

Figure 2.2: The implementation of the class changes, but since it is hidden from the user and the functionality was not changed, the user does not have to change how their code interacts with it

The set of functionalities the class exposes to the users is normally referred to as the **public interface**.

> **Note**
>
> Changing the implementation of a class is generally more convenient than to changing the interface of a class, which requires you to change all the users of the class to adapt to the new interface. Getting the design of the public interface of a class right is the first step to creating a class that is easy to use and requires low maintenance.

- **Encapsulation**: This is the principle of grouping the data and the operations we can perform on it together. Since the data is hidden in the class, the user cannot access or operate on it. The class must provide functionality to interact with it. C++ enables encapsulation by letting the user put the operations to interact with a class and the data that is used to implement such operations in the same unit: **class**.

Let's explore the structure of a class in C++ and the information associated with it. The following is the basic structure of a class:

```
class ClassName {

  // class body

};
```

> **Note**
>
> It is common to forget the last **semicolon** after closing curly brackets. Always make sure that you add it.

C++ Data Members and Access Specifiers

Inside the body of a class, we can define the following class members:

- **Data members**: These are variables that live inside a class, which look like a **variable declaration**, but are inside the class body. They are also called **fields**.

- **Member functions**: These are functions that can access the variables inside a class. They look like a **function declaration** but are inside the class body. They are also called **methods**.

As we mentioned before, classes support information hiding by denying users of the class to access information. The programmer uses **access specifiers** to specify which parts of the class are available for the user to be accessed.

There are the following three access specifiers in C++:

- **Private**: Members declared as `private` can only be accessed by the functions inside the class and are not allowed to be accessed directly outside the class

- **Protected**: Members declared as `protected` can only be accessed by the functions inside the class and the derived classes. We will learn more about in the last chapter of this book

- **Public**: Members declared as `public` can be accessed from anywhere in the program

Access specifiers followed by a colon delimit an area in the class, and any member defined in that area has the access specifier that precedes it. Here's the syntax:

```
class ClassName {

  private:

    int privateDataMember;

    int privateMemberFunction();


  protected:

    float protectedDataMember;

    float protectedMemberFunction();


  public:

    double publicDataMember;

    double publicMemberFunction();

};
```

> **Note**
>
> By default, class members have the `private` access modifier.

In C++, we can also use the **struct** keyword to define a class. A **struct** is identical to a class, with the only exception that, by default, the access modifier is **public**, while for the class it is **private**.

The following side-by-side code snippets are equivalent:

```struct Name {``` ```// body``` ```};```	```class Name {``` ```public:``` ```// body``` ```};```
```struct Name {``` ```private:``` ```// body``` ```};```	```Class Name {``` ```// body``` ```};```

Figure 3.2: The difference between the code snippets of class and struct

Whether to use **struct** or **class** depends on convention used: usually, we use **structs** when we want a collection of data members that should be accessible from anywhere in the code; on the other hand, we use classes when we are modelling a more complex concept.

We have learned how to define a class. Now, let's understand how to use one in a program.

A class defines a blueprint or the design of an object. Like a blueprint, we can create multiple objects from the same class. These objects are called **instances**.

We can create an instance in the same way that we create any basic type: define the type of the variable followed by the name of the variable. Let's explore the following example.

```
class Coordinates {
  public:
    float latitude;
    float longitude;

    float distance(const Coordinates& other_coordinate);
};
```

Here's an example that shows a class that has multiple instances:

```
Coordinates newYorkPosition;

Coordinates tokyoPosition;
```

Here, we have two instances of the **Coordinates** class, each with their **latitude** and **longitude**, which can change independently. Once we have an instance, we can access its members.

When we declare a class, we create a new scope called the **class scope**. The names defined inside the class scope are accessible only inside the same class scope. The operator for accessing members of a **class** or a **struct** from a scope outside the class is the dot (.) operator.

For the previously defined variables, we can access their **latitude** using the following code:

```
float newYorkLatitude = newYorkPosition.latitude;
```

If we want to call a member function instead, we can invoke it like this:

```
float distance = newYorkPosition.distance(tokyoPosition);
```

On the other hand, when we are writing the body of a **class** method, we are inside the class's scope. This means that we can access the other members of the class by using their names directly, without having to use the *dot* operator. The members of the current instance are going to be used.

Let's assume that the **distance** method is implemented as follows:

```
float Coordinates::distance(const Coordinates& other_coordinate) {

  return pythagorean_distance(latitude, longitude, other_coodinate.latitude,
other_coordinate.longitude);

}
```

When we call **newYorkPosition.distance(tokyoPosition);**, the **distance** method is called on the **newYorkPosition** instance. This means that **latitude** and **longitude** in the **distance** method refer to **newYorkPosition.latitude** and **newYorkPosition.longitude**, while **other_coordinate.latitude** refers to **tokyoPosition.latitude**.

If we had called **tokyoPosition.distance(newYorkPosition);** instead, the current instance would have been **tokyoPosition**, and **latitude** and **longitude** would have referred to the **tokyoPosition**, and **other_coordinate** to **newYorkPosition**.

Static Members

In the previous section, we learned that a class defines the fields and methods that compose an object. It is like a blueprint, specifying what the object looks like, but it does not actually build it. *An instance is the object that's built from the blueprint that's defined by the class.* Instances contain data and we can operate on instances.

Imagine the blueprint of a car. It specifies the engine of the car and that the car will have four wheels. The blueprint is the class of the car, but we cannot turn on and drive a blueprint. A car that's built by following the blueprint is an instance of the class. The built car has four wheels and an engine, and we can drive it. In the same way, an instance of a class contains the fields that are specified by the class.

This means that the value of each field is connected to a specific instance of a class and evolves independently from the fields of all the other instances. At the same time, it also means that a field cannot exist without the associated instance: there would be no object that would be able to provide the storage (the space in memory) to store the value of the field!

However, sometimes, we want to share the same value across all instances. In those cases, we can associate the field with the class instead of the instance by creating a **static** field. Let's examine the following syntax:

```
class ClassName {
    static Type memberName;
};
```

There will be only one **memberName** field, which is shared across all instances. Like any variable in C++, **memberName** needs to be stored in memory. We cannot use the storage of the instance object, since **memberName** is not associated with any specific instance. **memberName** is stored in a similar way to a *global variable*.

Outside of the class in which the static variable is declared, in a **.cpp** file, we can define the value of the **static** variable. The syntax to initialize the value is as follows:

```
Type ClassName::memberName = value;
```

> **Note**
>
> Note that we do not repeat the **static** keyword.
>
> It is important to define the values of the **static** variables in the **.cpp** file. If we define them inside the **header** file, the definition will be included anywhere inside the header, which will create multiple definitions, and the **linker** will complain.

A class static variable's lifetime lasts for the complete duration of the program, like global variables.

Let's see an example of how a static field in a class can be defined in the header and how to assign a value to it in the **.cpp** file:

```cpp
// In the .h file
class Coordinates {
  // Data member
  float latitude_ = 0;

  // Data member
  float longitude_ = 0;

public:
  // Static data member declaration
  static const Coordinates hearthCenter;

  // Member function declaration
  float distanceFrom(Coordinates other);

  // Member function definition
  float distanceFromCenter() {
    return distanceFrom(hearthCenter);
  }
};


// In the .cpp file
// Static data member definition
const Coordinates Coordinates::hearthCenter = Coordinates(0, 0);
```

When accessing the members of an instance, we learned to use the dot operator.

When accessing a static member, we might not have an instance to use the dot operator on. C++ gives us the ability to access the static members of a class by using the **scope resolution operator**, which is, a double colon (::), after the class name.

> **Note**
>
> Always use **const** when declaring a static field. Any instance can access the static fields of its class; if they are **mutable**, it becomes extremely hard to track down which instances is modifying the value. In programs that use multiple threads, it is common to create bugs by modifying the static fields from different threads at the same time.

Let's examine the following exercise to understand how static variables work.

Exercise 7: Working with Static Variables

Let's write a program to print and find the square of numbers from 1 to 10:

1. Include the required header files.

2. Write the **squares()** function and the following logic:

```cpp
void squares()
{
    static int count = 1;
    int x = count * count;
    x = count * count;
    std::cout << count << "*" << count;
    std::cout << ": " << x <<std::endl;
    count++;
}
```

3. Now, in the **main** function, add the following code:

```cpp
int main()
{
    for (int i=1; i<11; i++)
        squares();
    return 0;
}
```

The output is as follows:

```
1*1:  1
2*2:  4
3*3:  9
4*4:  16
5*5:  25
6*6:  36
7*7:  49
8*8:  64
9*9:  81
10*10:  100
```

In addition to static fields, classes can also have static methods.

A static method is associated with a class; it can be invoked without an instance. Since the fields and members of a class are associated with an instance, while static methods are not, static methods cannot invoke them. Static methods can be invoked using the scope resolution operator: `ClassName::staticMethodName();`.

> **Note**
> Static methods can only call other static methods and static fields inside a class.

Member Functions

Member functions are functions that are used to manipulate the data members of a class, and they define the properties and behavior of the objects of the class.

Declaring a member function is just a matter of declaring a function inside the body of a class. Let's examine the following syntax:

```
class Car
{
  public:
  void turnOn() {}
};
```

Member functions, like the data members of a class, can be accessed using the dot (.) operator that's applied on the object:

```
Car car;
car.turnOn();
```

Let's understand how to declare a member function outside the class scope.

Declaring a Member Function

Member functions, like data members, must be declared inside the class. However, a member function's implementation can be placed either inside or outside the class, body.

The following is a definition of a member function outside of the class, scope. This is done by using the scope resolution operator (::) to declare that the function that's being referred to is a member of the class. In the class, body, the function is declared with its prototype:

```
class Car
{
  public:
  void turnOn();
};


void Car::turnOn() {}
```

Using const Member Functions

The member functions of a class can be qualified as **const**, which means that the function limits its access to be read-only. Moreover, a member function is required to be **const** when it accesses **const** member data. So, **const** member functions are not allowed to modify the state of an object or call another function that does so.

To declare a member function as **const**, we use the **const** keyword in the function declaration after the function name and before its body:

```
const std::string& getColor() const
{
  // Function body
}
```

In addition to the overloading rules that we learned in the previous chapter that member functions can be overloaded in their const-ness, which means that two functions can have identical signatures except for one being **const** and the other not. The **const** member function will be called when an object is declared **const**; otherwise, the non-const function is called. Let's examine the following code:

```
class Car
{
  std::string& getColor() {}
  const std::string& getColor() const {}
};
Car car;
// Call std::string& getColor()
car.getColor();
const Car constCar;
// Call const Color& getColor() const
constCar.getColor();
```

> **Note**
>
> It is important to distinguish between a **const** function and a function returning a **const** type. Both make use of the same **const** keyword, but in different places in the function prototype. They express a different concept and are independent.

The following examples show three versions of the **const** function:

- The first one is a **const** member function
- The second returns a **const** reference
- The third one is a **const** function that returns a **const** reference:

```
type& function() const {}

const type& function() {}

const type& function() const {}
```

The this Keyword

When the **this** keyword is used in the **class** context, it represents a pointer whose value is the address of the object on which the member function is called. It can appear within the body of any non-static member function.

In the following example, **setColorToRed()** and **setColorToBlue()** perform the same action. Both set a data member, but the former uses the **this** keyword to refer to the current object:

```
class Car
{
  std::string color;

  void setColorToRed()
  {
    this->color = "Red";
    // explicit use of this
  }

  void setColorToBlue()
  {
    color = "Blue";
    // same as this->color = "Blue";
  }
};
```

> **Note**
>
> **pointer->member** is a convenient way to access the member of the **struct** pointed by **pointer**. It is equivalent to **(*pointer).member**.

Exercise 8: Creating a Program Using the this Keyword to Greet New Users

Let's write a program that asks users for their names and greets them with a welcoming message:

1. First, include the required header files.

2. Then, add the following functions to print the required output:

```cpp
class PrintName {
    std::string name;


};
```

3. Now, let's complete the program with a closing message using the **this** keyword. Define the following methods inside the previous class:

```cpp
public:
    void set_name(const std::string &name){
        this->name = name;
    }
    void print_name() {
        std::cout << this->name << "! Welcome to the C++ community :)" <<
std::endl;
    }
```

4. Write the **main** function, as follows:

```cpp
int main()
{
PrintName object;
object.set_name("Marco");
object.print_name();
}
```

The output is as follows:

```
Marco! Welcome to the C++ community :)
```

> **Note**
>
> A function argument that has the same name as a data member of a class can shadow its visibility. In this case, the **this** keyword is required for disambiguation.

Non-Member Class-Related Functions

Defined as functions or operations that conceptually belong to the interface of a class, non-member class-related functions are not part of a class itself. Let's examine the following example:

```
class Circle{
  public:
    int radius;
};


ostream& print(ostream& os, const Circle& circle) {
  os << "Circle's radius: " << circle.radius;
  return os;
}
```

The print function writes the radius of the circle on the given stream, which is most commonly the standard output.

Activity 7: Information Hiding Through Getters and Setters

In this activity, you are being asked to define a class named **Coordinates**, which contains two data members, and **latitude** and **longitude**, both of type **float** and not publicly accessible.

There are four operations that are associated with the **Coordinates** class: **set_latitude**, **set_longitude**, **get_latitude**, and **get_longitude**.

> **Note**
>
> The **set_latitude** and **set_longitude** operations are used to **set** the x and y coordinates (also referred to as **setters**), while **get_latitude** and **get_longitude** are used to **retrieve** them (sometimes called **getters**).

Performing encapsulation using the member functions through getter and setters.

To perform this activity, follow these steps:

1. Define a class with the name **Coordinates**, with its members under a **private** access specifier.

2. Add the four operations previously specified and make them publicly accessible by preceding their declaration by the **public** access specifier.

3. The setters (**set_latitude** and **set_longitude**) should take a float as a parameter and return **void**, while the getters do not take any parameters and return a **float**.

4. The four methods should now be implemented. The setters assign the given value to the corresponding member they are supposed to set; the getters return the values that are stored.

> **Note**
>
> The solution for this activity can be found on page 288.

Constructors and Destructors

Up until now, we have learned how to declare data members, how to use them in functions with a **public** specifier, and how to access them. Now, let's explore how to set a value to them.

In the following example, we'll declare a **struct** by the name of **Rectangle**, and set a value to it as follows:

```
struct Rectangle {
  int height;
  int width;
};


Rectangle rectangle;


// What will the following print function print?
std::cout << "Height: " << rectangle.height << std::endl;
```

This line will print a random value because we never set the value of **int**. The C++ rule for the initialization of basic types is that they get non-specified values.

> **Note**
>
> In some situations, the values of variables are set to **0** when they are not initialized. This might happen because of some details in the implementation of the operating system, the standard library, or the compiler, and the C++ standard does not guarantee it. A program will have strange bugs when it relies on this behavior, since it is unpredictable when variables are initialized to **0**. Always explicitly initialize variables with basic types.

Constructors

The way to initialize data members is by using a **constructor**. A constructor is a special member function that has the *same name* as the class and *no return type*, and it is called automatically by the compiler when a new object of the class is created.

Like any other function, a constructor can accept parameters and has a function body. We can invoke a constructor by adding a parameter list after the name of the variable:

```
Rectangle rectangle(parameter1, paramter2, ..., parameterN);
```

When there are no parameters, we can avoid using parentheses, which is what we did in the previous example.

An example of a constructor with no parameters for the **Rectangle** struct would look as follows:

```
struct Rectangle {
  int height, width;
  Rectangle() {
    height = 0;
    width = 0;
  }
};
```

> **Note**
>
> When the only operation the constructor does is initialize the data members, opt for using the initialization list, which we will show you later in this chapter.

In addition to assigning values to data members, a constructor can also execute code, similar to a normal function body. This is important for the concept of the *class invariant*.

A key advantage of hiding the implementation of a class in *private* members and only exposing *public* methods to interact with the concept represented by the class is the ability to enforce a class invariant.

A class invariant is a property or a set of properties of a class that should be **true** for any given instance of the class, at any point. It is called **invariant** because the set of properties do not vary; they are always **true**.

Let's look at an example of a class that requires a class invariant. Imagine that we want to create a class that represents a date. The date would contain a year, month, and day, all represented as integers.

Implement it as a **struct** with all the fields as **public**. Refer to the following code:

```
struct Date {
    int day;
    int month;
    int year;
};
```

Now, the user could easily do the following:

```
Date date;
date.month = 153;
```

The previous code does not make any sense, as there are only 12 months in the Gregorian calendar.

A class invariant for the date would be that the month is always between 1 and 12, and that the day is always between 1 and 31, and depending on the month, even less.

Independently of any change the user performs on the **Date** object, the invariant must always hold.

A class can hide the detail that the date is stored as three integers and expose the functions to interact with the **Date** object. Functions can expect to find the dates to always be in a valid state (the invariant is satisfied at the start of the function), and they need to make sure to leave the class in a valid state (the invariant is satisfied at the end of the function).

The constructor does not only initialize the data members but also ensure that the class respects the invariant. After the constructor is executed, the invariant must be **true**.

> **Note**
>
> The concept of an invariant is not specific to the C++ language, and there is no dedicated facility to specify the invariant of a class. A best practice is to document the expected invariant of the class together with the class code so that the developers working with the class can easily check what the expected invariant is and make sure they respect it.

Using assertions in code also helps in identifying when the invariant is not respected. This probably means there is a bug in the code.

Overloading Constructor

Similar to other functions, we can overload the constructor by accepting different parameters. This is useful when an object can be created in several ways, since the user can create the object by providing the expected parameter, and the correct constructor is going to be called.

We showed an example of a default constructor for the **Rectangle** class earlier in this chapter. If we want to add a constructor that creates a rectangle from a square, we could add the following constructor to the **Rectangle** class:

```
class Rectangle {
  public:
    Rectangle(); // as before
    Rectangle (Square square);
};
```

The second constructor is an overloaded constructor and will be invoked according to the way the class object is initialized.

In the following example, the first line will call the constructor with empty parameters, while the second line will call the overloaded constructor:

```
Rectangle obj; // Calls the first constructor
Rectangle obj(square); // Calls the second overloaded constructor
```

> **Note**
>
> A constructor with a single non-default parameter is also called a **converting constructor**. This kind of constructor specifies an implicit conversion, from the type of the argument to the class type.

The following conversion is possible according to the previous definitions:

```
Square square;
Rectangle rectangle(square);
```

The constructor is initialized, and it converts from type **Square** to **Rectangle**.

Similarly, the compiler can create implicit conversions when calling functions, as shown in the following example:

```
void use_rectangle(Rectangle rectangle);


int main() {
  Square square;
  use_rectangle(square);
}
```

When calling **use_rectangle**, the compiler creates a new object of type **Rectangle** by calling the conversion constructor, which accepts a **Square**.

One way to avoid this is to use the **explicit** specifier before the constructor definition:

```
explicit class_name(type arg) {}
```

Let's look at a different implementation of **Rectangle**, which has an explicit constructor:

```
class ExplicitRectangle {
  public:
    explicit ExplicitRectangle(Square square);
};
```

When we use try to use **Square** to call a function that takes **ExplicitRectangle**, we get an error:

```
void use_explicit_rectangle(ExplicitRectangle rectangle);


int main() {
    Square square;
    use_explicit_rectangle(square); // Error!
}
```

Constructor Member Initialization

Constructors, as we've seen already, are used to initialize members. Up until now, we have initialized the members inside the body of the function by assigning values to members directly. C++ provides a feature to initialize the values of fields of the class in a more ergonomic way: initialization lists. Initialization lists allow you to call the constructor of the data members of class before the constructor body is executed. To write an initializer list, insert a colon (:) and a comma-separated list of initializations for class members before the constructor's body.

Let's look at the following example:

```
class Rectangle {
  public:
    Rectangle(): width(0), height(0) { } //Empty function body, as the
variables have already been initialized
  private:
    int width;
    int height;
};
```

Note how, in this last case, the constructor does nothing other than initialize its members. Hence, it has an empty function body.

Now, if we try to print the width and the height of the **Rectangle** object, we will notice that they are correctly initialized to **0**:

```
Rectangle rectangle;
std::cout << "Width: " << rectangle.width << std::endl;  // 0
std::cout << "Height: " << rectangle.height << std::endl; // 0
```

Initializer lists are the recommended way to initialize member variables in C++, and they are necessary when a data member is **const**.

When using an initializer list, the order in which the members are constructed is the one in which they are declared inside the class; not the one in which they appear in the initializer list. Let's look at the following example:

```
class Example {
    Example() : second(0), first(0) {}
    int first;
    int second;
};
```

When calling the default constructor of the **Example** class, the **first** method will be initialized first, and the **second** method after it, even if they appear in a different order in the initializer list.

> **Note**
>
> You should always write the members in the initializer list in the same order as they are declared; compilers will help you by warning you when the order differs from the expected one.

Aggregate Classes Initialization

Classes or structs with no user-declared constructors, no private or protected specifiers non-static data members, no base classes, and no virtual functions are considered aggregate.

> **Note**
>
> We will talk about base classes and virtual functions in chapter 6.

These types of classes can be initialized, even though they do not have a constructor, by using a brace-enclosed comma-separated list of initializer-clauses, as shown here:

```
struct Rectangle {
    int length;
    int width;
};


Rectangle rectangle = {10, 15};


std::cout << rectangle.length << "," << rectangle.width;
// Prints: 10, 15
```

Destructors

A *destructor* function is called automatically when the object goes out of scope and is used to destroy objects of its class type.

Destructors have the same name as the class preceded by a tilde (~) and do not take any argument nor return any value (not even void). Let's examine the following example:

```
class class_name {
    public:
        class_name() {} // constructor
        ~class_name() {} // destructor
};
```

After executing the body of the destructor and destroying any automatic objects allocated within the body, a destructor for a class calls the destructors for all the direct members of the class. Data members are destroyed in reverse order of their construction.

Exercise 9: Creating a Simple Coordinate Program to Demonstrate the Use of Constructors and Destructors

Let's write a simple program to demonstrate the use of constructors and destructors:

1. First, include the required header files.

2. Now, add the following code to the **Coordinates** class:

```cpp
class Coordinates {
    public:
    Coordinates(){
        std::cout << "Constructor called!" << std::endl;
    }

    ~Coordinates(){
        std::cout << "Destructor called!" << std::endl;
    }

};
```

3. In the **main** function, add the following code:

```cpp
int main()
{

    Coordinates c;
    // Constructor called!
    // Destructor called!

}
```

The output is as follows:

```
Constructor called!
Destructor called!
```

Default Constructor and Destructor

All the classes needs constructor and destructor functions. When the programmer does not define these, the compiler automatically creates an implicitly defined constructor and destructor.

> **Note**
>
> The default constructor might not initialize data members. Classes that have members of a built-in or compound type should ordinarily either initialize those members inside the class or define their version of the default constructor.

Activity 8: Representing Positions in a 2D Map

Alice is building a program to show 2D maps of the world. Users need to be able to save locations, such as their house, a restaurant, or their workplace. To enable this functionality, Alice needs to be able to represent a position in the world.

Create a class named **Coordinates** whose data members are the 2D coordinates of a point. To ensure that the object is always properly initialized, implement a constructor to initialize the data members of the class.

Let's perform the following steps:

1. The first step is to create a class named **Coordinates** containing the coordinates as data members.

2. Now, there are two floating-point values, **_latitude** and **_longitude**, which identify the coordinates on a geographic coordinate system. Additionally, these data members are defined with the **private** access specifier.

3. Extend the class with a **public** constructor that takes two arguments, **latitude** and **longitude**, which are used to initialize the data members of the class.

4. Alice can now use this **Coordinates** class to represent 2D positions on the map.

> **Note**
>
> The solution for this activity can be found on page 289.

Resource Acquisition Is Initialization

Resource Acquisition Is Initialization, or just **RAII**, is a programming idiom that is used to manage the life cycle of a resource automatically by binding it to the lifetime of an object.

Through the smart use of the constructor and destructor of an object, you can achieve RAII. The former acquires the resource, while the latter takes care of realizing it. The constructor is allowed to throw an exception, when a resource cannot be acquired, while the destructor must never throw exceptions.

Typically, it is a good practice to operate on a resource via an instance of a RAII class when its usage involves **open()/close()**, **lock()/unlock()**, **start()/stop()**, **init()/ destroy()**, or similar function calls.

The following is a way to open and close a file using an RAII-style mechanism.

> **Note**
>
> C++, like many languages, represents input/output operations as streams, where data can be written to or read from.

The constructor of the class opens the file into a provided stream, while the destructor closes it:

```
class file_handle {
  public:
    file_handle(ofstream& stream, const char* filepath) : _stream(stream) {
      _stream.open(filepath);
    }

    ~file_handle {
      _stream.close();
```

```
    }
  private:
    ofstream& _stream;
};
```

To open the file, it is sufficient to provide the file path to the **file_handle** class. Then, for the entire lifetime of the **file_handle** object, the file will not be closed. Once the object reaches the end of the scope, the file is closed:

```
ofstream stream;
{
  file_handle myfile(stream, "Some path"); // file is opened
  do_something_with_file(stream);
}                                           // file is closed here
```

This is used instead of the following code:

```
ofstream stream;
{
  stream.open("Some path");    // file is opened
  do_something_with_file(stream);
  stream.close();              // file is closed here
}
```

Even though the benefit provided by applying the RAII idiom seems to be just to reduce code, the real improvement is having safer code. It is common for a programmer to write a function that correctly opens a file but never closes it or allocates memory that never gets destroyed.

RAII makes sure that these operations cannot be forgotten, as it automatically handles them.

Activity 9: Storing Multiple Coordinates of Different Positions on a Map

In the 2D map program, the user can save multiple positions on the map. We need to be able to store multiple coordinates to keep track of the positions saved by the user. To do so, we need a way to create an array that can store them:

1. Using the RAII programming idiom, write a class that manages memory allocation and the deletion of an array of values . The class has an array of integers as member data, which will be used to store the values .

2. The constructor takes the size of the array as a parameter.

3. The constructor also takes care of allocating memory, which is used to store the coordinates.

4. To allocate the memory use the function **allocate_memory** (number of elements) which returns a pointer to an array of Coordinates of the requested size.
    To release the memory, call **release_memory** (array) which takes an array of Coordinates and releases the memory.

5. Finally, define a destructor and make sure to free the previously allocated array in its implementation:

> ### Note
>
> The solution for this activity can be found on page 290.

Nested Class Declarations

Inside the scope of a class, we can declare more than just data members and member functions; we can declare a class inside another class. These classes are called **nested classes**.

Since a nested class declaration happens inside the *outer class*, it has access to all the declared names as if it were part of the outer class: it can access even **private declarations**.

On the other hand, a nested class is not associated with any instance, so it can only access *static members*.

To access a nested class, we can use the double colon (::), similar to accessing static members of the outer class. Let's examine the following example:

```
// Declaration
class Coordinate {

...

  struct CoordinateDistance {
    float x = 0;
    float y = 0;
    static float walkingDistance(CoordinateDistance distance);
  }
};
// Create an instance of the nested class CoordinateDistance
Coordinate::CoordinateDistance distance;


/* Invoke the static method walkingDistance declared inside the nested class
CoordinateDistance */
Coordinate::CoordinateDistance::walkingDistance(distance);
```

Nested classes are useful for two main reasons:

- When implementing a class, we need an object that manages some of the logic of the class. In such cases, the nested class is usually **private**, and is not exposed through the **public interface** of the class. It is mostly used to ease the implementation of the class.

- When designing the functionality of a class, we want to provide a different class, closely related to the original one, which provides part of that functionality. In that case, the class is accessible by the users of the class and is usually an important part of the interaction with the class.

Imagine a list – a sequence of objects. We would like the user to be able to iterate over the items contained in the list. To do so, we need to keep track of which items the user has already iterated over and which are remaining. This is typically done with an **iterator**, which is a *nested class*. The iterator is an integral part of interacting with the **List** class.

We will look at iterators more in detail in *Lesson 5*, *Standard Library Containers and Algorithms*.

Friend Specifier

As we have already seen, private and protected members of a class are not accessible from within other functions and classes. A class can declare another function or class as a friend: this function or class will have access to the private and protected members of the class which declares the **friend relationship**.

The user has to specify the **friend** declaration within the body of the class.

Friend Functions

Friend functions are non-member functions that are entitled to access the private and protected members of a class. The way to declare a function as a **friend** function is by adding its declaration within the class and preceding it by the **friend** keyword. Let's examine the following code:

```
class class_name {
    type_1 member_1;
    type_2 member_2;

    public:
        friend void print(const class_name &obj);
};


friend void print(const class_name &obj){
    std::cout << obj.member_1 << " " << member_2 << std::endl;
}
```

In the previous example, the function declared outside of the class scope has the right to access the class data members because it is declared as a **friend** function.

Friend Classes

Similarly, like a **friend** function, a class can also be made a friend of another class by using the **friend** keyword.

Declaring a class as a **friend** is like declaring all of its methods as friend functions.

> **Note**
>
> Friendship is not mutual. If a class is a friend of another, then the opposite is not automatically true.

The following code demonstrates the concept of how friendship is not mutual:

```
class A {
    friend class B;
    int a = 0;
};

class B {
    friend class C;
    int b = 0;
};

class C {
    int c = 0;

    void access_a(const A& object) {
        object.a;
        // Error! A.a is private, and C is not a friend of A.
    }
};
```

Friendship is not transitive; so, in the previous example, class C is not a friend of class A, and the methods of class C cannot access the protected or private members of class A. Additionally, A cannot access B's private members, since B is a friend of A, but friendship is not mutual.

Exercise 10: Creating a Program to Print the User's Height

Let's write a program that collects height input from the user in inches and, after performing a calculation, prints the height of the user in feet:

1. First, let's add all the required header files to the program.

2. Now, create the **Height** class with one **public** method, as illustrated:

    ```
    class Height {
        double inches;
        public:
            Height(double value): inches(value) { }
            friend void print_feet(Height);
    };
    ```

3. As you can see, in the previous code, we used a friend function named **print_feet**. Now, let's declare it:

    ```
    void print_feet(Height h){
        std::cout << "Your height in inches is: " << h.inches<< std::endl;
        std::cout << "Your height in feet is: " << h.inches * 0.083 <<
        std::endl;
    }
    ```

4. Invoke the class in the **main** function, as shown here:

    ```
    int main(){
        IHeight h(83);
        print_feet(h);
    }
    ```

    The output is as follows:

    ```
    Your height in inches is: 83
    Your height in feet is: 6.889
    ```

Activity 10: The AppleTree Class, which Creates an Apple Instance

Sometimes, we would like to prevent the creation of an object of a specific type except for a limited number of classes. This usually happens when the classes are strictly related.

Create an **Apple** class that does not provide a **public** constructor and an **AppleTree** class that is in charge of creating the former object.

Let's execute the following steps:

1. First, we need to create a class with a **private** constructor. In this way, the object cannot be constructed, because the constructor is not publicly accessible:

```
class Apple
{
  private:
    Apple() {}
    // do nothing
};
```

2. The **AppleTree** class is defined and contains a method called **createFruit**, which is in charge of creating an **Apple** and returning it:

```
class AppleTree
{
  public:
    Apple createApple(){
      Apple apple;
      return apple;
    }
};
```

3. If we compile this code, we will get an error. At this point, the **Apple** constructor is **private**, so the **AppleTree** class cannot access it. We need to declare the **AppleTree** class as a **friend** of **Apple** to allow **AppleTree** to access the private methods of **Apple**:

```
class Apple
{
  friend class AppleTree;
  private:
    Apple() {}
    // do nothing
}
```

4. The **Apple** object can now be constructed using the following code:

```
AppleTree tree;
Apple apple = tree.createFruit();
```

> **Note**
>
> The solution for this activity can be found on page 291.

Copy Constructors and Assignment Operators

One special type of constructor is the **copy constructor**. It initializes the data members of one object to another object. The object that's used to copy the member's value is passed as an argument to the copy constructor, typically of *type reference* to the class itself, and possibly **const** qualified.

The following code refers to a class with a user-defined copy constructor, which copies the data member of the other object into the current one:

```
class class_name {

  public:

    class_name(const class_name& other) : member(other.member){}


  private:

    type member;

};
```

A copy constructor is declared *implicitly* by the compiler when the class definition does not explicitly declare a copy constructor and all the data members have a copy constructor. This implicit copy constructor performs a copy of the class members in the *same order* of initialization.

Let's look at an example:

```
struct A {
  A() {}
  A(const A& a) {
    std::cout << "Copy construct A" << std::endl;
  }
};

struct B {
  B() {}
  B(const B& a) {
    std::cout << "Copy construct B" << std::endl;
  }
};

class C {
  A a;
  B b;
  // The copy constructor is implicitly generated
};

int main() {
  C first;
  C second(first);
  // Prints: "Copy construct A", "Copy construct B"
}
```

When **C** is copy constructed, the members are copied in order: first, **a** is copied and then **b** is copied. To copy **A** and **B**, the compiler calls the copy constructor defined in those classes.

> **Note**
>
> When a pointer is copied, we are not copying the object pointed to, but simply the address at which the object is located.
>
> This means that when a class contains a **pointer** as a data member, the implicit copy constructor only copies the pointer and not the pointed object, so the copied object and the original one will share the object that's pointed to by the pointer. This is sometimes called a **shallow copy**.

The copy Assignment Operator

An alternative way to copy an object is by using the **copy assignment operator**, which, contrary to the construct operator, is called when the object has been already initialized.

The assignment operator signature and implementation look quite similar to the copy constructor, with the only difference being that the former is an overload of the = operator and it generally returns a reference to ***this**, although it's not required.

Here's an example of the use of the copy assignment operator:

```
class class_name {
  public:
    class_name& operator= (const class_name & other) {
      member = other.member;
    }

  private:
    type member;
};
```

Also, for the copy assignment operator, the compiler generates an *implicit* one when it is not explicitly declared. As for the copy constructor, the members are copied in the same order of initialization.

In the following example, the copy constructor and the copy assignment operator will output a sentence when they are called:

```
class class_name {

  public:

    class_name(const class_name& other) : member(other.member){

      std::cout << "Copy constructor called!" << std::endl;

    }


    class_name& operator= (const class_name & other) {

      member = other.member;

      std::cout << "Copy assignment operator called!" << std::endl;

    }


  private:

    type member;

};
```

The following code shows two ways of copying an object. The former uses the copy constructor, while the latter uses the copy assignment operator. The two implementations will print a sentence when they are called:

```
class_name obj;


class_name other_obj1(obj);

\\ prints "Copy constructor called!"


class_name other_obj2 = obj;

\\ prints "Copy assignment operator called!"
```

The move-constructor and move-assignment Operator

Like copying, moving also allows you to set the data members of an object to be equal to those of another data member. The only difference with copying lies in the fact that the content is transferred from one object to another, removing it from the source.

The move-constructor and move-assignment are members that take a parameter of type **rvalue** reference to the **class** itself:

```
class_name (class_name && other);

// move-constructor


class_name& operator= (class_name && other);

// move-assignment
```

> **Note**
>
> For clarity, we can briefly describe an **rvalue** reference (formed by placing an **&&** operator after the type of the function argument) as a value that does not have a memory address and does not persist beyond a single expression, for example, a **temporary object**.

A move constructor and a move assignment operator enable the resources owned by an **rvalue** object to be moved into an **lvalue** without copying.

When we move a construct or assign a source object to a destination object, we transfer the content of the source object into the destination object, but the source object needs to remain valid. To do so, when implementing such methods, it is fundamental to reset the data members of the source object to a valid value. This is necessary to prevent the destructor from freeing the resources (such as memory) of the class multiple times.

Let's assume that there is a **Resource** that can be acquired, released, reset, and checked if it's reset.

Here is an example of a **WrongMove** constructor:

```
class WrongMove {
  public:
    WrongMove() : _resource(acquire_resource()) {}


    WrongMove(WrongMove&& other) {
      _resource = other._resource;
```

```
      // Wrong: we never reset other._resource
   }


   ~WrongMove() {
     if (not is_reset_resource(_resource)) {
       release_resource(_resource);
     }
   }


 private:
   Resource _resource;
}
```

The move-constructor of the **WrongMove** class will release the resource twice:

```
{
  WrongMove first;
  // Acquires the resource
  {
  /* Call the move constructor: we copy the resource to second, but we are
not resetting it in first */
    WrongMove second(std::move(first));
  }
  /* Second is destroyed: second._resource is released here. Since we copied
the resource, now first._resource has been released as well. */
}
// First is destroyed: the same resource is released again! Error!
```

Instead, the move constructor should have reset the **_resource** member of other, so that the destructor would not call **release_resource** again:

```
WrongMove(WrongMove&& other) {
  _resource = other._resource;
  other._resource = resetted_resource();
}
```

The move constructor and move assignment operator can be implicitly generated by the compiler if no user-defined ones are provided and there are no user-declared destructors, copy constructors, or copy or move assignment operators:

```
struct MovableClass {

  MovableClass(MovableClass&& other) {

    std::cout << "Move construct" << std::endl;

  }


  MovableClass& operator=(MovableClass&& other) {

    std::cout << "Move assign" << std::endl;

  }
};


MovableClass first;
// Move construct
MovableClass second = std::move(first);
// Or: MovableClass second(std::move(first));
MovableClass third;
// Move assignment
second = std::move(third);
```

Preventing Implicit Constructors and Assignment Operators

The compiler will implicitly generate the copy constructor, copy assignment, move constructor, and move assignment if our class respects all the required conditions.

For cases in which our class should not be copied or moved, we can prevent that.

To prevent the generation of implicit constructors and operators, we can write the declaration of the constructor or operator and add **= delete**; at the end of the declaration.

Let's examine the following example:

```
class Rectangle {
  int length;
  int width;

  // Prevent generating the implicit move constructor
  Rectangle(Rectangle&& other) = delete;

  // Prevent generating the implicit move assignment
  Rectangle& operator=(Rectangle&& other) = delete;
};
```

Operator Overloading

C++ classes represent user-defined types. So, the need arises to be able to operate with these types in a different way. Some operator functions may have a different meaning when operating on different types. **Operator overloading** lets you define the meaning of an operator when applied to a class type object.

For example, the + operator applied to numerical types is different than when it is applied to the following **Point** class, which is constituted of coordinates. The language cannot specify what the + operator should do for user-defined types such as **Point**, as it is not in control of such types and does not know what the expected behavior is. Because of that, the language does not define the operators for user-defined types.

However, C++ allows the user to specify the behavior of most operators for user-defined types, including classes.

Here is an example of the + operator, defined for the **Point** class:

```
class Point
{
  Point operator+(const Point &other)
  {
    Point new_point;
    new_point.x = x + other.x;
    new_point.y = y + other.y;
    return new_point;
```

```
    }
  private:
      int x;
      int y;
  }
```

Here is a list of all the operators that can and cannot be overloaded:

- The following are the operators that can be overloaded:

+	-	*	/	%	^
+=	-=	*=	/=	%=	^=
<	>	<=	>=	++	--
<<	>>	==	!=	&&	||
&=	|=	<<=	>>=	[]	()
,	=	&	!	|	~
->*	->	new	delete	new[]	delete[]

Figure 3.4: Operators that can be overloaded

- The following are the operators that cannot be overloaded:

::	.*	.	?:

Figure 3.5: Operators that cannot be overloaded

Operators that expect two operands are called **binary operators**. Examples are +, -, *, and /.

A method overloading a binary operator needs to accept a single parameter. When the compiler encounters the use of the operator, it will call the method on the variable on the left-hand side of the operator, while the variable on the right-hand side will be passed as parameter to the method.

We saw in the previous example that **Point** defines the + operator, which takes a parameter. When using the addition operation on a **Point**, the code would look like this:

```
Point first;
Point second;
Point sum = first + second;
```

The last line from the code example is equivalent to writing the following:

```
Point sum = first.operator+(second);
```

The compiler automatically rewrites the first expression to the second one.

Operators that expect only one operand are called **<u>unary operators</u>**. Examples are --, ++, and !.

A method overloading a unary operator must not accept any parameters. When the compiler encounters the use of the operator, it will call the method on the variable to which the operator is assigned.

As an example, let's say we are given an object that's defined as follows:

```
class ClassOverloadingNotOperator {
  public:
    bool condition = false;

    ClassOverloadingNotOperator& operator!() {
      condition = !condition;
    }
};
```

We would write the following:

```
ClassOverloadingNotOperator object;
!object;
```

The code is therefore rewritten as follows:

```
ClassOverloadingNotOperator object;

object.operator!();
```

> **Note**
>
> Operator overloading is possible in two ways: either as a member function or as a non-member function. The two end up producing the same effect.

Activity 11: Ordering Point Objects

In the 2D map application, we want to be able to display the locations that have been saved by the user in order: from South-West to North-East. To be able to show the locations in order, we need to be able to sort the location points representing the locations in such an order.

Remember that the **x** coordinate represents the location along the West-East axis and the **y** coordinate represents the location along the North-South axis.

In a real-life scenario, to compare two points, we need to compare their **x** and **y** coordinates. To do so in code, we need to overload the **<** operator for the **Point** class. This new function we're defining returns a **bool**, either **true** or **false**, according to the order of **p_1** and **p_2**.

The **p_1** point comes before than **p_2** in the order if the **x** coordinate of **p_1** is less than the **x** coordinate of **p_2**. If they are equal, then we need to compare their **y** coordinates.

Let's perform the following steps:

1. We need to add an overload for the **<** operator to the **Point** class that we previously defined, which takes another object of type **Point** as an argument and returns a **bool** indicating whether the object is less than the one provided as a parameter, using the previous definition for how to compare two points:

2. At this point, we are able to compare two **Point** objects:

3. Since, in our example, **p_1.x** is initialized to **1** and **p_2.x** to **2**, the result of the comparison will be **true**, which indicates that **p_1** comes earlier than **p_2** in the order.

> **Note**
>
> The solution for this activity can be found on page 293.

Introducing Functors

A **Functor** (function object) is similar to a class. The class that overloads the `operator()` function is also known as the **function call operator**.

The syntax that's used to define a **functor** is as follows:

```
class class_name {
  public:
    type operator()(type arg) {}
};
```

The function call operator has a return type and takes any number of arguments of any type. To invoke the call operator of an object, we can write the name of the object, followed by parentheses containing the arguments to pass to the operator. You can imagine that an object that provides a call operator can be used in the same way as you would use a function. Here's an example of a **functor**:

```
class_name obj;

type t;

/* obj is an instance of a class with the call operator: it can be used as
if it was a function */

obj(t);
```

They are particularly useful in places where you can pass a function object to an algorithmic template that accepts an object with `operator()` defined. This exploits code reusability and testability. We will see more on this in chapter 5 when we talk about **lambda**.

The following is a simple example of a **functor** that prints a string before appending a new line at the end of it:

```
class logger{
  public:
    void operator()(const std::string &s) {
      std::cout << s << std::endl;
    }
};


logger log;
log ("Hello world!");
log("Keep learning C++");
```

Activity 12: Implementing Functors

Write a function object that takes a number when constructed and defines an operator call that takes another number and returns the sum of the two.

Let's perform the following steps to achieve the desired output:

1. Define a class by the name of **AddX**, constituted by a **private** data member of type **int**, and a constructor that is used to initialize it.

2. Extend it with the call operator, **operator()**, which takes an **int** as a parameter and returns an **int**. The implementation in the function body should return the addition of the previously defined **x** value and the parameter of the function named **y**.

3. Instantiate an object of the class we just defined and invoke the calling operator:

```
class AddX {
  public:
    explicit AddX(int v) : value(v) {}
    int operator()(int other_value) {
Indent it to the right, same as above
}
```

```
    private:
        int value;
};

AddX add_five(5);
std::cout << add_five(4) << std::endl; // prints 9
```

> **Note**
>
> The solution for this activity can be found on page 294.

Summary

In this chapter, we saw how the concept of classes can be used in C++. We started by delineating the advantages of using classes, describing how they can help us to create powerful abstractions.

We outlined the access modifiers a class can use to control who has access to class fields and methods.

We continued by exploring the conceptual differences between a class and its instances, along with the implications this has when implementing static fields and static methods.

We saw how constructors are used to initialize classes and their members, while destructors are used to clean up the resources that are managed by a class.

We then explored how constructors and destructors can be combined to implement the fundamental paradigm C++ is famous for: RAII. We showed how RAII makes it easy to create classes that handle resources and make programs safer and easier to work with.

Finally, we introduced the concept of operator overloading and how it can be used to create classes that are as easy to use as built-in types.

In the next chapter, we'll focus on templates. We'll primarily look at how to implement template functions and classes, and write code that works for multiple types.

Generic Programming and Templates

Lesson Objectives

By the end of this chapter, you will be able to:

- Understand how templates work and when to use them
- Identify and implement templated functions
- Implement template classes
- Write code that works for multiple types

In this chapter, you will learn how to use templates effectively in your program.

Introduction

When programming, it is common to face problems that are recurring for different types of objects, such as storing a list of objects, or searching elements in a list, or finding the maximum between two elements.

Let's say that in our program we want to be able to find the maximum between two elements, either integers or doubles. With the features we have learned so far, we could write the following code:

```
int max(int a, int b) {
  if ( a > b) return a;
  else return b;
}


double max(double a, double b) {
  if ( a> b) return a;
  else return b;
}
```

In the previous code, the two functions are identical except for the *types* of the parameters and the *return type*. Ideally, we would like to write these kind of operations only once and reuse them in the entire program.

Moreover, our **max()** function can only be called with types for which an overload exists: **int** and **double** in this case. If we wanted it to work with any numerical type, we would need to write an **overload** for each of the numerical types: we would need to know in advance about all the types that will be used to call it, especially when the function is part of a library that is intended to be used by other developers, as it becomes impossible for us to know the types that will be used when calling the function.

We can see that there is nothing specific to integers being required to find the maximum elements; if the elements implement **operator<**, then it is possible to find the greater of the two numbers, and the algorithm does not change. In these situations, C++ offers an effective tool–**templates**.

Templates

Templates are a way to define functions or classes that can work for many different types, while still writing them only once.

They do so by having special kinds of parameters—**type parameters**.

When writing the template code, we can use this type parameter as if it were a real type, such as **int** or **string**.

When the templated function is called or the template class is instantiated, the type parameter is substituted with the real type that's used by the calling code.

Now let's look at an example of a template in C++ code:

```
template<typename T>
T max(T a, T b) {
  if(a>b) {
    return a;
  } else {
    return b;
  }
}
```

A template always starts with the **template** keyword, followed by the list of template parameters enclosed in *angle* brackets.

A template parameter list is a list of comma-separated parameters. In this case, we only have one—**typename T**.

The **typename** keyword tells the template that we are writing a templated function that uses a generic type, which we are going to name **T**.

> **Note**
>
> You can also use the **class** keyword in place of **typename**, since there is no difference between them.

Then, the definition of the function follows. In the function definition, we can use the name **T** when we want to refer to the generic type.

To call the template, we specify the name of the template, followed by the list of types we want to use as *type arguments*, enclosed in angle brackets:

```
max<int>(10, 15);
```

This calls the templated function **max**, specifying **int** as the type parameter. We say that we instantiated the templated function **max** with type **int**, and then called that instance.

We do not always need to specify the type parameters of a template; the compiler can deduce them from the calling code. A later section will describe this feature.

Because of how powerful templates are, the big part of the C++ standard library is based on templates, as we will see in *Chapter 5, Standard Library Containers and Algorithms*.

Now we'll explore in depth what happens when we compile the code that contains templates.

Compiling the Template Code

Similar to functions and classes, a template needs to be *declared* before being used.

When the compiler first encounters a template definition in the program, it parses it and performs only *part* of the checks it usually does on the rest of the code.

This happens because the compiler does not know which type is going to be used with the template when it parses it, since the types are parameters themselves. This prevents the compiler from performing checks that involve the parameter types, or anything that depends on them.

Because of this, you get notified of some errors in the template only when you instantiate it.

Once we define a template, we can instantiate it in our code.

When a template is instantiated, the compiler looks at the definition of the template and uses it to generate a new instance of the code, where all the references to the type parameters are replaced by the types that are provided when instantiating it.

For example: when we call **max<int>(1,2)**, the compiler looks at the template definition we specified earlier and generates code as if we wrote the following:

```
int max(int a, int b) {
  if(a>b) {
    return a;
  } else {
    return b;
  }
}
```

> **Note**
>
> Since the compiler generates the code from the template definition, it means that the full definitions need to be visible to the calling code, not only the declaration, as was the case for functions and classes.

The template can still be forward declared, but the compiler must also see the definition. Because of this, when writing templates that should be accessed by several files, both the definition and the declaration of the templates must be in the **header** file.

This restriction does not apply if the template is used only in one file.

Exercise 11: Finding the Bank Account of the User with the Highest Balance

Write a template function that accepts details of two bank accounts (of the same type) and returns the balance of the bank account with the highest balance.

For this exercise, perform the following steps:

1. Let's create two structs named **EUBankAccount** and **UKBankAccount** to represent the **European Union** bank account and the **United Kingdom** bank account with the required basic information, as shown in the following code:

    ```
    #include <string>
    struct EUBankAccount {
        std::string IBAN;
        int amount;
    };
    ```

```
struct UKBankAccount {
    std::string sortNumber;
    std::string accountNumber;
    int amount;
};
```

2. The template function will have to compare the amount of the bank accounts. We want to work with different bank account types, so we need to use a template:

```
template<typename BankAccount>
int getMaxAmount(const BankAccount& acc1, const BankAccount& acc2) {
    // All bank accounts have an 'amount' field, so we can access it safely
    if (acc1.amount > acc2.amount) {
        return acc1.amount;
    } else {
        return acc2.amount;
    }
}
```

3. Now, in the **main** function, call both the structs and the template function, as shown here:

```
int main() {
    EUBankAccount euAccount1{"IBAN1", 1000};
    EUBankAccount euAccount2{"IBAN2", 2000};
    std::cout << "The greater amount between EU accounts is " <<
getMaxAmount(euAccount1, euAccount2) << std::endl;

    UKBankAccount ukAccount1{"SORT1", "ACCOUNT_NUM1", 2500};
    UKBankAccount ukAccount2{"SORT2", "ACCOUNT_NUM2", 1500};
    std::cout << "The greater amount between UK accounts is " <<
getMaxAmount(ukAccount1, ukAccount2) << std::endl;
}
```

The output is as follows:

```
The greater amount between EU accounts is 2000
The greater amount between UK accounts is 2500
```

Using Template Type Parameters

As we saw earlier, the compiler uses the template as a guide to generate a template instance with some concrete type when the template is used.

This means that we can use the type as a *concrete* type, including applying type modifiers to it.

We saw earlier, a type can be modified by making it constant with the **const** modifier, and we can also take a reference to an object of a specific type by using the *reference* modifier:

```
template<typename T>
T createFrom(const T& other) {
    return T(other);
}
```

Here, we can see a **template** function that creates a new object from a different instance of an object.

Since the function does not modify the original type, the function would like to accept it as a **const** reference.

Since we are declaring the type **T** in the template, in the function definition we can use the modifiers on the type to accept the parameter in the way we deem more appropriate.

Notice that we used the type two times: once with some modifiers and once with no modifiers.

This gives a lot of flexibility when using templates and writing functions, as we can liberally modify the type to suit our needs.

Similarly, we have a lot of freedom in where we can use the template arguments.

Let's see two templates with a multiple template type argument:

```
template<typename A, typename B>
A transform(const B& b) {
    return A(b);
}
```

```
template<typename A, typename B>
A createFrom() {
  B factory;
  return factory.getA();
}
```

We can see that we can use the template argument in the function parameter, in the return type, or instantiate it directly in the function body.

Also, the order in which the template arguments are declared does not impact where and how the template parameters can be used.

Requirements of Template Parameter Types

In the code snippet at the beginning of this chapter, we wrote some templates that accept any kind of type. In reality, our code does not work for any kind of type; for example: **max()** requires the types to support the < operation.

We can see that there were some requirements on the type.

Let's try to understand what having a requirement on a type means when using templates in C++ code. We will do so by using the following template code:

```
template<typename Container, typename User>
void populateAccountCollection (Container& container, const User& user) {
  container.push_back(user.getAccount());
}
```

We can then write the following function as main and compile the program:

```
int main() {
  // do nothing
}
```

When we compile this program, the compilation ends successfully without any error.

Let's say we change the **main** function to be the following:

```
int main() {
    std::string accounts;
    int user;
    populateAccountCollection(accounts, user);
}
```

> **Note**
>
> We did not specify the type to the template. We will see later in this chapter when the compiler can automatically deduce the types from the call.

The compiler will give us an error when we compile it:

```
error: request for member 'getAccount' in 'user', which is of non-class type
'const int'
```

Note how the error appeared when we used the template function, and that it was not detected before.

The error is telling us that we tried to call the **getAccount** method on an integer, which does not have such a method.

Why didn't the compiler tell us this when we were writing the template?

The reason for this is that the compiler does not know what type **User** will be; therefore, it cannot tell whether the **getAccount** method will exist or not.

When we tried to use the template, we tried to generate the code with two specific types, and the compiler checked that these two types were suitable for the template; they were not, and the compiler gave us an error.

The types we used were not satisfying the requirements of the template types.

Unfortunately, there is no easy way in the current C++ standard, even the most recent C++17, to specify the requirements of templates in the code—for that, we need good documentation.

The template has two type arguments, so we can look at the requirements for each type:

- **User requirements**: The `User` object must have a `getAccount` method
- **Container requirements**: The `Container` object must have a `push_back` method

The compiler finds the first problem when we call the `getAccount()` function and it notifies us.

To solve this issue, let's declare a suitable class, as shown here:

```cpp
struct Account {
  // Some fields
};
class User {
public:
  Account getAccount() const{
    return Account();
  }
};
```

Now, let's call the template with the help of the following code:

```cpp
int main() {
  std::string accounts;
  User user;
  populateAccountCollection(accounts, user);
}
```

We still get an error:

```
error: no matching function for call to 'std::__cxx11::basic_
string<char>::push_back(Account)'
```

This time, the error message is less clear, but the compiler is telling us that there is no method called **push_back** that accepts an account in **basic_string<char>** (`std::string` is an alias for it). The reason for this is that `std::string` has a method called **push_back**, but it only accepts characters. Since we are calling it with an **Account**, it fails.

We need to be more precise in the requirements for our template:

- **User requirements**: The user object must have a **getAccount** method that returns an object

- **Container requirements**: The container object must have a **push_back** method that accepts objects of the type returned by **getAccount** on the user

> **Note**
>
> The **std::vector** type in the C++ standard library allows to store sequences of elements of an arbitrary type. **push_back** is a method that's used for adding a new element at the end of the vector. We will see more about vectors in *Chapter 5, Standard Library Containers and Algorithms*.

We now change the calling code to consider all the requirements:

```
#include <vector>
int main(){
    std::vector<Account> accounts;
    User user;
    populateAccountCollection(accounts, user);
}
```

This time, the code compiles correctly!

This shows us how the compiler checks most of the errors, but only when we instantiate the template.

It is also very important to clearly document the requirements of the template so that the user does not have to read complicated error messages to understand which requirement is not respected.

> **Note**
>
> To make it easy to use our templates with many types, we should try to set the least requirements we can on the types.

Defining Function and Class Templates

In the previous section, we saw the advantages of templates in writing abstractions. In this section, we are going to explore how we can effectively use templates in our code to create **templated functions** and **templated classes**.

Function Template

In the previous section, we learned how function templates are written.

In this section, we will learn about the two features that were introduced by C++11 that make it easier to write template functions. These two functions are trailing return types and `decltype`.

Let's start with the `decltype`. The `decltype` is a keyword that accepts an expression and returns the type of that expression. Let's examine the following code:

```
int x;
decltype(x) y;
```

In the previous code, **y** is declared as an integer, because we are using the type of the expression **x**, which is **int**.

Any expression can be used inside `decltype`, even complex ones, for example:

```
User user;
decltype(user.getAccount()) account;
```

Let's look at the second feature—**trailing return types**.

We saw that a function definition starts with the return type, followed by the name of the function and then the parameters. For example:

```
int max(int a, int b);
```

Starting from C++11, it is possible to use a trailing return type: specifying the return type at the end of the function signature. The syntax to declare a function with a trailing return type is to use the keyword **auto**, followed by the name of the function and the parameters, and then by an *arrow* and the *return type*.

The following is an example of a trailing return type:

```
auto max(int a, int b) -> int;
```

This is not beneficial when writing regular functions, but it becomes useful when writing templates and when combined with `decltype`.

The reason for this is that **decltype** has access to the variables defined in the parameters of the function, and the return type can be computed from them:

```
template<typename User>
auto getAccount(User user) -> decltype(user.getAccount());
```

This is an example of a **forward declaration** of a function template.

> **Note**
>
> When the user wants to provide a definition, it needs to provide the same template declaration, followed by the body of the function.

Without the trailing return type, we would have to know what the type returned by **user.getAccount()** is to use it as the return type of the **getAccount()** function. The return type of **user.getAccount()** can be different depending on the type of the template parameter **User**, which in turn means that the return type of the **getAccount** function could change depending on the **User** type. With the trailing return type, we don't need to know what type is returned by **user.getAccount()**, as it is determined automatically. Even better, when different types are used in our function or a user changes the return type of the **getAccount** method in one of the types that's used to instantiate the template, our code will handle it automatically.

More recently, C++14 introduced the ability to simply specify **auto** in the function declaration, without the need for the trailing return type:

```
auto max(int a, int b)
```

The return type is automatically deduced by the compiler, and to do so, the compiler needs to see the definition of the function—we cannot forward declare functions that return **auto**.

Additionally, **auto** always returns a value—it never returns a reference: this is something to be aware of when using it, as we could unintentionally create copies of the returned value.

One last useful feature of function templates is how to reference them without calling them.

Up until now, we have only seen how to call the function templates, but C++ allows us to pass functions as parameters as well. For example: when sorting a container, a custom comparison function can be provided.

We know that a template is just a blueprint for a function, and the real function is going to be created only when the template is instantiated. C++ allows us to instantiate the template function even without calling it. We can do this by specifying the name of the template function, followed by the template parameters, without adding the parameters for the call.

Let's understand the following example:

```
template<typename T>
void sort(std::array<T, 5> array, bool (*function)(const T&, const T&));
```

The **sort** is a function that takes an array of five elements and a pointer to the function to compare two elements:

```
template<typename T>
bool less(const T& a, const T& b) {
   return a < b;
}
```

To call **sort** with an instance of the **less** template for integers, we would write the following code:

```
int main() {
   std::array<int, 5> array = {4,3,5,1,2};
   sort(array, &less<int>);
}
```

Here, we take a pointer to the instance of **less** for integers. This is particularly useful when using the Standard Template Library, which we will see in *Chapter 5, Standard Library Containers and Algorithms.*

Class Templates

In the previous section, we learned how to write template functions. The syntax for class templates is equivalent to the one for functions: first, there is the template declaration, followed by the declaration of the class:

```
template<typename T>
class MyArray {
   // As usual
};
```

And equivalently to functions, to instantiate a class template, we use the angle brackets containing a list of types:

```
MyArray<int> array;
```

Like functions, class template code gets generated when the template is instantiated, and the same restrictions apply: the definition needs to be available to the compiler and some of the error-checking is executed when the template is instantiated.

As we saw in *Lesson 3*, *Classes*, while writing the body of a class, the name of the class is sometimes used with a special meaning. For example, the name of the constructor functions must match the name of the class.

In the same way, when writing a class template, the name of the class can be used directly, and it will refer to the specific template instance being created:

```
template<typename T>

class MyArray {

    // There is no need to use MyArray<T> to refer to the class, MyArray
    automatically refers to the current template instantiation

    MyArray();
    // Define the constructor for the current template T


    MyArray<T>();
    // This is not a valid constructor.
};
```

This makes writing template classes a similar experience to writing regular classes, with the added benefit of being able to use the template parameters to make the class work with generic types.

Like regular classes, template classes can have fields and methods. The field can depend on the type declared by the template. Let's review the following code example:

```
template<typename T>

class MyArray {
    T[] internal_array;
};
```

Also when writing methods, the class can use the type parameter of the class:

```
template<typename T>
class MyArray {
  void push_back(const T& element);
};
```

Classes can also have templated methods. Templated methods are similar to template functions, but they can access the class instance data.

Let's review the following example:

```
template<typename T>
class MyArray {
  template<typename Comparator>
  void sort (const Comparator & element);
};
```

The **sort** method will accept any type and will compile if the type satisfies all the requirements that the method imposes on the type.

To call the method, the syntax follows the one for calling functions:

```
MyArray<int> array;
MyComparator comparator;
array.sort<MyComparator>(comparator);
```

> **Note**
>
> The method template can be part of a non-template class.

In these situations, the compiler can sometimes deduce the type of the parameter, where the user does not have to specify it.

If a method is only declared in the class, as we did in the example with **sort**, the user can later implement it by specifying the template types of both the class and the method:

```
template<typename T> // template of the class

template<typename Comparator> // template of the method

MyArray<T>::sort(const Comparator& element) {

  // implementation

}
```

The name of the types does not have to match, but it is a good practice to be consistent with the names.

Similar to methods, the class can also have templated overloaded operators. The approach is identical to writing the operator overloads for regular classes, with the difference that the declaration of a template must precede the overload declaration like we saw for method templates.

Finally, something to be aware of is how static methods and static fields interact with the class template.

We need to remember that the template is a guide on the code that will be generated for the specific types. This means that when a template class declares a static member, the member is shared only between the instantiations of the template with the same template parameters:

```
template<typename T>

class MyArray {

  const Static int element_size = sizeof(T);

};

MyArray<int> int_array1;

MyArray<int> int_array2;

MyArray<std::string> string_array;
```

int_array1 and **int_array2** will share the same static variable, **element_size**, since they are both of the same type: **MyArray<int>**. On the other hand, **string_array** has a different one, because its class type is **MyArray<std::string>**. **MyArray<int>** and **MyArray<std::string>**, even if generated from the same class template, are two different classes, and thus do not share static fields.

Dependent Types

It's fairly common, especially for code that interacts with templates, to define some public aliases to types.

A typical example would be the **value_type type alias** for containers, which specifies the type contained:

```
template<typename T>
class MyArray {
public:
  using value_type = T;
};
```

Why is this being done?

The reason for this is that if we are accepting a generic array as a template parameter, we might want to find out the contained type.

If we were accepting a specific type, this problem would not arise. Since we know the type of vector, we could write the following code:

```
void createOneAndAppend(std::vector<int>& container) {
  int new_element{}; // We know the vector contains int
  container.push_back(new_element);
}
```

But how can we do this when we accept any container that provides the **push_back** method?

```
template<typename Container>
void createOneAndAppend(Container& container) {
  // what type should new_element be?
  container.push_back(new_element);
}
```

We can access the **type alias** declared inside the container, which specifies which kind of values it contains, and we use it to instantiate a new value:

```
template<typename Container>
void createOneAndAppend(Container& container) {
  Container::value_type new_element;
  container.push_back(new_element);
}
```

This code, unfortunately, does not compile.

The reason for this is that **value_type** is a **dependent type**. A dependent type is a type that is derived from one of the template parameters.

When the compiler compiles this code, it notices that we are accessing the **value_type** identifier in the **Container** class.

That could either be a static field or a **type alias**. The compiler cannot know when it parses the template, since it does not know what the **Container** type will be and whether it has a **type alias** or a static variable. Therefore, it assumes we are accessing a static value. If this is the case, the syntax we are using is not valid, since we still have **new_element{}** after access to the field.

To solve this issue, we can tell the compiler that we are accessing a type in the class, and we do so by prepending the **typename** keyword to the type we are accessing:

```
template<typename Container>
void createOneAndAppend(Container& container) {
  typename Container::value_type new_element{};
  container.push_back(new_element);
}
```

Activity 13: Reading Objects from a Connection

The user is creating an online game which require to send and receive its current state over an internet connection. The application has several types of connections (TCP, UDP, socket) each of them has a **readNext()** method which returns an **std::array** of 100 chars containing the data inside the connection, and a **writeNext()** method which takes an **std::array** of 100 characters which puts data into the connection.

Let's follow these steps to create our online application:

1. The objects that the application wants to send and receive over the connection have a **serialize()** static method which takes an instance of the object and return an **std::array** of 100 characters representing the object.

```cpp
class UserAccount {
public:
    static std::array<char, 100> serialize(const UserAccount& account) {
        std::cout << "the user account has been serialized" << std::endl;
        return std::array<char, 100>();
    }

    static UserAccount deserialize(const std::array<char, 100>& blob) {
        std::cout << "the user account has been deserialized" <<
std::endl;
        return UserAccount();
    }
};

class TcpConnection {
public:
    std::array<char, 100> readNext() {
        std::cout << "the data has been read" << std::endl;
        return std::array<char, 100>{};
    }
    void writeNext(const std::array<char, 100>& blob) {
        std::cout << "the data has been written" << std::endl;
    }
};
```

2. The **deserialize()** static method takes an **std::array** of 100 characters representing the object, and creates an object from it.

3. The connection objects are already provided. Create the header **connection.h** with the following declarations:

```cpp
template<typename Object, typename Connection>
Object readObjectFromConnection(Connection& con) {
  std::array<char, 100> data = con.readNext();
  return Object::deserialize(data);
}
```

4. Write a function template called **readObjectFromConnection** that takes a connection as the only parameter and the type of the object to read from the connection as a template type parameter. The function returns an instance of the object constructed after deserializing the data in the connection.

5. Then, call the function with an instance of the **TcpConnection** class, extracting an object of type **UserAccount**:

```
TcpConnection connection;
UserAccount userAccount =
readObjectFromConnection<UserAccount>(connection);
```

The aim is to be able to send the information on the account of a user to the other users connected to the same online game, so that they can see the user information like their username and the level of their character.

> **Note**
>
> The solution for this activity can be found on page 295.

Activity 14: Creating a User Account to Support Multiple Currencies

Write a program that supports and stores multiple currencies. Follow these steps:

1. We want to create an **Account** class that stores the account balance in different currencies.

2. A **Currency** is a class that represents a certain value in a specific currency. It has a public field called **value** and a template function called **to()** that takes the argument as a **Currency** type and returns an instance of that currency with the value set to the appropriate conversion of the current value of the class:

```
struct Currency {
    static const int conversionRate = CurrencyConversion;
    int d_value;
    Currency(int value): d_value(value) {}
};

template<typename OtherCurrency, typename SourceCurrency>
OtherCurrency to(const SourceCurrency& source) {
    float baseValue = source.d_value / float(source.conversionRate);
    int otherCurrencyValue = int(baseValue *
OtherCurrency::conversionRate);
    return OtherCurrency(otherCurrencyValue);
```

```
      }

      using USD = Currency<100>;
      using EUR = Currency<87>;
      using GBP = Currency<78>;

      template<typename Currency>
      class UserAccount {
      public:
        Currency balance;
      };
```

3. Our aim is to write an **Account** class that stores the current balance in any currency provided by the **template** parameter.

4. The user account must provide a method called **addToBalance** that accepts any kind of currency, and after converting it to the correct currency that's used for the account, it should sum the value to the balance:

```
      template<typename OtherCurrency>
        void addToBalance(OtherCurrency& other) {
          balance.value += to<Currency>(other).value;
        }
```

5. The user now understands how to write class templates, how to instantiate them, and how to call their templates.

> **Note**
>
> The solution for this activity can be found on page 296.

Non-Type Template Parameters

We learned how templates allow you to provide the types as parameters and how we can make use of this to write generic code.

Templates in C++ have an additional feature—**non-type template parameters**.

A non-type template parameter is a template parameter that is not a type—it is a value.

We made use of such non-type template parameters many times when using `std::array<int, 10>;`.

Here, the second parameter is a non-type template parameter, which represents the size of the array.

The declaration of a non-type template parameter is in the parameter list of the template, but instead of starting with a **typename** keyword such as the type parameters, it starts with the type of the value, followed by the identifier.

There are strict restrictions on the types that are supported as non-type template parameters: they must be of integral type.

Let's examine the following example of the declaration of a non-type template parameter:

```
template<typename T, unsigned int size>
Array {
  // Implementation
};
```

For example: here, we declared a class template that takes a type parameter and a non-type parameter.

We already saw that functions can take parameters directly and classes can accept parameters in the constructor. Additionally, the type of regular parameters is not restricted to be an integral type.

What is the difference between template and non-template parameters? Why would we use a non-type template parameter instead of a regular parameter?

The main difference is when the parameter is known to the program. Like all the template parameters and unlike the non-template parameters, the value must be known at compile time.

This is useful when we want to use the parameters in expressions that need to be evaluated at compile time, as we do when declaring the size of an array.

The other advantage is that the compiler has access to the value when compiling the code, so it can perform some computations during compilation, reducing the amount of instruction to execute at runtime, thus making the program faster.

Additionally, knowing some values at compile time allows our program to perform additional checks so that we can identify problems when we compile the program instead of when the program is executed.

Activity 15: Writing a Matrix Class for Mathematical Operations in a Game

In a game, it is common to represent the orientation of a character in a special kind of matrix: a *quaternion*. We would like to write a **Matrix** class that will be the base of the mathematical operations inside our game.

Our **Matrix** class should be a template that accepts a type, a number of rows, and a number of columns.

We should store the elements of the matrix inside an **std::array**, stored inside the class.

The class should have a method called **get()** that takes a row and a column, and returns a reference to the element in that position.

If the row or column is outside of the matrix, we should call **std::abort()**.

Let's follow these steps:

1. The **Matrix** class takes three template parameters—one type and the two dimensions of the **Matrix** class. The dimensions are of type **int**.

```
template<typename T, int R, int C>
class Matrix {
    // We store row_1, row_2, ..., row_C
    std::array<T, R*C> data;
    public:
        Matrix() : data({}) {}
};
```

2. Now, create a **std::array** with a size of the number of rows times the number of columns so that we have enough space for all the elements of the matrix.

3. Add a constructor to initialize the array:

4. We add a **get()** method to the class to return a reference to the element **T**. The method needs to take the row and column we want to access.

5. If the index are outside of the bounds of the matrix, we call **std::abort()**. In the array, we store all the elements of the first row, then all the elements of the second row, and so on. So, when we want to access the elements of the nth row, we need to skip all the elements of the previous rows, which are going to be the number of elements per row (so the number of columns) times the previous rows:

```
T& get(int row, int col) {
  if (row >= R || col >= C) {
    std::abort();
  }
```

```
        return data[row*C + col];
    }
```

The output is as follows:

```
Initial matrix:
1 2
3 4
5 6
```

> **Note**
>
> The solution for this activity can be found on page 298.

Bonus step:

In games, multiplying a matrix by a vector is a common operation.

Add a method to the class that takes a **std::array** containing elements of the same type of the matrix, and returns a **std::array** containing the result of the multiplication. See the definition of a matrix-vector product at https://mathinsight.org/matrix_vector_multiplication.

Bonus step:

We add a new method, **multiply**, which takes a **std::array** of type **T** with the length of **C** by const reference, since we are not modifying it.

The function returns an array of the same type, but a length of **R**?

We follow the definition of the matrix-vector multiplication to compute the result:

```
std::array<T, R> multiply(const std::array<T, C>& vector){
    std::array<T, R> result = {};
    for(int r = 0; r < R; r++) {
        for(int c = 0; c < C; c++) {
            result[r] += get(r, c) * vector[c];
        }
    }
    return result;
}
```

Making Templates Easier to Use

We always said that we need to provide the template arguments to the parameters of a template function or class. Now, in this section, we are going to see two features that C++ offers to make it easier to use templates.

These features are default template arguments and template argument deduction.

Default Template Arguments

Like function arguments, template arguments can also have default values, both for type and non-type template parameters.

The syntax for default template arguments is to add after the template identifier the equal, followed by the value:

```
template<typename MyType = int>

void foo();
```

When a template provides a default value for a parameter, the user does not have to specify the parameter when instantiating the template. The default parameter must come after the parameters that do not have a default value.

Additionally, you can reference the previous template parameters when defining the default type for a subsequent template parameter.

Let's see some examples of both errors and valid declarations:

```
template<typename T = void, typename A>
void foo();
```

- **Error**: The template parameter **T**, which has a default type, comes before the template parameter **A**, which does not have a default parameter:

```
template<typename T = A, typename A = void>
void foo();
```

- **Error**: The template parameter **T** references the template parameter **A**, which comes after **T**:

```
template<typename T, typename A = T >
void foo();
```

- **Correct**: **A** has a default value, and no other template parameter without default value comes after it. It also references **T**, which is declared before the template parameter **A**.

The reason to use the default arguments is to provide a sensible option for the template, but still allowing the user to provide their own type or value when needed.

Let's see an example of type arguments:

```
template<typename T>
struct Less {
  bool operator()(const T& a, const T& b) {
    return a < b;
  }
};
template<typename T, typename Comparator= Less<T>>
class SortedArray;
```

The hypothetical type **SortedArray** is an array that keeps its elements always sorted. It accepts the type of the elements it should hold and a comparator. To make it easy to use for the user, it sets the comparator to use the **less** operator by default.

The following code shows how a user can implement it:

```
SortedArray<int> sortedArray1;
SortedArrat<int, Greater<int>> sortedArray2;
```

We can also see an example of a default non-type template parameter:

```
template<size_t Size = 512>
struct MemoryBuffer;
```

The hypothetical type **MemoryBuffer** is an object that reserves an amount of memory on the stack; the program will then allocate objects into that memory. By default, it uses 512 bytes of memory, but the user can specify a different size:

```
MemoryBuffer<> buffer1;
MemoryBuffer<1024> buffer2;
```

Note the empty angle brackets in the **buffer1** declaration. They are needed to signal to the compiler that we are making use of a template. This requirement has been removed in C++17, and we can write **MemoryBuffer buffer1;**.

Template Argument Deduction

All the template parameters need to be known to instantiate a template, but not all of them need to be explicitly provided by the caller.

Template argument deduction refers to the ability of the compiler to automatically understand some of the types that are used to instantiate the template, without the user having to explicitly type them.

We are going to see them for functions as that is supported by most of the versions of C++. C++17 introduced **deduction guides**, which allow the compiler to perform template argument deduction for class templates from the constructor, but we are not going to see them.

The detailed rules for template argument deduction are very complex, and so we are going to see them by example so that we can understand them.

In general, the compiler tries to find the type for which the provided argument and the parameter match the closest.

The code we are going to analyze is as follows:

```
template<typename T>
void foo(T parameter);
```

The calling code is as follows:

```
foo(argument);
```

Parameter and Argument Types

We are going to see how, based on different pairs of parameters and arguments, the type is deduced:

	foo(1): int	int x; foo(x): int&	const int x; foo(x): const int&
void foo(T)	T = int	T = int	T = int
void foo(T&)	Error	T = int	T = const int
void foo(const T&)	T = int	T = int	T = int

Figure 4.1: Different parameter and argument types

The error happens because we cannot bind a temporary value, like 1, to a non-**const** reference.

As we can see, the compiler tries to deduce a type so that when it is substituted in the parameter, it matches the argument as best as possible.

The compiler cannot always find such a type; in those situations, it gives an error and it's up to the user to provide the type.

The compiler cannot deduce a type for any of the following reasons:

The type is not used in the parameters. For example: the compiler cannot deduce a type if it is only used in the return type, or only used inside the body of the function.

The type in the parameter is a derived type. For example: **template<typename T> void foo(T::value_type a)**. The compiler cannot find the type **T** given the parameter that's used to call the function.

Knowing these rules, we can derive a best practice for the order of the template parameters when writing templates: the types that we expect the user to provide need to come before the types that are deduced.

The reason for this is that a user can only provide the template arguments in the same order they have been declared.

Let's consider the following template:

```
template<typename A, typename B, typename C>
C foo(A, B);
```

When calling **foo(1, 2.23)**, the compiler can deduce **A** and **B**, but cannot deduce **C**. Since we need all the types, and the user has to provide them in order, the user has to provide all of the types: **foo<int, double, and float>(1, 2.23);**.

Let's say we put the types that cannot be deduced before the types that can be deduced, as in the following example:

```
template< typename C, typename A, typename B>
C foo(A, B);
```

We could call the function with **foo<float>(1, 2.23)**. We would then provide the type to use for **C** and the compiler would automatically deduce **A** and **B**.

In a similar way, we need to reason about default template arguments.

Since they need to come last, we need to make sure to put the types that the user is more likely to want to modify first, since that will force them to provide all the template arguments up to that parameter.

Activity 16: Making the Matrix Class Easier to Use

The **Matrix** class we created in *Activity 15: Writing a Matrix Class for Mathematical Operations in a Game*, requires that we provide three template parameters.

Now, in this activity, we want to make the class easier to use by requiring that the user is required to only pass two parameters: the number of rows and the number of columns in the **Matrix** class. The class should also take a third argument: the type contained in the **Matrix** class. If not provided, it should default to **int**.

In the previous activity, we added to the matrix a **multiply** operation. We now want to let the user customize the function by specifying how the multiplication between the types should be executed. By default, we want to use the * operator. For that, a **class** template named **std::multiplies** from the **<functional>** header exists. It works like the **Less** class we saw previously in this chapter:

1. We start by importing **<functional>** so that we have access to **std::multiplies**.

2. We then change the order of the template parameters in the class template so that the size parameters come first. We also add a new template parameter, **Multiply**, which is the type we use for computing the multiplication between the elements in the vector by default, and we store an instance of it in the class.

3. We now need to make sure that the **multiply** method uses the **Multiply** type provided by the user to perform the multiplication.

4. To do so, we need to make sure we call **multiplier(operand1, operand2)** instead of **operand1 * operand2** so that we use the instance we stored inside the class:

```
std::array<T, R> multiply(const std::array<T, C>& vector) {
    std::array<T, R> result = {};
    for(int r = 0; r < R; r++) {
        for(int c = 0; c < C; c++) {
            result[r] += multiplier(get(r, c), vector[c]);
        }
    }
    return result;
}
```

5. Add an example of how we can use the class:

```
// Create a matrix of int, with the 'plus' operation by default
Matrix<3, 2, int, std::plus<int>> matrixAdd;
matrixAdd.setRow(0, {1,2});
matrixAdd.setRow(1, {3,4});
matrixAdd.setRow(2, {5,6});

std::array<int, 2> vector = {8, 9};
// This will call std::plus when doing the multiplication
std::array<int, 3> result = matrixAdd.multiply(vector);
```

The output is as follows:

```
Initial matrix:
1 2
3 4
5 6


Result of multiplication (with plus instead of multiply): [20, 24, 28]
```

> **Note**
>
> The solution for this activity can be found on page 300.

Being Generic in Templates

So far, we have learned how the compiler can make our templated functions easier to use by automatically deducing the types used. The template code decides whether to accept a parameter as a value or a reference, and the compiler finds the type for us. But what do we do if we want to be agnostic regarding whether an argument is a value or a reference, and we want to work with it regardless?

An example would be **std::invoke** in C++17. **std::invoke** is a function that takes a function as the first argument, followed by a list of arguments, and calls the function with the arguments. For example:

```
void do_action(int, float, double);

double d = 1.5;

std::invoke(do_action, 1, 1.2f, d);
```

Similar examples would apply if you wanted to log before calling a function, or you wanted to execute the function in a different thread, such as **std::async** does.

Let's demystify the difference by using the following code:

```
struct PrintOnCopyOrMove {
  PrintOnCopyOrMove(std::string name) : _name(name) {}
  PrintOnCopyOrMove(const PrintOnCopyOrMove& other) : _name(other._name) {
std::cout << "Copy: " << _name << std::endl; }
  PrintOnCopyOrMove(PrintOnCopyOrMove&& other) : _name(other._name) {
std::cout << "Move: " << _name << std::endl; }


  std::string _name;
};
void use_printoncopyormove_obj(PrintOnCopyOrMove obj) {}
```

> **Note**
>
> **use_printoncopyormove_obj** always accepts the parameter by value.

Let's say we execute the following code:

```
PrintOnCopyOrMove local{"l-value"};
std::invoke(use_printoncopyormove_obj, local);
std::invoke(use_printoncopyormove_obj, PrintOnCopyOrMove("r-value"));
```

The code would print the following:

```
Copy: l-value
Move: r-value
```

How can we write a function such as **std::invoke** that works regardless of the kind of reference (colloquially referred to as "ref-ness", similarly to how "const-ness" is used to talk about whether a type is const qualified) of the parameters?

The answer to that is **forwarding references**.

Forwarding references look like r-value references, but they only apply where the type is deduced by the compiler:

```
void do_action(PrintOnCopyOrMove&&)
// not deduced: r-value reference
template<typename T>
void do_action(T&&) // deduced by the compiler: forwarding reference
```

> **Note**
>
> If you see a type identifier declared in the template, the type is deduced, and the type has &&, then it is a forwarding reference.

Let's see how the deduction works for forwarding references:

	foo(1): Int	int x; foo(x): int&	const int x; foo(x): const int&
void do_action(T&&)	T = int	T = int&	T = const int&

Figure 4.2: Forward reference function.

> **Note**
>
> Let's say the type is not deduced, but, it is provided explicitly, for example:
>
> ```
> int x = 0;
> ```
>
> ```
> do_action<int>(x);
> ```
>
> Here, **T** will be **int**, since it was explicitly stated.

The advantage, as we saw before, is that we work with any kind of reference, and when the calling code knows it can move the object, then we can make use of the additional performance provided by the move constructor, but when a reference is preferred, then the code can use it as well.

Additionally, some types do not support copying, and we can make our template work with those types as well.

When we write the body of the template function, the parameter is used as an **1-value** reference, and we can write code ignoring whether **T** is an **1-value** reference or an **r-value** one:

```
template<typename T>

void do_action(T&& obj) { /* forwarding reference, but we can access obj as
if it was a normal l-value reference */

  obj.some_method();

  some_function(obj);

}
```

In *Chapter 3, Classes*, we learned that **std::move** can make our code more efficient when we need to use an object that we are not going to access after the call happens.

But we saw that we should never move objects we receive as an **1-value** reference parameter, since the code that called us might still use the object after we return.

When we are writing templates using a forwarding reference, we are in front of a dilemma: our type might be a value or a reference, so how do we decide whether we can use **std::move**?

Does it mean we cannot make use of the benefit that **std::move** brings us?

The answer, of course, is *no*:

```
template<typename T>

void do_action(T&& obj) {

  do_something_with_obj(???);

// We are not using obj after this call.

}
```

Should we use move or not in this case?

The answer is *yes*: we should move if **T** is a value, and, no, we should not move if **T** is a reference.

C++ provides us with a tool to do exactly this: **std::forward**.

std::forward is a function template that always takes an explicit template parameter and a function parameter: **std::forward<T>(obj)**.

Forward looks at the type of **T**, and if it's an **l-value** reference, then it simply returns a reference to the **obj**, but if it's not, then it is equivalent to calling **std::move** on the object.

Let's see it in action:

```
template<typename T>
void do_action(T&& obj) {
  use_printoncopyormove_obj(std::forward<T>(obj));
}
```

Now, we call it by using the following code:

```
PrintOnCopyOrMove local{"l-value"};
do_action(local);
do_action(PrintOnCopyOrMove("r-value"));
do_action(std::move(local));
// We can move because we do not use local anymore
```

When executed, the code will print the following output:

```
Copy: l-val
Move: r-val
Move: l-val
```

We successfully managed to write code that is independent on whether the type is passed as reference or value, removing a possible requirement on the template type parameter.

> **Note**
>
> A template can have many type parameters. Forwarding references can apply to any of the type parameters independently.

This is important because the caller of the templated code might know whether it is better to pass values or pass references, and our code should work regardless of whether there is a requirement to ask for a specific ref-ness.

We also saw how we can still maintain the advantages of moving, which is required for some types that do not support copying. This can make our code run much faster, even for types that support copying, without complicating our code: when we have forwarding references we use **std::forward** where we would have used **std::move**.

Activity 17: Ensuring Users are Logged in When Performing Actions on the Account

We want to allow the users of our e-commerce website to perform arbitrary actions (for the scope of this activity, they will be adding and removing items) on their shopping carts.

Before performing any action, we want to make sure that the user is logged in. Now, let's follow these instructions:

1. Ensure that there is a **UserIdentifier** type for identifying the user, a **Cart** type that represents the shopping cart of the user, and a **CartItem** type that represents any item in the cart:

    ```cpp
    struct UserIdentifier {
        int userId = 0;
    };
    struct Cart {
        std::vector<Item> items;
    };
    ```

2. Ensure that there is also a function with the signature **bool isLoggedIn(const UserIdentifier& user)** and a function to retrieve the cart for an user, **Cart getUserCart(const UserIdentifier& user)**:

    ```cpp
    bool isLoggedIn(const UserIdentifier& user) {
        return user.userId % 2 == 0;
    }

    Cart getUserCart(const UserIdentifier& user) {
        return Cart();
    }
    ```

3. In most of our code, we only have access to the `UserIdentifier` for a user, and we want to make sure that we always check whether the user is logged in before doing any action on the cart.

4. To solve this problem, we decide to write a function template called `execute_on_user_cart`, which takes the user identifier, an action, and a single parameter. The function will check if the user is logged in and if so, retrieve their cart, then perform the action of passing the cart and the single parameter:

```
template<typename Action, typename Parameter>
void execute_on_user_cart(UserIdentifier user, Action action, Parameter&&
parameter) {
    if(isLoggedIn(user)) {
        Cart cart = getUserCart(user);
        action(cart, std::forward<Parameter>(parameter));
    } else {
        std::cout << "The user is not logged in" << std::endl;
    }
}
```

5. One of the actions we want to perform is **void remove_item(Cart, CartItem)**. A second action we want to perform is **void add_items(Cart, std::vector<CartItem>)**:

```
void removeItem(Cart& cart, Item cartItem) {
    auto location = std::find(cart.items.begin(), cart.items.end(),
cartItem);
    if (location != cart.items.end()) {
        cart.items.erase(location);
    }
    std::cout << "Item removed" << std::endl;
}
```

```
void addItems(Cart& cart, std::vector<Item> items) {
    cart.items.insert(cart.items.end(), items.begin(), items.end());
    std::cout << "Items added" << std::endl;
}
```

> **Note**
>
> A parameter of a function template can be used to accept functions as parameters.

The aim is to create a function that performs the necessary checks on whether the user is logged in so that throughout our program we can use it to perform safely any actions that are required by our business on the user cart, without the risk of forgetting to check the logged status of the user.

6. We can also move the types that are not forwarding references:

```
template<typename Action, typename Parameter>
void execute_on_user_cart(UserIdentifier user, Action action, Parameter&&
parameter) {
    if(isLoggedIn(user)) {
        Cart cart = getUserCart(user);
        action(std::move(cart), std::forward<Parameter>(parameter));
    }
}
```

7. Examples of how the **execute_on_user_cart** function can be used with the actions we described earlier in the activity is as follows:

```
UserIdentifier user{/* initialize */};
execute_on_user_cart(user, remove_item, CartItem{});
std::vector<CartItem> items = {{"Item1"}, {"Item2"}, {"Item3"}}; // might
be very long
execute_on_user_cart(user, add_items, std::move(items));
```

8. The developers in our software can write the functions they need to execute on the cart, and call **execute_on_user_cart** to safely execute them.

> **Note**
>
> The solution for this activity can be found on page 302.

Variadic Templates

We just saw how we can write a template that accepts parameters independently from their ref-ness.

But the two functions we talked about from the standard library, **std::invoke** and **std::async**, have an additional property: they can accept any number of arguments.

In a similar way, **std::tuple**, a type similar to a **std::array** but that can contain values of different types, can contain an arbitrary number of types.

How is it possible for a template to accept an arbitrary number of arguments of different types?

In the past, a solution to this problem was to provide a great number of overloads for the same function, or multiple implementations of the class or struct, one for each number of the parameters.

This is clearly code that is not easy to maintain, as it forces us to write the same code multiple times. Another drawback is that there is a limit to the number of template parameters, so if your code requires more parameters than what is provided, you do not have a way to use the function.

C++11 introduced a nice solution for this problem: **parameter pack**.

A parameter pack is a template parameter that can accept zero or more template arguments.

A parameter pack is declared by appending ... to the type of the template parameter.

Parameter packs are a functionality that works with any template: both functions and classes:

```
template<typename... Types>
void do_action();
template<typename... Types>
struct MyStruct;
```

A template that has a parameter pack is called a **variadic template**, since it is a template that accepts a varying number of parameters.

When instantiating a variadic template, any number of arguments can be provided to the parameter pack by separating them with a comma:

```
do_action<int, std:string, float>();
do_action<>();
MyStruct<> myStruct0;
MyStruct<float, int> myStruct2;
```

Types will contain the list of arguments that are provided when instantiating the template.

A parameter pack by itself is a list of types and the code cannot interact with it directly.

The variadic template can use the parameter pack by expanding it, which happens by appending ... to a pattern.

When a pattern is expanded, it is repeated as many times as there are types in its parameter pack, separating it with a comma. Of course, to be expanded, a pattern must contain at least a parameter pack. If multiple parameters are present in the pattern, or the same parameter is present several times, they are all expanded at the same time.

The simplest pattern is the name of the parameter pack: **Types...**

For example: to let a function accept multiple arguments, it would expand the parameter pack in the function arguments:

```
template<typename... MyTypes>
void do_action(MyTypes... my_types);
do_action();
do_action(1, 2, 4.5, 3.5f);
```

When we call the function, the compiler automatically deduces the types of the parameter pack. In the last call, **MyTypes** will contain **int**, **double**, and **float**, and the signature of the generated function would be **void do_action(int __p0, int __p1, double __p2, float __p3)**.

> **Note**
>
> A parameter pack in the list of template parameters can only be followed by template parameters that have a default value, or those that are deduced by the compiler.
>
> Most commonly, the parameter pack is the last in the list of template parameters.

The function parameter **my_types** is called a **function parameter pack** and needs to be expanded as well so that it can access the single parameters.

For example: let's write a variadic struct:

```
template<typename... Ts>
struct Variadic {
  Variadic(Ts... arguments);
};
```

Let's write a function that creates the struct:

```
template<typename… Ts>
Variadic<Ts…> make_variadic(Ts… args) {
  return Variadic<Ts…>(args…);
}
```

Here, we have a variadic function that takes a parameter pack and expands it when calling the constructor of another variadic struct.

The function **parameter packs**, which is the function variadic parameter, can be expanded only in some locations–the most common is as parameters when calling a function.

The template **parameter packs**, which is a type variadic parameter, can be expanded in template argument lists: the list of arguments between **<>** when instantiating a template.

As we mentioned previously, the pattern for the expansion might be more complex than just the name of the argument.

For example: we can access type aliases declared in the type or we can call a function on the parameter:

```
template<typename… Containers>
std::tuple<typename Containers::value_type…> get_front(Containers…
containers) {
  return std::tuple<typename Containers::value_type…>(containers.front()…);
}
```

We call it like so:

```
std::vector<int> int_vector = {1};
std::vector<double> double_vector = {2.0};
std::vector<float> float_vector = {3.0f};
get_front(int_vector, double_vector, float_vector) // Returns a tuple<int,
double, float> containing {1, 2.0, 3.0}
```

Alternatively, we can pass the parameter as an argument to a function:

```
template<typename... Ts>
void modify_and_call (Ts... args) {
  do_things(modify (args)...));
}
```

This will call the **modify** function for each argument and pass the result to **do_things**.

In this section, we saw how the variadic parameter functionality of C++ lets us write functions and classes that work with any number and type of parameters.

While it is not a common everyday task to write variadic templates, almost every programmer uses a variadic template in their day-to-day coding, since it makes it so much easier to write powerful abstractions, and the standard library makes vast use of it.

Additionally, in the right situation, variadic templates can allow us to write expressive code that works in the multitude of situations we need.

Activity 18: Safely Performing Operations on the User Cart with an Arbitrary Number of Parameters

In the previous activity, we saw a function, **execute_on_user_cart**, which allows us to execute arbitrary functions that take an object of type **Cart** and a single parameter.

In this activity, we want to expand on the supported types of actions we can perform on the shopping cart of the user by allowing any function that takes an object of type **Cart** and an arbitrary number of arguments:

1. Expand the previous activity to accept any number of the parameter with any kind of ref-ness and pass it to the action provided.

2. Write variadic templates and learn how to expand them:

    ```
    template<typename Action, typename... Parameters>
    void execute_on_user_cart(UserIdentifier user, Action action,
    Parameters&&... parameters) {
        if(isLoggedIn(user)) {
            Cart cart = getUserCart(user);
    ```

```
        action(std::move(cart), std::forward<Parameters>(parameters)...);
    }
}
```

Note

The solution for this activity can be found on page 303.

Writing Easy-to-Read Templates

Up until now, we have seen many features that we can use to write powerful templates that allow us to create high-level abstractions over the specific problems we face.

But, as usual, code is more often read than written, and we should optimize for readability: the code should express the intentions of the code more than what operation is achieved.

Template code can sometimes make that hard to do, but there are a few patterns that can help.

Type Alias

Type **aliases** allow the user to give a name to a type. They are declared with using **name = type**.

After the declaration, everywhere *Name* is used is going to be equivalent to having used *Type*.

This is very powerful for three reasons:

- It can give a shorter and more meaningful name to complex types
- It can declare a nested type to simplify access to it
- It allows you to avoid having to specify the **typename** keyword in front of a dependent type

Let's see examples for these two points.

Imagine we have a type, **UserAccount**, which contains several fields on the user, such as user ID, user balance, user email, and more.

We want to organize the user accounts into a high scoreboard based on their account balances to visualize which users are most actively using our service.

To do so. we can use a data structure that requires a few parameters: the type to store, a way for ordering the types, a way to compare the types, and possibly others.

The type could be as follows:

```
template<typename T, typename Comparison = Less<T>, typename Equality =
Equal<T>>

class SortedContainer;
```

To be easy to use, the template correctly provided some default values for **Comparison** and **Equality**, which use the **<** and **==** operators, but our **UserAccount** type does not implement the **<** operator, as there is no clear ordering, and the **==** operator does not do what we want, as we are only interested in comparing balances. To solve this, we implemented two structures to provide the functionality we need:

```
SortedContainer<UserAccount, UserAccountBalanceCompare,
UserAccountBalanceEqual> highScoreBoard;
```

The creation of a high scoreboard is both verbose.

Using a type alias, we could write the following:

```
using HighScoreBoard = SortedContainer<UserAccount,
UserAccountBalanceCompare, UserAccountBalanceEqual>;
```

Following this, we could create instances of **HighScoreBoard** directly, with little typing and clearly specify the intent:

```
HighScoreBoard highScoreBoard;
```

We now also have a single place to update if we want to change the way in which we want to sort the accounts. For example: if we also wanted to consider how long the user has been registered in the service, we could change the comparator the comparator. Every user of the type alias will be updated, without the risk of forgetting to update one location.

Additionally, we clearly have a location where we can put the documentation on the decision made for using the type we picked.

> **Note**
>
> When using type aliases, give a name that represents what the type is for, not how it works. **UserAccountSortedContainerByBalance** is a not a good name because it tells us how the type works instead of what its intention is.

The second case is extremely useful for allowing code to introspect the class, that is, looking into some of the details of the class:

```
template<typename T>
class SortedContainer {
public:
  T& front() const;
};
template<typename T>
class ReversedContainer {
public:
  T& front() const;
}
```

We have several containers, which mostly support the same operations. We would like to write a template function that takes any container and returns the first element, **front**:

```
template<typename Container>
??? get_front(const Container& container);
```

How can we find out what type is returned?

A common pattern is to add a type alias inside the class, like so:

```
template<typename T>
class SortedContainer {
  using value_type = T; // type alias
  T& front() const;
};
```

Now the function can access the type of the contained element:

```
template<typename Container>
typename Container::value_type& get_front(const Container& container);
```

> **Note**
>
> Remember that **value_type** depends on the **Container** type, so it is a dependent type. When we use dependent types, we must use the **typename** keyword in **front**.

This way, our code can work with any type that declares the nested type **value_type**.

The third use case, that is, to avoid having to type the **typename** keyword repeatedly, is common when interacting with code that follows the previous pattern.

For example: we can have a class that accepts a type:

```
template<typename Container>
class ContainerWrapper {
  using value_type = typename Container::value_type;
}
```

In the rest of the class, we can use **value_type** directly, without having to type **typename** anymore. This allows us to avoid a lot of repetitions.

The three techniques can also be combined. For example: you can have the following:

```
template<typename T>
class MyObjectWrapper {
  using special_type = MyObject<typename T::value_type>;
};
```

Template Type Alias

The ability to create type aliases, as described in the previous part of this chapter, is already very useful for improving the readability of our code.

C++ gives us the ability to define generic type aliases so that they can simply be reused by the users of our code.

A template alias is a template that generates aliases.

Like all the templates we saw in this chapter, they start with a template declaration and follow with the alias declaration, which can depend on the type that's declared in the template:

```
template<typename Container>
using ValueType = typename Container::value_type;
```

A **ValueType** is a template alias that can be instantiated with the usual template syntax: **ValueType<SortedContainer> myValue;**.

This allows the code to just use the alias **ValueType** whenever they want to access the **value_type** type inside any container.

Template aliases can combine all the features of templates: they can accept multiple parameters, accept non-type parameters, and even use parameter packs.

Summary

In this chapter, the students were introduced to templates in C++. We saw that templates exist to create high-level abstractions that work independently from the types of the objects at zero overhead at runtime. We explained the concept of type requirements: the requirements a type must satisfy to work correctly with the templates. We then showed the students how to write function templates and class templates, mentioning dependent types as well, to give the students the tools to understand a class of errors that happen when writing template code.

We then showed how templates can work with non-type parameters, and how templates can be made easier to use by providing default template arguments, thanks to template argument deduction.

We then showed the students how to write more generic templates, thanks to the forwarding reference, **std::forward**, and the template parameter pack.

Finally, we concluded with some tools to make templates easier to read and more maintainable.

In the next chapter, we will cover standard library containers and algorithms.

5

Standard Library Containers and Algorithms

Chapter Objectives

By the end of this chapter, you will be able to:

- Explain what iterators are
- Demonstrate the use of sequential containers, container adaptors, and associative containers
- Understand and use unconventional containers
- Explain cases of iterator invalidation
- Discover algorithms implemented in the standard library
- Use user-defined operations on algorithms with lambda expressions

Introduction

The core of C++ is its **<u>Standard Template Library</u>** (**<u>STL</u>**), which represents a set of important data structures and algorithms that facilitates the programmer's task and improves code efficiency.

The components of the STL are parametric so that they can be reused and combined in different ways. The STL is mainly made up of container classes, iterators, and algorithms.

Containers are used to store collections of elements of a certain type. Usually, the type of the container is a template parameter, which allows the same container class to support arbitrary elements. There are several container classes, each of them with different characteristics and features.

Iterators are used to traverse the elements of a container. Iterators offer the programmer a simple and common interface to access containers of a different type.

Iterators are similar to raw pointers, which can also iterate through elements using the increment and the decrement operators, or can access a specific element using the de-reference (*) operator.

Algorithms are used to perform standard operations on the elements stored in the containers. They use iterators to traverse the collections, since their interface is common to all the containers, so that the algorithm can be agnostic about the container it's operating on.

Algorithms treat functions as parameters that are provided by the programmer in order to be more flexible in the operation that's being performed. It is common to see an algorithm applied to a container of objects of a user-defined type. This algorithm, to execute correctly, needs to know how to treat the object in detail. For this reason, the programmer provides a function to the algorithm to specify the operations to be executed on the objects.

Sequence Containers

Sequence containers, sometimes referred to as **<u>sequential containers</u>**, are a particular class of containers where the order in which their elements are stored is decided by the *programmer* rather than by the values of the elements. Every element has a certain position that is independent of its value.

The STL contains five sequence container classes:

Sequence Container	Description
Array	Fixed-size array Fast random access No addition or deletion operation
Vector	Variable-size array Fast random access Addition and deletion operations supported Append is fast, while inserting at a given position is slow
Deque	Double-ended queue Fast random access Insertion and deletion operations only at front and back of the queue
Forward-list	Singly linked list Sequential access in the forward direction Insertion and deletion operations are fast
List	Doubly linked list Sequential access in both directions Insertion and deletion operations are fast

Figure 5.1: Table presenting the sequence container classes and their descriptions

Array

The array container is a fixed-size data structure of contiguous elements. It recalls the static array that we saw in *Chapter 1, Getting Started*:

Array

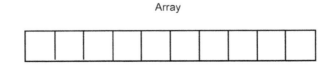

Figure 5.2: Array elements are stored in contiguous memory

An array's size needs to be specified at compile time. Once defined, the size of the array *cannot be changed*.

When an array is created, the `size` elements it contains are initialized next to each other in memory. While elements cannot be added or removed, their values can be modified.

Arrays can be randomly accessed using the access operator with the corresponding element's index. To access an element at a given position, we can use the operator `[]` or the `at()` member function. The former does not perform any range checks, while the latter throws an exception if the index is out of range. Moreover, the first and the last element can be accessed using the `front()` and `back()` member functions.

These operations are fast: since the elements are contiguous, we can compute the position in memory of an element given its position in the array, and access that directly.

The size of the array can be obtained using the `size()` member function. Whether the container is empty can be checked using the `empty()` function, which returns *true* if `size()` is zero.

The array class is defined in the `<array>` header file, which has to be included before usage.

Vector

The vector container is a data structure of contiguous elements whose size can be dynamically modified: it does not require to specify its size at creation time:

Vector

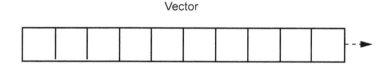

Figure 5.3: Vector elements are contiguous, and their size can grow dynamically

The **vector** class is defined in the `<vector>` header file.

A vector stores the elements it contains in a single section of memory. Usually, the section of memory has enough space for more elements than the number of elements stored in the vector. When a new element is added to the vector, if there is enough space in the section of memory, the element is added after the last element in the vector. If there isn't enough space, the vector gets a new, bigger section of memory and copies all the existing elements into the new section of memory, then it deletes the old section of memory. To us, it will seem like the size of the section of memory has increased:

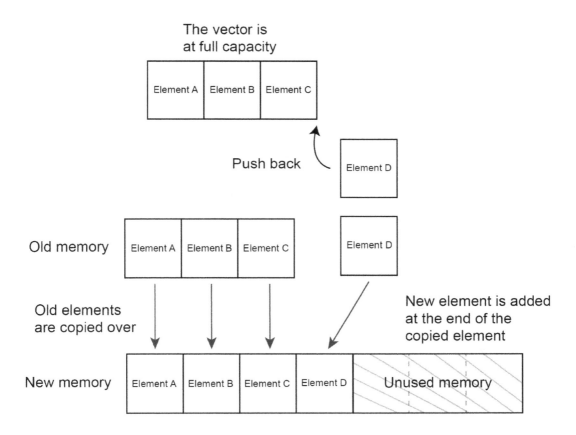

Figure 5.4: Memory allocation of vectors

When the vector is created, it is empty.

Most of the interface is similar to the array's, but with a few differences.

Elements can be appended using the **push_back()** function or inserted at a generic position using the **insert()** function. The last element can be removed using **pop_back()** or at a generic position using the **erase()** function.

Appending or deleting the last element is fast, while inserting or removing other elements of the vector is considered slow, as it requires moving all the elements to make space for the new element or to keep all the elements contiguous:

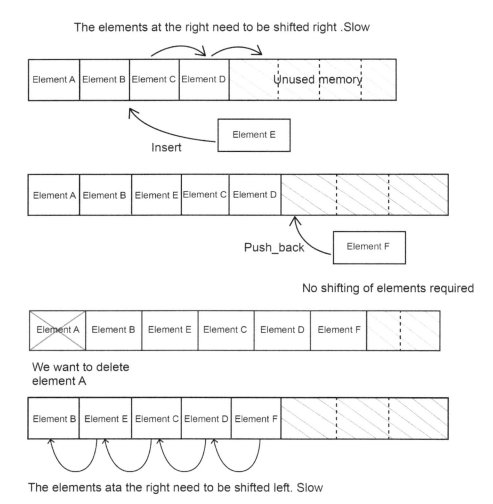

Figure 5.5: Elements being moved during insertions or deletions inside a vector

Vectors, just like arrays, allow efficient access of elements at random positions. A vector's size is also retrieved with the `size()` member function, but this should not be confused with `capacity()`. The former is the actual number of elements in the vector, and the latter returns the maximum number of elements that can be inserted in the current section of memory.

For example, in the preceding diagram, initially, the array had a size of 4 and a capacity of 8. So, even when an element had to be moved to the right, the vector's capacity did not change, as we never had to get a new, bigger section of memory to store the elements.

The operation of getting a new section of memory is called reallocation. Since reallocation is considered an expensive operation, it is possible to *reserve* enough memory for a given number of elements by enlarging a vector's capacity using the `reserve()` member function. The vector's capacity can also be reduced to fit the number of elements using the `shrink_to_fit()` function in order to release memory that is not needed anymore.

> **Note**
>
> Vector is the most commonly used container for a sequence of elements and is often the best one performance-wise.

Let's look at the following example to understand how `vector::front()` and `vector::back()` work in C++:

```cpp
#include <iostream>
#include <vector>
// Import the vector library


int main()
{
  std::vector<int> myvector;

  myvector.push_back(100);
  // Both front and back of vector contains a value 100


  myvector.push_back(10);
  // Now, the back of the vector holds 10 as a value, the front holds 100


  myvector.front() -= myvector.back();
  // We subtracted front value with back
```

```
std::cout << "Front of the vector: " << myvector.front() << std::endl;
std::cout << "Back of the vector: " << myvector.back() << std::endl;
}
```

```
Output:
Front of the vector: 90
Back of the vector: 10
```

Deque

The *deque* container (pronounced *deck*) is short for "double-ended queue." Like *vector*, it allows for fast, direct access of deque elements and fast insertion and deletion at the back. Unlike *vector*, it also allows for fast insertion and deletion at the front of the deque:

Deque

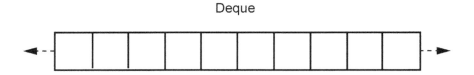

Figure 5.6: Deque elements can be added and removed at the start and the end

The **deque** class is defined in the **<deque>** header file.

Deque generally requires more memory than *vector*, and *vector* is more performant for accessing the elements and **push_back**, so unless it is required to insert at the front, *vector* is usually preferred.

List

The list container is a data structure of nonadjacent elements that can be dynamically grown:

List

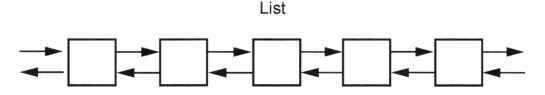

Figure 5.7: List elements are stored in different sections of memory, and have connecting links

The **list** class is defined in the **<list>** header file.

Each element in the list has its memory segment and a link to its predecessor and its successor. The structure containing the element, which is the link to its predecessor and to its successor, is called a **node**.

When an element is inserted in a list, the predecessor node needs to be updated so that its successor link points to the new element. Similarly, the successor node needs to be updated so that its predecessor link points to the new element:

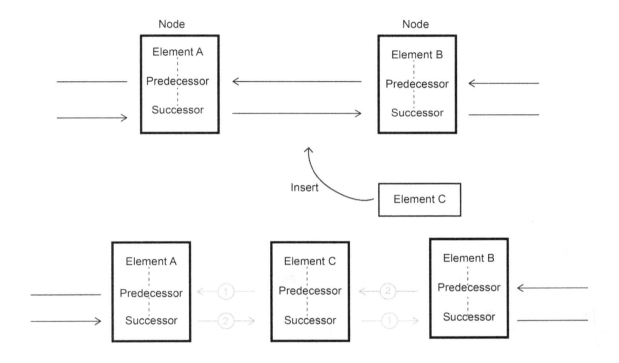

Figure 5.8: C is to be inserted between A and B. A's successor and B's predecessor link must be updated to point to C (orange). C's link to the predecessor and successor are updated to points A and B (green)

When an element is removed from the list, we need to update the successor link of the predecessor node to point to the successor of the removed node. Similarly, the predecessor link of the successor node needs to be updated to point to the predecessor of the removed node.

In the preceding diagram, if we were to remove **C**, we would have to update **A**'s successor to point to **C**'s successor (**B**), and **B**'s predecessor to point to **C**'s predecessor (**A**).

Unlike vectors, lists do not provide random access. Elements are accessed by linearly following the chain of elements: starting from the first, we can follow the successor link to find the next node, or from the last node we can follow the predecessor link to find the previous node, until we reach the element we are interested into.

The advantage of **list** is that insertion and removal are fast at any position, if we already know the node at which we want to insert or remove. The disadvantage of this is that getting to a specific node is slow.

The interface is similar to a vector, except that lists don't provide **operator[]**.

Forward-List

The **forward_list** container is similar to the list container, with the difference that its nodes only have the link to the successor. For this reason, it is not possible to iterate over a **forward_list** in backward order:

Forward-list

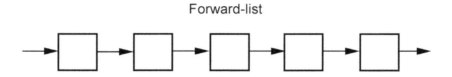

Figure 5.9: Forward-list elements are like List elements, but only have one-way connecting links

As usual, the **forward_list** class is defined in the **<forward_list>** header file.

The **forward_list** class does not even provide **push_back()** or **size()**. Inserting an element is done using **insert_after()**, which is a variation of the **insert()** function, where the new element is inserted after the provided position. The same idea applies to element removal, which is done through **erase_after()**, which removes the element after the provided position.

Providing Initial Values to Sequence Containers

All the sequence containers we have looked at are empty when they are first created.

When we want to create a container containing some elements, it can be repetitive to call the **push_back()** or **insert()** functions repeatedly for each element.

Fortunately, all the containers can be initialized with a sequence of elements when they are created.

The sequence must be provided in curly brackets, and the elements need to be comma-separated. This is called an initializer list:

```
#include <vector>

int main()
{
    // initialize the vector with 3 numbers
    std::vector<int> numbers = {1, 2, 3};
}
```

This works for any of the containers we have seen in this chapter.

Activity 19: Storing User Accounts

We want to store the account balance, stored as an **int** instance, for 10 users. The account balance starts with 0. We then want to increase the balance of the first and last user by 100.

These steps will help you complete the activity:

1. Include the header for the **array** class.

2. Declare an integer array of ten elements.

3. Initialize the array using the **for** loop. The **size()** operator to evaluate the size of the array and the **operator[]** to access every position of the array.

4. Update the value for the first and last user.

> **Note**
>
> The solution for this activity can be found on page 304.

Now let's do the same using a vector:

1. Include the **vector** header.

2. Declare a vector of integer type and reserve memory to store 100 users with resize it to be able to contain 10 users.

3. Use a for loop to initialize the vector.

With this activity, we learned how we can store an arbitrary number of accounts.

Associative Containers

Associative containers are containers that allow for the fast lookup of elements. Additionally, the elements are always kept in a sorted order. The order is determined by the value of the element and a comparison function. The comparison function is called a *comparator*, and by default this is the **operator<**, although the user can supply a **Functor** (function object) as a parameter to specify how the elements should be compared. The **<functional>** header contains many such objects that can be used to sort the associative containers, like **std::less** or **std::less**.

Associative Containers	Description
Set	Container in which elements are sorted according to their values; elements are all distinct values
Multiset	Same as a set, but duplicates are allowed
Map	Container in which elements are mapped as key-value pairs, sorted by key values; each key may occur only once
Multimap	Same as a map, but the keys can be duplicated

Figure 5.10: Table presenting associative containers and their descriptions

Typically, associative containers are implemented as variations of binary trees, providing fast element lookup by exploiting the logarithmic complexity of the underlying structure.

Set and Multiset

A **Set** is a container that contains a unique group of sorted elements. A **Multiset** is similar to *Set*, but it allows duplicate elements:

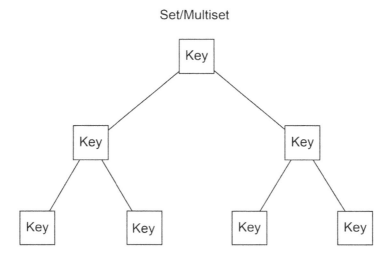

Figure 5.11: Set and Multiset store a sorted group of elements

Set and multiset have **size()** and **empty()** function members to check how many elements are contained and whether any elements are contained.

Insertion and removal is done through the **insert()** and **erase()** functions. Because the order of the elements is determined by the *comparator*, they do not take a position argument like they do for sequential containers. Both insertion and removal are fast.

Since sets are optimized for element lookup, they provide special search functions. The **find()** function returns the position of the first element equal to the provided value, or the position past the end of the set when the element is not found. When we look for an element with **find**, we should always compare it with the result of calling **end()** on the container to check whether the element was found.

Let's examine the following code:

```
#include <iostream>
#include <set>
int main() {
    std::set<int> numbers;
    numbers.insert(10);

    if (numbers.find(10) != numbers.end()) {
        std::cout << "10 is in numbers" << std::endl;
    }
}
```

Finally, **count()** returns the number of elements equal to the value provided.

The **set** and **multiset** classes are defined in the **<set>** header file.

Example of a set with a custom comparator:

```
#include <iostream>
#include <set>
#include <functional>

int main() {
    std::set<int> ascending = {5,3,4,2,1};
    std::cout << "Ascending numbers:";
    for(int number : ascending) {
        std::cout << " " << number;
    }
    std::cout << std::endl;
```

```
        std::set<int, std::greater<int>> descending = {5,3,4,2,1};
        std::cout << "Descending numbers:";
        for(int number : descending) {
            std::cout << " " << number;
        }
        std::cout << std::endl;
    }
```

Output:

Ascending numbers: 1 2 3 4 5

Descending numbers: 5 4 3 2 1

Map and Multimap

Map and **multimap** are containers that manage **key/value** pairs as elements. The elements are sorted automatically according to the provided comparator and applied to the *key*: the *value* does not influence the order of the elements:

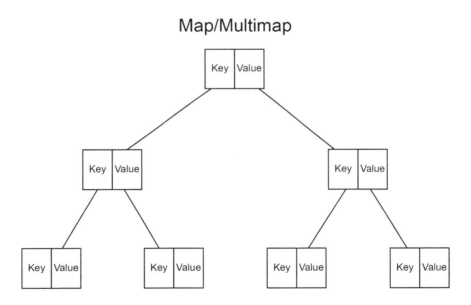

Figure 5.12: Map and multimap store a sorted group of keys, which is associated to a value

Map allows you to associate a single value to a key, while multimap allows you to associate multiple values to the same key.

The **map** and **multimap** classes are defined in the **<map>** header file.

To insert values into a map, we can call **insert()**, providing a **pair** containing the key and the value. Later in this chapter, we will see more about pairs. The function also returns a pair, containing the position at which the element was inserted, and a Boolean set to **true** if the element was inserted, or **false** if an element with the same key already exists.

Once values are inserted into the map, there are several ways to look up a key/value pair in a map.

Similar to set, map provides a **find()** function, which looks for a key in the map and returns the position of the key/value pair if it exists, or the same result of calling **end()**.

From the position, we can access the key with **position->first** and the value with **position->second**:

```
#include <iostream>

#include <string>

#include <map>


int main()
{
    std::map<int, std::string> map;
    map.insert(std::make_pair(1, "some text"));
    auto position = map.find(1);
    if (position != map.end() ) {
        std::cout << "Found! The key is " << position->first << ", the value
 is " << position->second << std::endl;
    }
}
```

An alternative to accessing a value from a key is to use **at()**, which takes a key and returns the associated value.

If there is no associated value, **at()** will throw an exception.

A last alternative to get the value associated with a key is to use **operator[]**.

The **operator[]** returns the value associated with a key, and if the key is not present, it inserts a new key/value pair with the provided key, and a default value for the value. Because **operator[]** could modify the map by inserting into it, it cannot be used on a *const* map:

```
#include <iostream>

#include <map>

int main()
{
    std::map<int, int> map;

    std::cout << "We ask for a key which does not exists: it is default
inserted: " << map[10] << std::endl;

    map.at(10) += 100;

    std::cout << "Now the value is present: " << map.find(10)->second <<
std::endl;
}
```

Activity 20: Retrieving a User's Balance from their Given Username

We'd like to be able to quickly retrieve the balance of a user given their username.

To quickly retrieve the balance from the username, we store the balance inside a map, using the name of the user as a key.

The name of the user is of type **std::string**, while the balance is an **int**. Add the balance for the users **Alice**, **Bob**, and **Charlie** with a balance of 50 each. Then, check whether the user **Donald** has a balance.

Finally, print the account balance of **Alice**:

1. Include the header file for the **map** class and the header for **string**:

    ```
    #include <string>
    #include <map>
    #include <string>
    ```

2. Create a map with the key being **std::string** and the value being **int**.

3. Insert the balances of the users inside the map by using **insert** and **std::make_pair**. The first argument is the **key**, while the second one is the **value**:

```
balances.insert(std::make_pair("Alice",50));
```

4. Use the **find** function, providing the name of the user to find the position of the account in the map. Compare it with **end()** to check whether a position was found.

5. Now, look for the account of Alice. We know Alice has an account, so there is no need to check whether we found a valid position. We can print the value of the account using **->second**:

```
auto alicePosition = balances.find("Alice");
std::cout << "Alice balance is: " << alicePosition->second << std::endl;
```

> **Note**
>
> The solution for this activity can be found on page 305.

Unordered Containers

Unordered associative containers differ from associative containers in that the elements have no defined order. Visually, unordered containers are often imagined as bags of elements. Because the elements are not sorted, unordered containers do not accept a comparator object to provide an order to the elements. On the other hand, all the unordered containers depend on a hash function.

he user can provide a **Functor** (function object) as a parameter to specify how the keys should be hashed:

Unordered Containers	Description
Unordered set	A container in which elements are unsorted; elements are all distinct values
Unordered multiset	Same as the unordered set, but duplicates are allowed
Unordered map	A container in which elements are unsorted key-values pairs; each key may occur only once
Unordered multimap	Same as the unordered map, but keys can be duplicated

Figure 5.13: Table presenting unordered containers and their descriptions

Typically, unordered containers are implemented as **hash tables**. The position in the array is determined using the hash function, which given a value returns the position at which it should be stored. Ideally, most of the elements will be mapped into different positions, but the hash function can potentially return the same position for different elements. This is called a *collision*. This problem is solved by using linked lists to chain elements that map into the same position, so that multiple elements can be stored in the same position. Because there might be multiple elements at the same position, the position is often called **bucket**.

Implementing unordered containers using a hash table allows us to find an element with a specific value in constant time complexity, which translates to an even faster lookup when compared to associative containers:

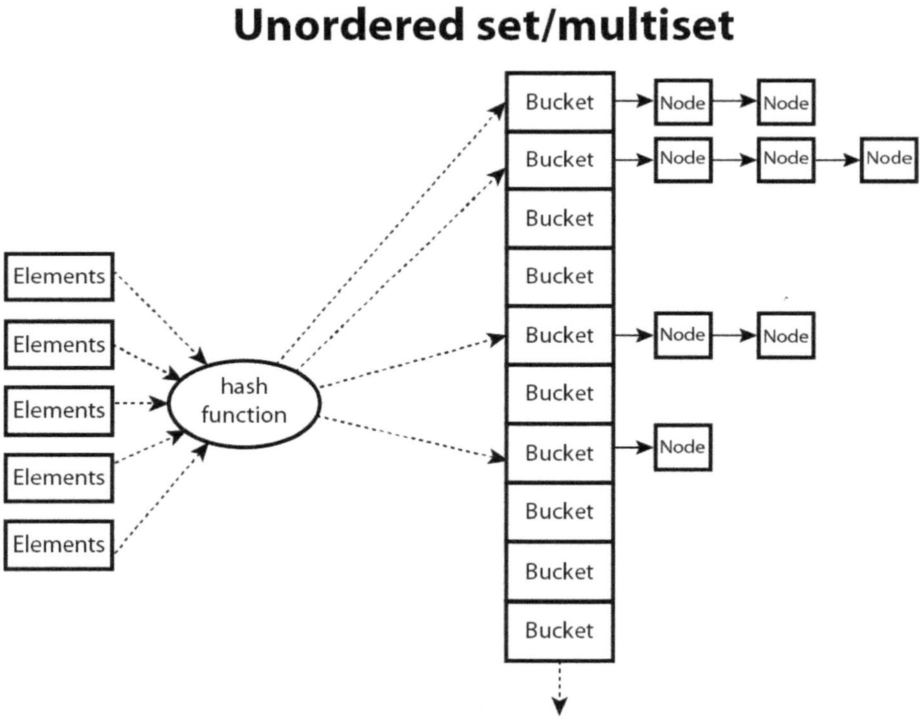

Figure 5.14: When an element is added to the set, its hash is computed to decide in which bucket the element should be added. The elements inside a bucket are stored as nodes of a list.

Container Adaptors | 199

When a key/value pair is added to the map, the hash of the key is computed to decide in which bucket the key/value pair should be added:

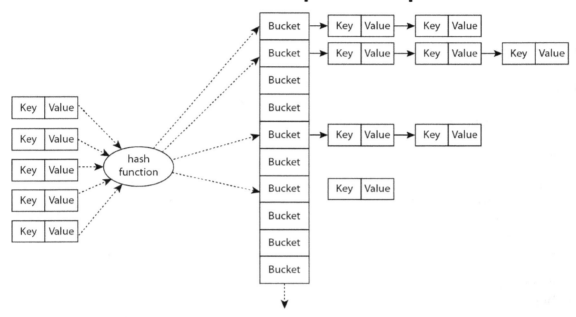

Figure 5.15: Representation of computing the bucket of an element from the key, and storing the key/ value pair as nodes in a list.

Unordered associative containers and ordered associative containers provide the same functionalities, and the explanations in the previous section apply to the unordered associative containers as well. Unordered associative containers can be used to get better performances when the order of the elements is not important.

Container Adaptors

Additional container classes that are provided by the STL library are container adaptors. Container adaptors provide constrained access policies on top of the containers we have looked at in this chapter.

Container adaptors have a template parameter that the user can provide to specify the type of container to wrap:

Container Adaptor	Description
Stack	Container with the LIFO (last-in-first-out) access policy. By default, it wraps a deque.
Queue	Container with the FIFO (first-in-first-out) access policy. By default, it wraps a deque.
Priority Queue	Container in which the elements have a priority associated; the container is accessed as a queue where the next element is the highest in priority. By default, it wraps a vector.

Figure 5.16: Table presenting container adaptors and their descriptions

Stack

The stack container implements the LIFO access policy, where the elements are virtually stacked one on the top of the other so that the last inserted element is always on top. Elements can only be read or removed from the top, so the last inserted element is the first that gets removed. A stack is implemented using a sequence container class internally, which is used to store all the elements and emulate the stack behavior.

The access pattern of the stack data structure happens mainly through three core member functions: **push()**, **top()**, and **pop()**. The **push()** function is used to insert an element into the stack, **top()** used to access the element on top of the stack, and **pop()** is used to remove the top element.

The **stack** class is defined in the **<stack>** header file.

Queue

The **queue** class implements the FIFO access policy, where the elements are enqueued one after the other, so that elements inserted before are ahead of elements inserted after. Elements are inserted at the end of the queue and removed at the start.

The interface of the queue data structure is composed of the **push()**, **front()**, **back()**, and **pop()** member functions.

The **push()** function is used to insert an element into the **queue()**; **front()** and **back()** return the next and last elements of the queue, respectively; the **pop()** is used to remove the next element from the queue.

The **queue** class is defined in the **<queue>** header file.

Priority Queue

Finally, the priority queue is a queue where the elements are accessed according to their priority, in descending order (highest priority first).

The interface is similar to the normal queue, where **push()** inserts a new element and **top()** and **pop()** access and remove the next element. The difference is in the way the next element is determined. Rather than being the first inserted element, it is the element that has the highest priority.

By default, the priority of the elements is computed by comparing the elements with the **operator<**, so that an element that is less than another comes after it. A user-defined sorting criterion can be provided to specify how to sort the elements by priority in regard to their priority in the queue.

The priority queue class is also defined in the **<queue>** header file.

Activity 21: Processing User Registration in Order

When a user registers to our website, we need to process the registration form at the end of the day.

We want to process the registration in *reverse* order of registration:

1. Assume that the class for the registration form is already provided:

   ```
   struct RegistrationForm {
       std::string userName;
   };
   ```

2. Create a **stack** to store the users.

3. We want to store the user registration form when the user registers, as well as process the registration at the end of the day. The function for processing the form is provided:

   ```
   void processRegistration(RegistrationForm form) {
       std::cout << "Processing form for user: " << form.userName <<
   std::endl;
   }
   ```

4. Additionally, there are already two functions that are called when a user registers.

5. Fill the code inside the following two functions to store the user form and process it:

```
void storeRegistrationForm(std::stack<RegistrationForm>& stack,
RegistrationForm form) {
}
void endOfDayRegistrationProcessing(std::stack<RegistrationForm>& stack) {
}
```

We'll see that the registration forms are processed in reverse order as the users are registered.

> **Note**
>
> The solution for this activity can be found at page 306.

Unconventional Containers

Up until now, we've seen containers that are used to store groups of elements of the same type.

The C++ standard defines some other types that can contain types but offer a different set of functionalities from the containers we saw previously.

These types are as follows:

1. String

2. Pair and tuple

3. Optional

4. Variant

Strings

A string is a data structure that's used to manipulate mutable sequences of contiguous characters. The C++ string classes are STL containers: they behave similarly to *vectors*, but provide additional functionalities that ease the programmer to perform common operations of sequences of characters easily.

There exist several string implementations in the standard library that are useful for different lengths of character sets, such as **string**, **wstring**, **u16string**, and **u32string**. All of them are a specialization of the **basic_string** base class and they all have the same interface.

The most commonly used type is **std::string**.

All types and functions for strings are defined in the **<string>** header file.

A string can be converted into a *null-terminating string*, which is an array of characters that terminate with the special null character (represented with '**\0**') via the use of the **data()** or **c_str()** functions. Null-terminating strings, also called *C-strings*, are the way to represent sequences of character in the C language and they are often used when the program needs to interoperate with a C library; they are represented with the **const char *** type and are the type of the *literal strings* in our programs.

Exercise 12: Demonstrating Working Mechanism of the c_str() Function

Let's examine the following code to understand how the **c_str()** function works:

1. First include the required header files as illustrated:

```
#include <iostream>
#include <string>
```

2. Now, in the **main** function add a constant char variable named **charString** with capacity as **8** characters:

```
int main()
{
  // Construct a C-string being explicit about the null terminator
  const char charString[8] = {'C', '+', '+', ' ', '1', '0', '1', '\0'};
  // Construct a C-string from a literal string. The compiler
automatically adds the \0 at the end
  const char * literalString = "C++ Fundamentals";
  // Strings can be constructed from literal strings.
  std::string strString = literalString;
```

3. Use the **c_str()** function and assign the value of **strString** to **charString2**:

```
const char *charString2 = strString.c_str();
```

4. Print the **charString** and **charString2** using the print function:

```
    std::cout << charString << std::endl;
    std::cout << charString2 << std::endl;
}
```

The output is as follows:

```
Output:
C++ 101
C++ Fundamentals
```

As for vectors, strings have **size()**, **empty()**, and **capacity()** member functions, but there is an additional function called **length()**, which is just an alias for **size()**.

Strings can be accessed in a character-by-character fashion using **operator[]** or the **at()**, **front()**, and **back()** member functions:

```
std::string chapter = "We are learning about strings";
```

```
std::cout << "Length: " << chapter.length() << ", the second character is "
<< chapter[1] << std::endl;
```

The usual comparison operators are provided for strings, thus simplifying the way two string objects can be compared.

Since strings are like vectors, we can add and remove characters from them.

Strings can be made empty by assigning an empty string, by calling the **clear()**, or **erase()** functions.

Let's look at the following code to understand the usage of the **clear()** and **erase()** functions:

```
#include <iostream>

#include <string>


int main()
{
  std::string str = "C++ Fundamentals.";
  std::cout << str << std::endl;


  str.erase(5,10);
```

```
    std::cout << "Erased: " << str << std::endl;


    str.clear();
    std::cout << "Cleared: " << str << std::endl;
}
```

Output:

```
C++ Fundamentals.
Erased: C++ Fs.
Cleared:
```

C++ also provides many convenience functions to convert a string into numeric values or vice versa. For example, the **stoi()** and **stod()** functions (which stand for *string-to-int* and *string-to-double*) are used to convert **string** to **int** and **double**, respectively. Instead, to convert a value into a string, it is possible to use the overloaded function **to_string()**.

Let's demystify these functions using the following code:

```
#include <iostream>
#include <string>
using namespace std;


int main()
{
  std::string str = "55";
  std::int strInt = std::stoi(str);
  double strDou = std::stod(str);
  std::string valToString = std::to_string(strInt);


  std::cout << str << std::endl;
  std::cout << strInt << std::endl;
  std::cout << strDou << std::endl;
  std::cout << valToString << std::endl;
}
```

Output:

55

55

55

55

Pairs and Tuples

The **pair** and **tuple** classes are similar to some extent, in the way they can store a collection of heterogeneous elements.

The **pair** class can store the values of two types, while the **tuple** class extended this concept to any length.

Pair is defined in the **<utility>** header, while tuple is in the **<tuple>** header.

The pair constructor takes two types as template parameters, used to specify the types for the first and second values. Those elements are accessed directly using the **first** and **second** data. Equivalently, these members can be accessed with the **get<0>()** and **get<1>()** functions.

The **make_pair()** convenience function is used to create a value pair without explicitly specifying the types:

```
std::pair<std::string, int> nameAndAge = std::make_pair("John", 32);

std::cout << "Name: " << nameAndAge.first << ", age: " << nameAndAge.second
<< std::endl;
```

The second line is equivalent to the following one:

```
std::cout << "Name: " << std::get<0>(nameAndAge) << ", age: " <<
std::get<1>(nameAndAge) << std::endl;
```

Pairs are used by unordered map, unordered multimap, map, and multimap containers to manage their key/value elements.

Tuples are similar to pairs. The constructor allows you to provide a variable number of template arguments. Elements are accessed with the **get<N>()** function only, which returns the nth element inside the tuple, and there is a convenience function to create them similar to that for pair, named **make_tuple()**.

Additionally, tuples have another convenience function that's used to extract values from them. The **tie()** function allows for the creation of a tuple of references, which is useful in assigning selected elements from a tuple to specific variables.

Let's understand how to use the **make_tuple()** and **get()** functions to retrieve data from a tuple:

```
#include <iostream>
#include <tuple>
#include <string>


int main()
{
  std::tuple<std::string, int, float> james = std::make_tuple("James", 7,
1.90f);
  std::cout << "Name: " << std::get<0>(james) << ". Agent number: " <<
std::get<1>(james) << ". Height: " << std::get<2>(james) << std::endl;
}


Output:
Name: James. Agent number: 7. Height: 1.9
```

std::optional

optional<T> is a that's used to contain a value that might be present or not.

The class takes a template parameter, **T**, which represents the type that the **std::optional** template class might contain. Value type means that the instance of the class contains the value. Copying **optional** will create a new copy of the contained data.

At any point in the execution of the program, **optional<T>** either contains nothing, when it's empty, or contains a value of type **T**.

Optional is defined in the **<optional>** header.

Let's imagine our application is using a class named **User** for managing registered users. We would like to have a function that gets us the information of a user from their email: **User getUserByEmail(Email email);**.

But what happens when a user is not registered? That is, when we can determine that our system does not have the associated **User** instance?

Some would suggest throwing an exception. In C++, exceptions are used for *exceptional* situations, ones that should almost never happen. A user not being registered on our website is a perfectly normal situation.

In these situations, we can use the **optional** template class to represent the fact that we might not have the data:

```
std::optional<User> tryGetUserByEmail(Email email);
```

The **optional** template provides two easy methods to work with:

- **has_value()**: This returns **true** if **optional** is currently holding a value, and **false** if the variant is empty.

- **value()**: This function returns the value currently held by **optional**, or throws an exception if it's not present.

- Additionally, **optional** can be used as a condition in an **if** statement: it will evaluate to **true** if it contains a value, or **false** otherwise.

Let's look at the following example to understand how the **has_value()** and **value()** functions work:

```cpp
#include <iostream>
#include <optional>

int main()
{
  // We might not know the hour. But if we know it, it's an integer
  std::optional<int> currentHour;
  if (not currentHour.has_value()) {
    std::cout << "We don't know the time" << std::endl;
  }
  currentHour = 18;
  if (currentHour) {
    std::cout << "Current hour is: " << currentHour.value() << std::endl;
  }
}
Output:
We don't know the time
Current hour is: 18
```

The **optional** template comes with additional convenience features. We can assign the **std::nullopt** value to **optional** to make it explicit when we want it empty, and we can use the **make_optional** value to create an optional from a value. Additionally, we can use the dereference operator, *****, to access the value of **optional** without throwing an exception if the value is not present. In such cases, we will access invalid data, so we need to be sure that **optional** contains a value when we use *****:

```
std::optional<std::string> maybeUser = std::nullopt;

if (not maybeUser) {

  std::cout << "The user is not present" << std::endl;

}

maybeUser = std::make_optional<std::string>("email@example.com");

if (maybeUser) {

  std::cout << "The user is: " << *maybeUser  << std::endl;

}
```

Another handy method is **value_or(defaultValue)**. This function takes a default value and returns the value contained by **optional** if it currently holds a value, otherwise it returns the default value. Let's explore the following example:

```
#include <iostream>

#include <optional>


int main()

{

  std::optional<int> x;

  std::cout << x.value_or(10) << std::endl;

  //Will return value of x as 10

  x = 15;

  std::cout << x.value_or(10)<< std::endl;

  //Will return value of x as 15

}
Output:
10
15
```

In addition to return values, **optional** is useful when accepting it as an argument to represent arguments that can be present or not.

Let's recall our **User** class that's composed of an email address, a phone number, and a physical address. Sometimes, users don't have a phone number and don't want to provide a physical address, so the only required field we have in **User** is the email address:

```
User::User(Email email, std::optional<PhoneNumber> phoneNumber =
std::nullopt, std::optional<Address> address = std::nullopt){

...

}
```

This constructor allows us to pass in all the information we have on the user. If, instead of using **optional**, we used multiple overloads, we would have had four overloads:

1. Only email

2. Email and phone number

3. Email and address

4. Email with phone number and address

You can see that the number of overloads grows quickly when there are more arguments that we might not want to pass.

std::variant

variant is a value type that's used to represent a *choice of types*. The class takes a list of types, and the variant will be able to contain one value of any of those types.

It is often referred to as **tagged union**, because similar to a union, it can store multiple types, with only one present at a time. It also keeps track of which type is currently stored.

During the execution of a program, **variant** will contain exactly one of the possible types at a time.

Like **optional**, **variant** is a value type: when we create a copy of **variant**, the element that is currently stored is copied into the new **variant**.

To interact with **std::variant**, the C++ standard library gives us two main functions:

- **holds_alternative<Type>(variant)**: It returns **true** if the variant is currently holding the provided type, if not then **false**.

- **get(variant)**: There are two versions: **get<Type>(variant)** and **get<Index>(variant)**.

get<Type>(variant) gets the value of the type that's currently stored inside the variant. Before calling this function, the caller needs to be sure that **holds_alternative<Type>(variant)** returns **true**.

get<Index>(variant) gets the value of the index type that's currently stored inside **variant**. Like before, the caller needs to be sure that **variant** is holding the correct type.

For example, with **std::variant<string, float> variant**, calling **get<0>(variant)** will give us the **string** value, but we need to be sure that **variant** is currently storing a string at the moment. Usually, it is preferable to access the elements with **get<Type>()** so that we are explicit on the type that we expect and that if the order of the types in the variant changes, we will still get the same result:

Exercise 13: Using Variant in the Program

Let's perform the following steps to understand how to use variant in the program:

1. Include the required header files:

    ```
    #include <iostream>
    #include <variant>
    ```

2. In the main function, add the variant with the value type as string and integer:

    ```
    int main()
    {
        std::variant<std::string, int> variant = 42;
    ```

3. Now using the two print statements call the variant in different ways:

    ```
    std::cout << get<1>(variant) << std::endl;
    std::cout << get<int>(variant) << std::endl;
    ```

The output is as follows:

```
Output:
42

42
```

An alternative way to get the content of **variant** is to use **std::visit(visitor, variant)**, which takes **variant** and a callable object. The callable objects need to support an overload of **operator()**, taking a type for each of the possible types stored inside **variant**. Then, **visit** will make sure to call the function that accepts the current type that's stored inside **variant**:

Exercise 14: Visitor Variant

Let's perform the following steps to understand how to use std::visit(visitor, variant) in the program:

1. Add the following header files at the start of the program:

```
#include <iostream>
#include <string>
#include <variant>
```

2. Now, add the struct Visitor as illustrated:

```
struct Visitor {
    void operator()(const std::string& value){
        std::cout << "a string: " << value << std::endl;
    }
    void operator()(const int& value){
        std::cout << "an int: " << value << std::endl;
    }
};
```

3. Now, in the main function, call the struct Visitor and pass values as illustrated:

```
int main()
{
    std::variant<std::string, int> variant = 42;
    Visitor visitor;
    std::cout << "The variant contains ";
    std::visit(visitor, variant);
    variant = std::string("Hello world");
    std::cout << "The variant contains ";
    std::visit(visitor, variant);
}
```

The output is as follows:

```
The variant contains an int: 42
The variant contains a string: Hello world
```

variant is incredibly valuable when we want to represent a set of values of different types. Typical examples are as follows:

- A function returning different types depending on the current state of the program

- A class that represents several states

Let's imagine our **std::optional<User> tryGetUserByEmail()** function, which we described earlier.

Thanks to **optional**, we could now write the function in a clear way, showing that sometimes we would not retrieve the user. It is likely that if the user is not registered, we might ask them whether they want to register.

Let's imagine we have **struct UserRegistrationForm**, which contains the information that's needed to let the user register.

Our function can now return **std::variant<User, UserRegistrationForm> tryGetUserByEmail()**. When the user is registered, we return **User**, but if the user is not registered, we can return the registration form.

Additionally, what should we do when there is an error? With **variant**, we could have **struct GetUserError** storing all the information we have so that our application will be able to recover from the error and add it to the return type: **std::variant<User, UserRegistrationForm, GetUserError>**, or **tryGetUserByEmail()**.

Now we can have the complete picture of what is going to happen when we call **getUserByEmail()** by just looking at the function signature, and the compiler will help us make sure that we handle all the cases.

Alternatively, **variant** can also be used to represent the various states in which a class can be. Each state contains the data that's required for that state, and the class only manages the transitions from one state to another.

Activity 22: Airport System Management

Let's write a program to create airport system management:

1. We want to represent the state of an airplane in an airport system. The airplane can be in three states: **at_gate**, **taxi**, or **flying**. The three states store different information.

2. With **at_gate**, the airplane stores the gate number at which it is. With **taxi**, we store which lane the airplane is assigned and how many passengers are on board. With **flying**, we store the speed:

   ```
   struct AtGate {
       int gate;
   };

   struct Taxi {
       int lane;
       int numPassengers;
   };

   struct Flying {
       float speed;
   };
   ```

3. The airplane should have three methods:

   - **startTaxi()**: This method takes the lane the airplane should go on and the number of passengers on board. The airplane can start taxi only if it is at the gate.

   - **takeOff()**: This method takes the speed at which the airplane should fly. The airplane can start flying only if it is in the taxi state.

   - **currentStatus()**: This method prints the current status of the airplane.

   Note

   The solution for this activity can be found on page 306.

Iterators

In this chapter, we've mentioned multiple times that elements have a position in a container: for example, we said that we can insert an element in a specific position in a list.

Iterators are the way in which the position of an element in a container is represented.

They provide a consistent way to operate on elements of the container, abstracting the details of the container to which the elements belong.

An iterator always belongs to a range. The iterator representing the start of the range, can be accessed by the **begin()** function, while the iterator representing the end of the range, non-inclusive, can be obtained with the **end()** function. The range where the first element is included, but where the last one is excluded, is referred to as half-open.

The interface that the iterator must offer is composed of four functions:

1. The * operator provides access to the element at the position currently referenced by the iterator.

2. The ++ operator is used to move forward to the next element.

3. Then, the == operator is used to compare two iterators to check whether they are pointing to the same position.

   Note that two iterators can only be compared if they are part of the same range: they must represent the position of elements of the same container.

4. Finally, the = operator is used to assign an iterator.

Every container class in C++ must specify the type of iterator that it provides to access its elements as a member type alias named **iterator**. For example, for a vector of integer, the type would be **std::vector<int>::iterator**.

Let's see how we could use iterators to iterate over all the elements of a container (a vector, in this case):

```
#include <iostream>
#include <vector>

int main()
{
```

```
    std::vector<int> numbers = {1, 2, 3};

    for(std::vector<int>::iterator it = numbers.begin(); it != numbers.
end(); ++it) {

        std::cout << "The number is: " << *it << std::endl;

    }

}
```

This looks complex for such an operation, and we saw in *Chapter 1, Getting Started* how we can use *range-based for*:

```
for(int number: numbers) {

    std::cout << "The number is: " << number << std::endl;

}
```

Range-based for works thanks to iterators: the compiler rewrites our *range-based for* to look like the one we wrote with iterators. This allows the *range-based for* to work with any type that provides **begin()** and **end()** functions and returns iterators.

The way operators provided by the iterators are implemented depends on the container on which the iterator operates.

Iterator can be grouped into four categories. Each category builds on the previous category, thus offering additional functionality:

Iterator	Description
Input	Iterator that can step forward. It can be used only in a single pass.
Forward	Iterator that can step forward and can be used in multiple passes.
Bidirectional	Iterator that can step forward and backward.
Random-access	Iterator that can step forward and backward to arbitrary positions in constant time.

Figure 5.17: Table presenting iterators and their descriptions

The following diagram gives more detail about C++ iterators:

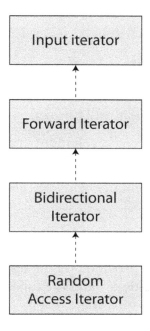

Figure 5.18: Representation of iterators hierarchy in C++

Let's understand each of these iterators in more detail:

- **Input iterator** can step forward and allow you to read the element it is pointing to. The iterator can be copied, but when one copy is incremented or dereferenced to access the element, all the other copies are invalidated and cannot be incremented or dereferenced anymore. Conceptually, it means that elements in a sequence that are accessed through an input iterator can only be read once at most.

  Input iterators are usually used in a pattern where access to elements is always followed by a position increment.

  Additionally, input iterators provide the == and != operators to check whether the iterator is equal to the **end()** value.

  Typically, input iterators are used to access elements from a stream of elements, where the whole sequence is not stored in memory, but we are obtaining one element at a time.

- **Forward iterators** are very similar to input iterators but provide additional guarantees.

  The same iterator can be dereferenced several times to access the element it points to.

  Additionally, when we increment or dereference a forward iterator, the other copies are not invalidated: if we make a copy of a forward iterator, we can advance the first one, and the second can still be used to access the previous element.

  Two iterators that refer to the same element are guaranteed to be equal.

- **Bidirectional iterators** are also forward iterators with the additional ability to iterate backward over the elements using the `operator--` (position decrement) member function.

- **Random-access iterators** are also bidirectional iterators with the additional ability to directly access any position without the need of a linear scan, in constant time. Random-access iterators are provided by the `operator[]` member function to access elements at generic indexes and the binary `operator+` and `operator-` to step forward and backward of any quantity.

Exercise 15: Exploring Iterator

Perform the following steps to explore the four categories discussed in the previous section and writing to the element it points to, it is also an Output Iterator:

1. Add the following header files at the start of the program:

    ```
    #include <iostream>
    #include <vector>
    ```

2. In the main function declare the vector named number:

    ```
    int main()
    {
        std::vector<int> numbers = {1, 2, 3, 4, 5};
        auto it = numbers.begin();
    ```

3. Perform the various arithmetic operations as illustrated:

    ```
    std::cout << *it << std::endl; // dereference: points to 1
    it++; // increment: now it points to 2
    std::cout << *it << std::endl;
    // random access: access the 2th element after the current one
    std::cout << it[2] << std::endl;
    --it; // decrement: now it points to 1 again
    ```

```
        std::cout << *it << std::endl;
        it += 4; // advance the iterator by 4 positions: now it points to 5
        std::cout << *it << std::endl;
        it++; // advance past the last element;
        std::cout << "'it' is after the past element: " << (it == numbers.
    end()) << std::endl;
    }
```

The output is as follows:

```
1

2

4

1

5

'it' is after the past element: 1
```

Many of the iterators we will talk about are defined in the **<iterator>** header.

Reverse Iterators

Sometimes, we need to iterate though a collection of elements in reverse order.

C++ provides an iterator that allows us to do this: the *reverse iterator*.

A *reverse iterator* wraps a *bidirectional iterator* and swaps the operation increment with the operation of decrement, and vice versa.

Because of this, when we are iterating a reverse iterator in the forward direction, we are visiting the elements in a range in backward order.

We can reverse the range of a container by calling the following methods on a container:

Iterator functions	Description
rbegin()	Returns the position of the last element of the container
rend()	Returns the position before the first element of the container

Figure 5.19: Table presenting iterator functions and their descriptions

Code that works on normal iterators, it will also work with reverse iterators.

For example, we can see how similar the code is to iterate in reverse order.

Exercise 16: Exploring Functions of Reverse Iterator

Let's perform the following steps to understand how functions in reverse iterator works:

1. Add the following header files at the start of the program:

    ```
    #include <iostream>
    #include <vector>
    ```

2. In the main function, add the vector named numbers as illustrated:

    ```
    int main()
    {
        std::vector<int> numbers = {1, 2, 3, 4, 5};
    ```

3. Now iterate through the number vector as illustrated:

    ```
    for(auto rit = numbers.rbegin(); rit != numbers.rend(); ++rit) {
        std::cout << "The number is: " << *rit << std::endl;
    }
    }
    ```

The output is as follows:

```
The number is: 5
The number is: 4
The number is: 3
The number is: 2
The number is: 1
```

Insert Iterators

Insert iterators, also called **inserters**, are used to insert new values into a container rather than overwrite them.

There exist three types of inserters, which differ on the position in the container at which they insert the elements.

The following table summarizes the different categories:

Iterator functions	Description
Back inserter	Appends a value at the end of the container by calling the push_back() function
Front inserters	Inserts a value at the beginning of the container by calling the push_front() function
General inserts	Inserts a value at a provided position of the container by calling the insert() function

Figure 5.20: Table presenting iterator functions and their descriptions

Some algorithms, which we are going to see later in this chapter, require an iterator for storing data. Insert iterators are usually used with such algorithms.

Stream Iterators

Stream iterators allow us to use streams as a source to read elements from or as a destination to write elements to:

Iterator Functions	Description
IStream	Reads elements from an input stream
OStream	Writes values to an output stream

Figure 5.21: Table presenting iterator functions and their descriptions

Because we don't have a container in this case, we cannot call the **end()** method to get the **end** iterator. A default constructed stream iterator counts as the end of any stream range.

Let's look at a program that reads space-separated integers from the standard input.

Exercise 17: Stream Iterator

Let's perform the following steps to understand how functions in reverse stream works:

1. Add the required header files as illustrated:

```
#include <iostream>
#include <iterator>
```

2. Now, in the main function, add the istream iterator as illustrated:

```
int main()
{
    std::istream_iterator<int> it = std::istream_iterator<int>(std::cin);
    std::istream_iterator<int> end;
    for(; it != end; ++it) {
        std::cout << "The number is: " << *it << std::endl;
    }
}
```

The output is as follows (input: 10):

```
The number is: 10
```

Iterator Invalidation

As we said, iterators represent the position of elements in a container.

This means that they are tightly tied with the container, and changes to the container might move the elements: this means that iterators pointing to such an element can no longer be used – they are **invalidated**.

It is extremely important to always check the invalidation contract when using iterators with containers, as it is not specified what happens when using an invalidated iterator. More commonly, invalid data is accessed or the program crashes, leading to bugs that are hard to find.

If we keep in mind how the containers are implemented, as we saw earlier in this chapter, we can more easily remember when an iterator is invalidated.

For example, we said that when we insert an element in a vector, we might have to get more memory to store the element, in which case all the previous elements are moved to the newly obtained memory. This means that all the iterators pointing to the elements are now pointing to the old location of the elements: they are invalidated.

On the other hand, we saw that when we insert an element into the list, we only have to update the predecessor and successor nodes, but the elements are not moved. This means that the iterators to the elements remain valid:

```
#include <iostream>

#include <vector>

#include <list>


int main()
```

```
{
    std::vector<int> vector = {1};
    auto first_in_vec = vector.begin();
    std::cout << "Before vector insert: " << *first_in_vec << std::endl;
    vector.push_back(2);
    // first_number is invalidated! We can no longer use it!
    std::list<int> list = {1};
    auto first_in_list = list.begin();
    list.push_back(2);
    // first_in_list is not invalidated, we can use it.
    std::cout << "After list insert: " << *first_in_list << std::endl;
}
```

Output:

```
Before vector insert: 1
After list insert: 1
```

When there is a need to store iterators to elements, iterator invalidation is an important consideration to make when deciding which container to use.

Exercise 18: Printing All of the Customers' Balances

We want to print the balances for all of the customers of our application. The balances are already stored inside a vector as integers.

We want to use iterators to traverse the vector of balances. Follow these steps to do so:

1. Initially, we include the header file for the **vector** class, and we declare a vector of 10 elements of type **int**:

   ```
   #include <vector>
   std::vector<int> balances = {10, 34, 64, 97, 56, 43, 50, 89, 32, 5};
   ```

2. The **for** loop has been modified to iterate using the vector's iterator, starting from the position returned by **begin()** until it reaches the one returned by **end()**:

   ```
   for (auto pos = numbers.begin(); pos != numbers.end(); ++pos)
   {
       // to be filled
   }
   ```

3. The element of the array is accessed using the dereference operator (*) on the iterator:

```
for (auto pos = numbers.begin(); pos != numbers.end(); ++pos)
{
    std::cout << "Balance: " << *pos << std::endl;
}
```

Algorithms Provided by the C++ Standard Template Library

Algorithms are a way to operate on containers in an abstract way.

The C++ standard library provides a wide range of algorithms for all the common operations that can be performed on ranges of elements.

Because algorithms accept iterators, they can operate on any container, even user-defined containers, as long as they provide iterators.

This allows us to have a large number of algorithms that work with a large number of containers, without the need for the algorithm to know how the container is implemented.

The following are some of the most important and common algorithms that are provided by the STL.

Note

Algorithms operate on ranges, so they normally take a pair of iterators: *first* and *last*.

As we said earlier in this chapter, the *last* iterator denotes the element past the end of the range – it is not part of the range.

This means that when we want to operate on a full container, we can pass **begin()** and **end()** as arguments to the algorithm, but if we want to operate on a shorter sequence, we must be sure that our *last* iterator is past the last item we want to include in the range.

Lambda

Most of the algorithms accept a unary or binary predicate: a **Functor** (function object), which accepts either one or two parameters. These predicates allow the user to specify some of the actions that the algorithm requires. What the actions are vary from algorithm to algorithm.

As we saw at the end of *Chapter 3, Classes*, to write a function object, we have to create a class and overload the **operator()**.

This can be very verbose, especially when the functor should perform a simple operation.

To overcome this with C++, the user has to write a **lambda expression**, also called just a *lambda*.

A *lambda expression* creates a special function object, with a type known only by the compiler, that behaves like a function but can access the variables in the scope in which it is created.

It is defined with a syntax very similar to the one of functions:

```
[captured variables] (arguments) { body }
```

This creates a new object that, when called with the arguments specified in the lambda expression, executes the body of the function.

Arguments is the list of arguments the function accepts, and *body* is the sequence of statements to execute when the function is invoked. They have the same meaning that they have for functions, and the same rules we saw in *Chapter 2, Functions*, apply.

For example, let's create a lambda that takes two integers and returns their sum:

```cpp
#include <iostream>

int main()
{
    auto sum_numbers = [] (int a, int b) { return a + b; };
    std::cout << sum_numbers(10, 20) << std::endl;
}
```

```
Output:
30
```

By default, the body of the lambda can only reference the variables that are defined in the argument list and inside the body, like for functions.

Additionally, *lambdas* can **capture** a variable in the local scope, and use it in their body.

Captured variables entail a list of variable names that can be referenced in the body of the lambda.

When a variable is captured, it is stored inside the created function object, and it can be referenced in the body.

By default, the variables are *captured by value*, so they are copied inside the function object:

```
#include <iostream>


int main()
{
    int addend = 1;
    auto sum_numbers = [addend](int b) { return addend + b; };
    addend = 2;
    std::cout << sum_numbers(3) << std::endl;
}
Output:
4
```

When we created the lambda, we captured **addend** by value: it was copied into the **sum_numbers** object. Even if we modified the value of **addend**, we did not change the copy stored inside **sum_numbers**, so when **sum_numbers** is executed, it sums 1 to **b**.

In some situations, we want to be able to modify the value of a variable in the scope in which the *lambda* is created, or we want to access the actual value, not the value that the variable had when the lambda was created.

In that case, we can capture by reference by prepending **&** to the variable name.

> **Note**
>
> When we capture by reference, we need to make sure that the variable that's been captured by reference is still valid when the lambda is invoked, otherwise the body of the function accesses an invalid object, resulting in bugs.
> Prefer to capture by value when it is possible.

Let's look at an example:

```cpp
#include <iostream>

int main()
{
    int multiplier = 1;
    auto multiply_numbers = [&multiplier](int b) { return multiplier * b; };
    multiplier = 2;
    std::cout << multiply_numbers(3) << std::endl;
}
Output:
6
```

Here, we capture the **multiplier** variable by reference: only a reference to it was stored into **multiply_numbers**.

When we invoke **multiply_numbers**, the body accesses the current value of **multiplier**, and since **multiplier** was changed to 2, that is the value that's used by the *lambda*.

A lambda can capture multiple variables, and each one can be either captured by value or by reference, independently one from the other.

Read-Only Algorithms

Read-only algorithms are algorithms that inspect the elements stored inside a container but do not modify the order of the elements of the container.

The following are the most common operations that inspect the elements of a range:

all_of any_of none_of	These three functions all accept three arguments: the beginning of a range, the end of the range, and a unary predicate. They return true if the predicate returns true for all, at least one, or no element in the sequence, respectively.
for_each	Take the beginning of a range, the end of the range, and a unary predicate. Calls the unary predicate with each element in the sequence, in order of iteration.
count count_if	Take the beginning of a range, the end of the range, and a value or a unary predicate. Returns the number of elements which are equal to the value, or for which the predicate is true.
find find_if find_if_not	Take the beginning of a range, the end of the range, and a value or a unary predicate. Returns the iterator pointing at the position of the first element that is equal to the value, or the end of the range if the element is not found. In the variant with the predicate, it returns the first element for which the predicate is true, the end of the range otherwise.

Figure 5.22: Table presenting the operations that inspect elements of a range

Let's see how we can use these functions:

```
#include <iostream>
#include <vector>
#include <algorithm>


int main()
{
    std::vector<int> vector = {1, 2, 3, 4};
    bool allLessThen10 = std::all_of(vector.begin(), vector.end(), [](int
value) { return value < 10; });
    std::cout << "All are less than 10: " << allLessThen10 << std::endl;
    bool someAreEven = std::any_of(vector.begin(), vector.end(), [](int
value) { return value % 2 == 0; });
    std::cout << "Some are even: " << someAreEven << std::endl;
    bool noneIsNegative = std::none_of(vector.begin(), vector.end(), [](int
value) { return value < 0; });
    std::cout << "None is negative: " << noneIsNegative << std::endl;
```

```
    std::cout << "Odd numbers: " << std::count_if(vector.begin(), vector.
end(), [](int value) { return value % 2 == 1; }) << std::endl;


    auto position = std::find(vector.begin(), vector.end(), 6);
    std::cout << "6 was found: " << (position != vector.end()) << std::endl;
}
```

Output:

All are less than 10: 1

Some are even: 1

None is negative: 1

Odd numbers: 2

6 was found: 0

Modifying Algorithms

Modifying algorithms are algorithms that modify the collections they iterate on:

copy copy_if	Take the beginning of a range, the end of the range, and an output iterator. Copies the elements in the range into the output iterator. The copy_if variant additionally takes a unary predicate and copies the element only if the predicate is true.
transform	There are two overloads of this function, and which are commonly used. One takes the beginning of a range, the end of the range, an output iterator, and a unary predicate. It applies the unary predicate to each element in the range and outputs it into the output iterator. The second one takes the beginning of a range, the end of the range, the beginning of a second range, which needs to be at least as long as the first one, an output iterator, and a binary predicate. It applies the binary predicate, passing the elements at the same position in the two ranges, and outputs the returned value into the output iterator.
remove remove_if	Take the beginning of a range, the end of the range, a value or a unary predicate. Unlike the name suggests, the algorithm does not remove the element from the container, but it puts all the elements equal to a value, or for which the predicate is true, at the end of the container, and returns the iterator after the last element that should not be removed. The iterator cannot know how to remove elements, since the algorithm is not provided with iterators, so it groups them to make it easy to remove by calling the appropriate method in the container.

Figure 5.23: Table presenting the modifying algorithms

Let's see these algorithms in action:

```cpp
#include <iostream>
#include <vector>
#include <algorithm>
#include <iterator>

int main()
{
    std::vector<std::string> vector = {"Hello", "C++", "Morning",
"Learning"};
    std::vector<std::string> longWords;

    std::copy_if(vector.begin(), vector.end(), std::back_inserter(longWords),
[](const std::string& s) { return s.length() > 3; });
    std::cout << "Number of longWords: " << longWords.size() << std::endl;

    std::vector<int> lengths;
    std::transform(longWords.begin(), longWords.end(), std::back_
inserter(lengths), [](const std::string& s) { return s.length(); });

    std::cout << "Lengths: ";
    std::for_each(lengths.begin(), lengths.end(), [](int length) { std::cout
<< length << " "; });
    std::cout << std::endl;

    auto newLast = std::remove_if(lengths.begin(), lengths.end(), [](int
length) { return length < 7; });
    std::cout << "No element removed yet: " << lengths.size() << std::endl;

    // erase all the elements between the two iterators
    lengths.erase(newLast, lengths.end());
    std::cout << "Elements are removed now. Content: ";
    std::for_each(lengths.begin(), lengths.end(), [](int length) { std::cout
```

```
<< length << " "; });
    std::cout << std::endl;
}
```

Output:

```
Number of longWords: 3
Lengths: 5 7 8
No element removed yet: 3
Elements are removed now. Content: 7 8
```

Mutating Algorithms

Mutating algorithms are algorithms that change the order of elements:

reverse reverse_copy	Take the beginning of a range and the end of the range. Reverse the order of the elements in the two ranges. The reverse_copy variant also takes an output iterator and the output of the reversed range without modifying the source range.
shuffle	Take the beginning of a range, the end of the range, and a random number generator. Reorders the elements in the range in a random order.

Figure 5.24: Table presenting mutating algorithms

Let's see how we can use them:

```
#include <iostream>

#include <random>

#include <vector>

#include <algorithm>

#include <iterator>


int main()
{
    std::vector<int> vector = {1, 2, 3, 4, 5, 6};

    std::random_device randomDevice;
    std::mt19937 randomNumberGenerator(randomDevice());
    std::shuffle(vector.begin(), vector.end(), randomNumberGenerator);
    std::cout << "Values: ";
```

```
    std::for_each(vector.begin(), vector.end(), [](int value) { std::cout <<
value << " "; });
    std::cout << std::endl;

}
```

Output:

Values: 5 2 6 4 3 1

Sorting Algorithms

This class of algorithms rearranges the order of elements within a container in a specific order:

Functions	Description
sort	Takes the beginning of a range, the end of the range, and optionally a binary predicate. Change the order of the range to keep the element in sorted, ascending order. When the binary predicate is provided, the elements are compared by invoking it, and the first argument is moved before the second if it returns true. The operator< is used otherwise.

Figure 5.25: Table presenting sorting algorithms

Here is how to sort a vector:

```
#include <iostream>

#include <vector>

#include <algorithm>


int main()

{

    std::vector<int> vector = {5, 2, 6, 4, 3, 1};


    std::sort(vector.begin(), vector.end());

    std::cout << "Values: ";

    std::for_each(vector.begin(), vector.end(), [](int value) { std::cout <<
value << " "; });

    std::cout << std::endl;

}
```

Output:

Values: 1 2 3 4 5 6

Binary Search Algorithms

The following table explains the use of **binary_search**:

binary_search	Takes the beginning of a range, the end of the range, a value, and optionally a binary predicate. Looks for the value in the range and states whether it was found. The provided range must be sorted according to the binary predicate. If no predicate is provided, the range must be sorted according to operator<.

Figure 5.26: Table presenting the use of binary_search

Here's how you can utilize the binary search algorithm:

```cpp
#include <iostream>
#include <vector>
#include <algorithm>

int main()
{
    std::vector<int> vector = {1, 2, 3, 4, 5, 6};

    bool found = std::binary_search(vector.begin(), vector.end(), 2);
    std::cout << "Found: " << found << std::endl;
}
Output:
Found: 1
```

Numeric Algorithms

This class of algorithms combines numeric elements using a linear operation in different ways:

accumulate	Takes the beginning of a range, the end of the range, an initial value, and optionally a binary predicate. Combines all the elements in the range with the initial value using the binary predicate. If the binary predicate is not provided, operator+ is used.

Figure 5.27: Table presenting the numeric algorithm

Let's see how we can use **accumulate** in the following program:

```
#include <iostream>
#include <vector>
#include <algorithm>

int main()
{
    std::vector<int> costs = {1, 2, 3};

    int budget = 10;
    int margin = std::accumulate(costs.begin(), costs.end(), budget, [](int
a, int b) { return a - b; });
    std::cout << "Margin: " << margin << std::endl;
}
Output:
Margin: 4
```

Exercise 19: Customer Analytics

We have the information of many customers of our application and we want to compute analytics data on that.

Given a map that has a username as a key and a user account as a value, we would like to print the balances of the new users in descending order.

A user is considered new if they registered no more than 15 days ago. The struct representing the user's account is provided and is as follows:

```
struct UserAccount {
    int balance;
    int daysSinceRegistered;
};
```

Write the **void computeAnalytics(std::map<std::string, UserAccount>& accounts)** function, which prints the desired balances.

1. Make sure to include all the required headers for the solution:

    ```
    #include <iostream>
    #include <vector>
    #include <iterator>
    #include <map>
    #include <algorithm>
    ```

2. First, we need to extract **UserAccount** from the map. Remember that the element the map stores is **pair** containing a key and value. Since we need to transform the type into **UserAccount**, we can use **std::transform**, by passing a **lambda** that only returns the user account from the **pair**. To insert this into **vector**, we can use **std::back_inserter**. Make sure to use a **const** reference when accepting **pair** in the lambda that's passed to transform:

    ```
    void computeAnalytics(std::map<std::string, UserAccount>& accounts) {
        // Balance of accounts newer than 15 days, in descending order
        std::vector<UserAccount> newAccounts;
        std::transform(accounts.begin(), accounts.end(), std::back_
    inserter(newAccounts),
                    [](const std::pair<std::string, UserAccount>& user) {
    return user.second; });
        }
    ```

3. After we have extracted the accounts in **vector**, we can use **remove_if** to remove all accounts that are older than 15 days:

    ```
    auto newEnd = std::remove_if(newAccounts.begin(), newAccounts.end(),
    [](const UserAccount& account) { return account.daysSinceRegistered > 15;
    } );
        newAccounts.erase(newEnd, newAccounts.end());
    ```

4. After removing the old accounts, we need to sort the balances in descending order. By default, **std::sort** uses an ascending order, so we need to provide a **lambda** to change the order:

```
std::sort(newAccounts.begin(), newAccounts.end(), [](const
UserAccount& lhs, const UserAccount& rhs) { return lhs.balance > rhs.
balance; } );
Now that the data is sorted, we can print it:
    for(const UserAccount& account : newAccounts) {
        std::cout << account.balance << std::endl;
    }
}
```

5. We can now invoke our function with the following test data:

```
int main()
{
    std::map<std::string, UserAccount> users = {
        {"Alice", UserAccount{500, 15}},
        {"Bob", UserAccount{1000, 50}},
        {"Charlie", UserAccount{600, 17}},
        {"Donald", UserAccount{1500, 4}}
    };
    computeAnalytics(users);
}
```

Summary

In this chapter, we introduced sequential containers – containers whose elements can be accessed in sequence. We looked at the **array**, **vector**, **deque**, **list**, and **forward_list** sequential containers.

We saw what functionality they offer and how we can operate on them, and we saw how they are implemented and how storage works for vector and list.

We followed this up with associative containers, containers that allow the fast lookup of their elements, always kept in order. **Set**, **multiset**, **map**, and **multimap** are part of this category.

We looked at the operations they support and how map and multimap are used to associate a value to a key. We also saw their unordered version, which does not keep elements in order but provides higher performance. **Unordered_set** and **unordered_map** are in this category.

Finally, we looked at unconventional containers. **String** is used to manipulate sequences of characters, **pair** and **tuple** are used to hold various elements of different types, **optional** is used to add optionality to a type, and **variant** is used to store a value that could be of several types.

We then explored iterators and learned how they are used to abstract the concept of containers and provide a common set of functionalities.

We looked at the various types of iterators, and we learned what iterator invalidation is and why it is important to be aware of it.

We finally moved on to algorithms in the C++ standard, after explaining that **lambda** is a convenient way of defining a function that can also access variables in the scope in which it is created.

We divided the most common algorithms into various categories, and we looked at the most important algorithms in those categories, including **find**, **remove**, and **sort**.

In the next chapter, you will learn how to use the advanced features of C++ to create dynamic programs.

Object-Oriented Programming

Lesson Objectives

By the end of this chapter, you will be able to:

- Compose classes that inherit properties from other classes
- Implement polymorphism in C++ programs
- Implement interfaces
- Use best practices to manage dynamic memory

In this chapter, you will learn how to use the advanced features of C++ to create dynamic programs.

Introduction

In earlier chapters, we learned about templates that are used to create functions and classes that work with arbitrary types. This avoids duplication of work. However, using templates is not applicable in all cases, or may not be the best approach. The limitation of templates is that their types need to be known when the code is compiled.

In real-world cases, this is not always possible. A typical example would be a program that determines what logging infrastructure to use depending on the value of a configuration file.

Consider the following problems:

- While developing the application and executing tests, the application would use a logger that prints detailed information.

- On the other hand, when the application is deployed to the PCs of its users, the application would use a logger that prints **error summaries** and notifies the developers if there are any errors.

We can solve these problems using the concept of inheritance in C++.

Inheritance

Inheritance allows the combination of one or more classes. Let's look at an example of inheritance:

```cpp
class Vehicle {
  public:
    TankLevel getTankLevel() const;
    void turnOn();
};


class Car : public Vehicle {
  public:
    bool isTrunkOpen();
};
```

In this example, the **Car** class inherits from the **Vehicle** class, or, we can say **Car** derives from **Vehicle**. In C++ terminology, **Vehicle** is the *base* class, and **Car** is the *derived* class.

When defining a class, we can specify the classes it derives from by appending :, followed by one or more classes, separated by a comma:

```
class Car : public Vehicle, public Transport {

}
```

When specifying the list of classes to derive from, we can also specify the visibility of the inheritance – **private**, **protected**, or **public**.

The visibility modifier specifies who can know about the inheritance relationship between the classes.

The methods of the base class can be accessed as methods of the derived class based on the following rules:

```
Car car;

car.turnOn();
```

When the inheritance is **public**, the code external to the class knows that **Car** derives from **Vehicle**. All the public methods of the base class are accessible as *public* method of the derived class by the code in the program. The protected methods of the base class can be accessed as *protected* by the methods of the derived class. When inheritance is **protected**, all the public and protected members are accessible as *protected* by the derived class. Only the derived class and classes that derive from it know about inheritance; external code sees the two classes as unrelated.

Finally, when deriving with a **private** modifier, all the **public** and **protected** methods and fields of the base class are accessible by the derived class as **private**.

The private methods and fields of a class are *never accessible* outside of that class.

Accessing the fields of the base class follows the same rules.

Let's see a summary:

Base class methods	Derive as public	Derive as protected	Derive as private
public	Accessible as if it was declared public in the derived class	Accessible as if it was declared protected in the derived class	Accessible as if it was declared private in the derived class
protected	Accessible as if was declared protected in the derived class	Accessible as if it was declared protected in the derived class	Accessible as if it was declared private in the derived class
private	Accessible only by the base class	Accessible only by the base class	Accessible only by the base class

Figure 6.1: Base class methods and the access level they provide

Inheritance creates a hierarchy of derived and base classes.

The **Orange** class can be derived from a **Citrus** class, which is in turn derived from a **Fruit** class. Here is how it can be written:

```
class Fruit {
};
class Citrus: public Fruit {
};
class Orange: public Citrus {
};
```

The class **Citrus** can access the public and protected methods of class **Fruit**, whereas class **Orange** will be able to access both **Citrus**' and **Fruit**'s public and protected methods (**Fruit**'s public methods are accessible through **Citrus**).

Exercise 20: Creating a Program to Illustrate Inheritance in C++

Let's perform the following exercise to create a derived class that inherits from multiple base classes:

1. Add the header file at the start of the program:

   ```
   #include <iostream>
   ```

2. Add the first base class, named **Vehicle**:

   ```
   // first base class
   class Vehicle {
     public:
       int getTankCapacity(){
         const int tankLiters = 10;
         std::cout << "The current tank capacity for your car is " <<
   tankLiters << " Liters."<<std::endl;
         return tankLiters;
       }
   };
   ```

3. Now add the second base class, named `CollectorItem`:

```
// second base class
class CollectorItem {
  public:
    float getValue() {
      return 100;
    }
};
```

4. Add the derived class, named `Ferrari250GT`, as illustrated here:

```
// Subclass derived from two base classes
class Ferrari250GT: protected Vehicle, public CollectorItem {
  public:
    Ferrari250GT() {
      std::cout << "Thank you for buying the Ferrari 250 GT with tank
capacity " << getTankCapacity() << std::endl;
      return 0;
    }
};
```

5. Now, in the **main** function, instantiate the **Ferrari250GT** class and call the **getValue()** method:

```
int main()
{
  Ferrari250GT ferrari;
  std::cout << "The value of the Ferrari is " << ferrari.getValue() <<
std::endl;

  /* Cannot call ferrari.getTankCapacity() because Ferrari250GT inherits
  from Vehicle with the protected specifier */
  return 0;
}
```

The output will be as follows:

```
Output:
The current tank capacity for your car is 10 Liters.
Thank you for buying the Ferrari 250 GT with tank capacity 10
The value of the Ferrari is 100
```

The specifier is not mandatory. If it is omitted, it defaults to *public for structs* and to *private for classes*.

> **Note**
>
> If you use inheritance to group together some functionality when implementing a class, it is often correct to use **private inheritance**, as that is a detail of how you are implementing the class, and it is not part the **public interface** of the class. If, instead, you want to write a derived class that can be used in place of the base class, use public inheritance.

When inheriting from a class, the base class gets **embedded** into the derived class. This means that all the data of the base class also becomes part of the derived class in its **memory representation**:

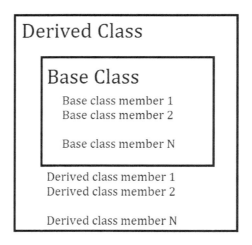

Figure 6.2: Representation of the derived class and the base class

A question might come up at this point – we are embedding the base class inside the derived class. This means that we need to initialize the base class when we initialize the derived class, otherwise, part of the class would be left uninitialized. When do we initialize the base class?

When writing the constructor of the derived class, the compiler will implicitly call the default constructor of the base class before any initialization takes place.

If the base class does not have a default constructor but has a constructor that accepts parameters, then the derived class constructor can explicitly call it in the initialization list. Otherwise, there will be an error.

In a similar way to how the compiler calls the constructor of the base class when the derived class is constructed, the compiler takes care of always calling the destructor of the base class after the destructor of the derived class has run:

```
class A {
  public:
    A(const std::string& name);
};


class B: public A {
  public:
    B(int number) : A("A's name"), d_number(number) {}


  private:
    int d_number;
};


}
```

When B's constructor is called, the A needs to be initialized. Since A doesn't have a default constructor, the compiler cannot initialize it for us: we have to call A's constructor explicitly.

The **copy constructor** and the **assignment operator** generated by the compiler take care of calling the constructor and operator of the base class.

When, instead, we write our implementation of the copy constructor and the assignment operators, we need to take care of calling the copy constructor and assignment operator.

Note

In many compilers, you can enable additional warnings that notify you if you forget to add the calls to the base constructor.

It is important to understand that inheritance needs to model an **is a** relationship: when you define a class, A to inherit from another class, B, you are saying that A **is a** B.

To understand this, a vehicle is a good example: a car is a vehicle, a bus is a vehicle, and a truck is also a vehicle. A bad example would be for a car to inherit from an engine. While the engine might have similar functionality to a car, such as a **start** method, it is wrong to say that a car is an engine. The relationship, in this case, is **has a**: the car has an engine; this relationship represents composition.

> **Note**
>
> Using an **is a** test to understand whether a relationship can use inheritance can fail in some cases: for example, a **square** inheriting from a **rectangle**. When the width of the rectangle is doubled, the area of the rectangle doubles, but the area of the square quadruples. This means that code that expects to interact with rectangles might get surprising results when using a square, even if the square, mathematically, is a rectangle.

A more general rule is to use the **Liskov Substitution Principle**: if the A class inherits from B, we could replace the A class anywhere the B class is used, and the code would still behave correctly.

Up to now, we have seen examples of single inheritance: a derived class has a single base class. C++ supports multiple inheritance: a class can derive from multiple classes. Let's look at an example:

```
struct A {
};


struct B {
};


struct C : A, B {
};
```

In this example, the C struct derives both from A and from B.

The rules on how inheritance works are the same for single and multiple inheritance: the methods of all the derived classes are visible based on the visibility access specified, and we need to make sure to call the appropriate constructors and assign an operator for all of the base classes.

> **Note**
>
> It is usually best to have a shallow inheritance hierarchy: there should not be many levels of derived classes.

When using a multi-level inheritance hierarchy or multiple inheritance, it's more likely that you'll encounter some problems, such as **ambiguous calls**.

A call is ambiguous when the compiler cannot clearly understand which method to call. Let's explore the following example:

```
struct A {
  void foo() {}
};


struct B {
  void foo() {}
};


struct C: A, B {
  void bar() { foo(); }
};
```

In this example, it is not clear which **foo()** to call, **A**'s or **B**'s. We can disambiguate that by prepending the name of the class followed by two columns: **A::foo()**.

Exercise 21: Using Multiple Inheritance to Create a "Welcome to the Community" Message Application

Let's use multiple inheritance to create an application to print a "welcome to the community" message:

1. First, add the required header files in the program, as illustrated:

```
#include <iostream>
```

2. Now, add the required classes, **DataScienceDev** and **FutureCppDev**, with the required print statement:

```cpp
class DataScienceDev {
public:
    DataScienceDev(){
        std::cout << "Welcome to the Data Science Developer Community." << std::endl;
    }
};

class FutureCppDev {
public:
    FutureCppDev(){
        std::cout << "Welcome to the C++ Developer Community." << std::endl;
    }
};
```

3. Now, add the **Student** class as illustrated here:

```cpp
class Student : public DataScienceDev, public FutureCppDev {
    public:
    Student(){
        std::cout << "Student is a Data Developer and C++ Developer." << std::endl;
    }
};
```

4. Now, invoke the **Student** class in the **main** function:

```cpp
int main(){
    Student S1;
    return 0;
}
```

The output will be as follows:

```
Welcome to the Data Science Developer Community.
Welcome to the C++ Developer Community.
Student is a Data Developer and C++ Developer.
```

Activity 23: Creating Game Characters

We want to write a new game, and in that game, create two types of characters – a hero and enemies. Enemies can swing their swords, and the hero can cast a spell.

Here is how you can achieve the task:

1. Create a **Character** class that has a public method, **moveTo**, that prints **Moved to position**.

2. Create a **Position** struct:

    ```
    struct Position {
        std::string positionIdentifier;
    };
    ```

3. Create two classes, **Hero** and **Enemy**, that are derived from the Character class:

    ```
    class Hero : public Character {
    };
    ```

    ```
    class Enemy : public Character {
    };
    ```

4. Create a **Spell** class with the constructor that takes the name of the spell:

    ```
    class Spell {
    public:
        Spell(std::string name) : d_name(name) {}

        std::string name() const {
            return d_name;
        }
    private:
        std::string d_name;
    }
    ```

5. The **Hero** class should have a **public** method to cast a spell. Use the value from the **Spell** class.

6. The **Enemy** class should have a **public** method to swing a sword, which prints **Swinging sword**.

7. Implement the main method, which calls these methods in various classes:

```
int main()
{
    Position position{"Enemy castle"};
    Hero hero;
    Enemy enemy;
}
```

The output will be as follows:

```
Moved to position Enemy castle
Moved to position Enemy castle
Casting spell fireball
Swinging sword
```

> **Note**
>
> The solution for this activity can be found on page 309.

Polymorphism

In the previous section, we mentioned that inheritance is a solution that allows you to change the behavior of code while a program is running. This is because inheritance enables polymorphism in C++.

Polymorphism means *many forms* and represents the ability of objects to behave in different ways.

We mentioned earlier that templates are a way to write code that works with many different types at compilation time and, depending on the types used to instantiate the template, the behavior will change.

This kind of pattern is called **static polymorphism** – static because it is known during compilation time. C++ also supports **dynamic polymorphism** – having the behavior of methods change while the program is running. This is powerful because we can react to information we obtain only after we have compiled our program, such as user input, values in configurations, or the kind of hardware the code is running on. This is possible thanks to two features – **dynamic binding** and **dynamic dispatch**.

Dynamic Binding

Dynamic binding is the ability for a reference or a pointer of a base type to point to an object of a derived type at runtime. Let's explore the following example:

```
struct A {
};

struct B: A{
};

struct C: A {
};

//We can write
B b;
C c;

A& ref1 = b;
A& ref2 = c;
A* ptr = nullptr;

if (runtime_condition()) {
  ptr = &b;
} else {
```

```
    ptr = &c;
}
```

> **Note**
>
> To allow dynamic binding, the code must *know* that the derived class derives from the base class.
>
> If the inheritance's visibility is **private**, then only code inside the derived class will be able to bind the object to a *pointer* or *reference* of the base class.
>
> If the inheritance is **protected**, then the derived class and every class deriving from it will be able to perform dynamic binding. Finally, if the inheritance is **public**, the dynamic binding will always be *allowed*.

This creates the distinction between the **static** type and the **dynamic** (or run-time) type. The static type is the type we can see in the source code. In this case, we can see that **ref1** has a static type of a reference to the **A** struct.

The dynamic type is the real type of the object: the type that has been constructed in the object's memory location at runtime. For example, the static type of both **ref1** and **ref2** is a reference to the **A** struct, but the **ref1** dynamic type is **B**, since **ref1** refers to a memory location in which an object of type **B** has been created, and the **ref2** dynamic type is **C** for the same reason.

As said, the dynamic type can change at runtime. While the static type of a variable is always the same, its dynamic type can change: **ptr** has a static type, which is a pointer to **A**, but its dynamic type could change during the execution of the program:

```
A* ptr = &b; // ptr dynamic type is B
ptr = &c; // ptr dynamic type is now C
```

It is important to understand that only references and pointers can be assigned values from a derived class safely. If we were to assign an object to a value type, we would get a surprising result – the object would get sliced.

We said earlier that a base class is **embedded** inside a derived class. Say, for example, we were to try and assign to a value, like so:

```
B b;
A a = b;
```

The code would compile, but only the embedded part of A inside of B would be copied – when we declare a variable of type A, the compiler dedicates an area of the memory big enough to contain an object of type A, so there cannot be enough space for B. When this happens, we say that we sliced the object, as we took only a part of the object when assigning or copying.

> **Note**
>
> It is not the intended behavior to slice the object. Be mindful of this interaction and try to avoid it.

This behavior happens because C++ uses *static dispatch* by default for function and method calls: when the compiler sees a method call, it will check the static type of the variable on which the method is called, and it will execute the **respective implementation**. In case of slicing, the copy constructor or assignment operator of A is called, and it only copies the part of A inside B, ignoring the remaining fields.

As said before, C++ supports dynamic dispatch. This is done by marking a method with a special keyword: **virtual**.

If a method is marked with the **virtual** keyword, when the method is called on a *reference* or a *pointer*, the compiler will execute the implementation of the dynamic type instead of the static type.

These two features enable *polymorphism* – we can write a function that accepts a reference to a base class, call methods on this base class, and the methods of the derived classes will be executed:

```
void safeTurnOn(Vehicle& vehicle) {
  if (vehicle.getFuelInTank() > 0.1 && vehicle.batteryHasEnergy()) {
    vehicle.turnOn();
  }
}
```

We can then call the function with many different types of vehicles, and the appropriate methods will be executed:

```
Car myCar;
Truck truck;
safeTurnOn(myCar);
safeTurnOn(truck);
```

A typical pattern is to create an interface that only specifies the methods that are required for some functionality.

Classes that need to be used with such functionality must derive the interface and implement all the required methods.

Virtual Methods

We've learned the advantages of dynamic dispatch in C++ and how it can enable us to execute the methods of a derived class by calling a method on a reference or pointer to a base class.

In this section, we will take an in-depth look at how to tell the compiler to perform dynamic dispatch on a method. The way to specify that we want to use dynamic dispatch for a method is to use the **virtual** keyword.

The **virtual** keyword is used in front of a method when declaring it:

```
class Vehicle {
  public:
    virtual void turnOn();
};
```

We need to remember that the compiler decides how to perform method dispatch based on the static type of the variable that is used when calling the method.

This means that we need to apply the virtual keyword to the type we are using in the code. Let's examine the following exercise to explore the virtual keyword.

Exercise 22: Exploring the Virtual Method

Let's create a program using the concept of inheritance using the virtual keyword:

1. First, make sure to add the required header file and namespace to compile the program.

2. Now, add the **Vehicle** class as illustrated:

    ```
    class Vehicle {
      public:
        void turnOn() {
          std::cout << "Vehicle: turn on" << std::endl;
        }
    };
    ```

3. In the **Car** class, add the **virtual** keyword as illustrated :

```
class Car : public Vehicle {
  public:
    virtual void turnOn()  {
      std::cout << "Car: turn on" << std::endl;
    }
};

void myTurnOn(Vehicle& vehicle) {
  std::cout << "Calling turnOn() on the vehicle reference" << std::endl;
  vehicle.turnOn();
}
```

4. Now, in the main function, invoke the **Car** class and pass the **car** object in the **myTurnOn()** function:

```
int main() {
  Car car;
  myTurnOn(car);
}
```

The output will be as follows:

```
Calling turnOn() on the vehicle reference
Vehicle: turn on
```

Here, the call will not be dynamically dispatched, and the call to the implementation of **Vehicle::turnOn()** will be executed. The reason is that the static type of the variable is **Vehicle**, and we did not mark the method as **virtual**, so the compiler uses static dispatch.

The fact that we wrote a **Car** class that declares the method virtual is not important, since the compiler only sees the **Vehicle** class being used in **myTurnOn()**. When a method is declared **virtual**, we can override it in a derived class.

To override a method, we need to declare it with the same signature as the parent class: the same return type, name, parameters (including **const**-ness and **ref**-ness), **const** qualifier, and the other attributes.

If the signature does not match, we will create an overload for the function. The overload will be callable from the derived class, but it will never be executed with a dynamic dispatch from a base class, for example:

```
struct Base {
  virtual void foo(int) = 0;
};
struct Derived: Base {
  /* This is an override: we are redefining a virtual method of the base
class, using the same signature. */
  void foo(int) { }


  /* This is an overload: we are defining a method with the same name of a
method of the base class, but the signature is different. The rules regarding
virtual do not apply between Base::foo(int) and Derived:foo(float). */
  void foo(float) {}
};
```

When a class overrides a virtual method of the base class, the method of the *most derived class* will be executed when the method is called on a base class. This is **true** even if the method is called from inside the base class, for example:

```
struct A {
  virtual void foo() {
    std::cout << "A's foo" << std::endl;
  }
};


struct B: A {
  virtual void foo() override {
    std::cout << "B's foo" << std::endl;
  }
};


struct C: B {
  virtual void foo() override {
```

```
        std::cout << "C's foo" << std::endl;
    }
};

int main() {
    B b;
    C c;
    A* a = &b;

    a->foo();  // B::foo() is executed
    a = &c;
    a->foo();
    /* C::foo() is executed, because it's the most derived Class overriding
    foo(). */
}
```

We can see a new keyword in the preceding example: the **override** keyword.

C++11 introduced this keyword to enable us to specify that we are overriding a method explicitly. This allows the compiler to give us an error message if we use the **override** keyword, but the signature does not match any base class' virtual method.

> **Note**
>
> Always use the **override** keyword when you are overriding a method. It is easy to change the signature of the base class and forget to update all the locations where we overrode the method. If we do not update them, they will become a new overload instead of an override!

In the example, we also used the **virtual** keyword for each function. This is not necessary, since a virtual method on a base class makes every method with the same signature in the derived classes virtual as well.

It is good to be explicit **virtual** keyword, but if we are already using the **override** keyword, it might be redundant – in these cases, the best way is to follow the coding standard of the project you are working on.

The `virtual` keyword can be applied to any method. Since the constructor is not a method, the constructor cannot be marked as virtual. Additionally, dynamic dispatch is disabled inside constructors and destructors.

The reason is that when constructing a hierarchy of derived classes, the constructor of the base class is executed before the constructor of the derived class. This means that if we were to call the virtual method on the derived class when constructing the base class, the derived class would not be initialized yet.

Similarly, when calling the destructor, the destructors of the whole hierarchy are executed in reverse order; first the derived and then the base class. Calling a `virtual` method in the destructor would call the method on a derived class that has already been destructed, which is an error.

While the constructor cannot be marked as virtual, the destructor can. If a class defines a virtual method, then it should also declare a virtual destructor.

Declaring a destructor virtual is extremely important when classes are created on dynamic memory, or the heap. We are going to see later in this chapter how to manage dynamic memory with classes, but for now, it is important to know that if a destructor is not declared virtual, then an object might be only partially destructed.

> **Note**
>
> If a method is marked virtual, then the destructor should also be marked virtual.

Activity 24: Calculating Employee Salaries

We are writing a system to compute the paycheques for the employees of a company. Each employee has a base salary plus a bonus.

For employee who are not managers, the bonus is computed from the performance of the department: they get 10% of the base salary if the department reached its goal.

The company also has managers, for whom the bonus is computed in a different way: they get 20% of the base salary if the department reached its goal, plus 1% of the difference between the achieved result of the department and the expected one.

We want to create a function that takes an employee and computes their total salary, summing the base salary and the bonus, regardless of whether they are a manager or not.

Perform the following steps:

1. The Department class accepts the expected earning and the effective earning when constructed, and stores them in two fields:

```
class Department {
public:

    Department(int expectedEarning, int effectiveEarning)
    : d_expectedEarning(expectedEarning), d_
effectiveEarning(effectiveEarning)
    {}

    bool hasReachedTarget() const {return d_effectiveEarning >= d_
expectedEarning;}
    int expectedEarning() const {return d_expectedEarning;}
    int effectiveEarning() const {return d_effectiveEarning;}
private:
    int d_expectedEarning;
    int d_effectiveEarning;
};
```

2. Define an **Employee** class with two **virtual** functions, **getBaseSalary()**, and **getBonus()**. Within it, implement the logic for employee bonus calculation if the department goal is met:

```
class Employee {
public:
    virtual int getBaseSalary() const { return 100; }

    virtual int getBonus(const Department& dep) const {
        if (dep.hasReachedTarget()) {
            return int(0.1 * getBaseSalary());
        }
        return 0;
    }

};
```

3. Create another function that provides the total compensation:

```
int getTotalComp(const Department& dep) {
        return getBaseSalary() + getBonus(dep);
}
```

4. Create a **Manager** class that derives from **Employee**. Again, create the same virtual functions, **getBaseSalary()** and **getBonus()**. Within it, implement the logic for a **Manager** bonus calculation if the department goal is met:

```
class Manager : public Employee {
public:
    virtual int getBaseSalary() const override { return 150; }

    virtual int getBonus(const Department& dep) const override {
        if (dep.hasReachedTarget()) {
            int additionalDeparmentEarnings = dep.effectiveEarning() -
dep.expectedEarning();
            return int(0.2 * getBaseSalary() + 0.01 *
additionalDeparmentEarnings);
        }
        return 0;
    }
};
```

5. Implement the **main** program, and run the program:

The output will be as follows:

```
Employee: 110. Manager: 181
```

> **Note**
>
> The solution for this activity can be found on page 311.

Interfaces in C++

In the previous section, we saw how to define a method that is virtual, and how the compiler will do dynamic dispatch when calling it.

We have also talked about interfaces throughout the chapter, but we never specified what an interface is.

An interface is a way for the code to specify a contract that the caller needs to provide to be able to call some functionality. We looked at an informal definition when talking about the templates and the requirements they impose on the types used with them.

Functions and methods which accepts parameters as interface are a way of saying: in order to perform my actions, I need these functionalities; it's up to you to provide them.

To specify an interface in C++, we can use an **Abstract Base Class (ABC)**.

Let's dive into the name; the class is:

- **Abstract**: This means that it cannot be instantiated

- **Base**: This means it is designed to be derived from

Any class that defines a pure virtual method is **abstract**. A pure virtual method is a virtual method that ends with **= 0**, for example:

```
class Vehicle {
  public:
    virtual void turnOn() = 0;
};
```

A pure virtual method is a method that does not have to be defined. Nowhere in the previous code have we specified the implementation of **Vehicle::turnOn()**. Because of this, the **Vehicle** class cannot be instantiated, as we do not have any code to call for its pure virtual methods.

We can instead derive from the class and override the pure virtual method. If a class derives from an abstract base class, it can be either of the following:

- Another abstract base class if it declares an additional pure virtual method, or if it does not override all the pure virtual methods of the base class

- A regular class if it overrides all the pure virtual methods of the base class

Let's continue with the previous example:

```
class GasolineVehicle: public Vehicle {
  public:
    virtual void fillTank() = 0;
};
class Car : public GasolineVehicle {
  virtual void turnOn() override {}
  virtual void fillTank() override {}
};
```

In this example, **Vehicle** is an abstract base class and **GasolineVehicle** is too, since it does not override all the pure virtual methods of **Vehicle**. It also defines an additional virtual method, which the **Car** class overrides together with the **Vehicle::turnOn()** method. This makes **Car** the only concrete class, a class that can be instantiated.

The same concept applies when a class is deriving from multiple abstract base classes: all the pure virtual methods of all the classes that need to be overridden in order to make the class concrete and thus instantiable.

While abstract base classes cannot be instantiated, we can define references and pointers to them.

> **Note**
>
> If you try to instantiate an abstract base class, the compiler will give an error specifying which methods are still pure virtual, thus making the class abstract.

Functions and methods that require specific methods can accept references and pointers to abstract base classes, and instances of concrete classes that derive from them can be bound to such references.

> **Note**
>
> It is good practice for the consumer of the interface to define the interface.
>
> A function, method, or class that requires some functionality to perform its actions should define the interface. Classes that should be used with such entities should implement the interface.

Since C++ does not provide a specialized keyword for defining interfaces and interfaces are simply abstract base classes, there are some guidelines that it's best practice to follow when designing an interface in C++:

- An abstract base class should *not* have any data members or fields.

  The reason for this is that an interface specifies behavior, which should be independent of the data representation. It derives that abstract base classes should only have a default constructor.

- An abstract base class should always define a **virtual destructor**.

  The definition of a destructor should be the default one: `virtual ~Interface() = default`. We are going to see why it is important for the destructor to be virtual later.

- All the methods of an abstract base class should be pure virtual.

  The interface represents an expected functionality that needs to be implemented; a method which is not pure is an implementation. The implementation should be separate from the interface.

- All of the methods of an abstract base class should be `public`.

  Similar to the previous point, we are defining a set of methods that we expect to call. We should not limit which classes can call the method only to classes deriving from the interface.

- All the methods of an abstract base class should be regarding a single functionality.

  If our code requires multiple functionalities, separate interfaces can be created, and the class can derive from all of them. This allows us to compose interfaces more easily.

Consider disabling the copy and move constructors and assignment operators on the interface. Allowing the interface to be copied can cause the slicing problem we were describing before:

```
Car redCar;
Car blueCar;

Vehicle& redVehicle = redCar;
Vehicle& redVehicle = blueCar;
redVehicle = blueVehicle;
// Problem: object slicing!
```

With the last assignment, we only copied the **Vehicle** part, since the copy constructor of the **Vehicle** class has been called. The copy constructor is not virtual, so the implementation in **Vehicle** is called, and since it only knows about the data members of the **Vehicle** class (which should be none), the ones defined inside **Car** have not been copied! This results in problems that are very hard to identify.

A possible solution is to disable the interface copy and move construct and assign operator: **Interface(const Interface&) = delete**; and similar. This has the drawback of disabling the compiler from creating the copy constructor and assign operators of the derived classes.

An alternative is to declare copy/move constructor/assignment protected so that only derived classes can call them, and we don't risk assigning interfaces while using them.

Activity 25: Retrieving User Information

We are writing an application to allow users to buy and sell items. When a user logs in, we need to retrieve several pieces of information to populate their profile, such as the URL for the profile picture and the full name.

Our service is running in many data centers around the world, to always be close to its customers. Because of that, sometimes we want to retrieve information for the user from a cache, but sometimes we want to retrieve it from our main database.

Perform the following:

1. Let's write the code, which can be independent of where the data is coming from, so we create an abstract **UserProfileStorage** class to retrieve the **CustomerProfile** from **UserId**:

```
struct UserProfile {};
struct UserId {};

class UserProfileStorage {
  public:
    virtual UserProfile getUserProfile(const UserId& id) const = 0;

    virtual ~UserProfileStorage() = default;

  protected:
    UserProfileStorage() = default;
    UserProfileStorage(const UserProfileStorage&) = default;
    UserProfileStorage& operator=(const UserProfileStorage&) = default;
};
```

2. Now, write the **UserProfileCache** class, which inherits from **UserProfileStorage**:

```cpp
class UserProfileCache : public UserProfileStorage {
public:
    UserProfile getUserProfile(const UserId& id) const override {
        std::cout << "Getting the user profile from the cache" <<
std::endl;
        return UserProfile();
    }
};
void exampleOfUsage(const UserProfileStorage& storage) {
    UserId user;
    std::cout << "About to retrieve the user profile from the storage" <<
std::endl;
    UserProfile userProfile = storage.getUserProfile(user);
}
```

3. In the **main** function, instantiate the **UserProfileCache** class and the call **exampleOfUsage** function as illustrated:

```cpp
int main()
{
    UserProfileCache cache;
    exampleOfUsage (cache);
}
```

The output is as follows:

```
About to retrieve the user profile from the storage
Getting the user profile from the cache
```

> **Note**
>
> The solution for this activity can be found at page 312.

Dynamic Memory

In this chapter, we have come across the term dynamic memory. Now let's understand in more detail what dynamic memory is, what problems it solves, and when to use it.

Dynamic memory is the part of the memory that the program can use to store objects, for which the program is responsible for maintaining the correct lifetime.

It is usually also called the **heap** and is often the alternative to the stack, which instead is handled automatically by the program. Dynamic memory can usually store much larger objects than the stack, which usually has a limit.

A program can interact with the operating system to get pieces of dynamic memory that it can use to store objects, and later it must take care to return such memory to the operating system.

Historically, developers would make sure they called the appropriate functions to get and return memory, but modern C++ automates most of this, so it is much easier to write correct programs nowadays.

In this section, we are going to show how and when it is recommended to use dynamic memory in a program.

Let's start with an example: we want to write a function that will create a logger. When we execute tests, we create a logger specifically for the test called **TestLogger**, and when we run our program for users, we want to use a different logger, called **ReleaseLogger**.

We can see a good fit for interfaces here – we can write a logger abstract base class that defines all the methods needed for logging and have **TestLogger** and **ReleaseLogger** derive from it.

All our code will then use a reference to the logger when logging.

How can we write such a function?

As we learned in *Chapter 2*, *Functions*, we cannot create the logger inside the function and then return a reference to it, since it would be an automatic variable and it would be destructed just after the return, leaving us with a dangling reference.

We cannot create the logger before calling the function and let the function initialize it either, since the types are different, and the function knows which type should be created.

We would need some storage that is valid until we need the logger, to put the logger in it.

Given only an interface, we cannot know the size of the classes implementing it, since multiple classes could implement it and they could have different sizes. This prevents us from reserving some space in memory and passing a pointer to such space to the function, so that it could store the logger in it.

Since classes can have different sizes, the storage not only needs to remain valid longer than the function, but it also needs to be variable. That is **dynamic memory**!

In C++, there are two keywords to interact with dynamic memory – **new** and **free**.

The **new** expression is used to create a new object in dynamic memory – it is composed by the **new** keyword, followed by the type of the object to create and the parameters to pass to the constructor, and returns a pointer to the requested type:

```
Car* myCar = new myCar();
```

The **new** expression requests a piece of dynamic memory big enough to hold the object created and instantiates an object in that memory. It then returns a pointer to such an instance.

The program can now use the object pointed to by `myCar` until it decides to delete it. To delete a pointer, we can use the delete expression: it is composed by the `delete` keyword followed by a variable, which is a pointer:

```
delete myCar;
```

The `delete` keyword calls the destructor of the object pointed to by the pointer provided to it, and then gives the memory we initially requested back to the operating system.

Deleting pointers to automatic variables lead to an error as follows:

```
Car myCar; // automatic variable

delete &myCar; // This is an error and will likely crash the program
```

It is of absolute importance that, for each new expression, we call the `delete` expression only once, with the same returned pointer.

If we forget to call the `delete` function on an object returned by calling the **new** function, we will have two major problems:

- The memory will not be returned to the operating system when we do not need it anymore. This is known as a **memory leak**. If this repeatedly happens during the execution of the program, our program will take more and more memory, until it consumes all the memory it can get.

- The destructor of the object will not be called.

We saw in previous chapters that, in C++, we should make use of RAII and get the resources we need in the constructor and return them in the destructor.

If we do not call the destructor, we might not return some resources. For example, a connection to the database would be kept open, and our database would struggle due to too many connections being open, even if we are using only one.

The problem that arises if we call **delete** multiple times on the same pointer is that all the calls after the first one will access memory they should not be accessing.

The result can range from our program crashing to deleting other resources our program is currently using, resulting in incorrect behavior.

We can now see why it is extremely important to define a virtual destructor in the base class if we derive from it: we need to make sure that the destructor of the runtime type is called when calling the **delete** function on the base object. If we call **delete** on a pointer to the base class while the runtime type is the derived class, we will only call the destructor of the base class and not fully destruct the derived class.

Making the destructor of the base class virtual will ensure that we are going to call the derived destructor, since we are using dynamic dispatch when calling it.

> **Note**
>
> For every call to the **new** operator, there must be exactly one call to **delete** with the pointer returned by **new**!

This error is extremely common and leads to many errors.

Like single objects, we can also use dynamic memory to create arrays of objects. For such use cases, we can use the **new[]** and **delete[]** expressions:

```
int n = 15;
Car* cars = new Car[n];
delete[] cars;
```

The **new[]** expression will create enough space for **n** **Car** instances and will initialize them, returning a pointer to the first element created. Here, we are not providing the arguments to the constructor, so the class must have a default constructor.

With **new[]**, we can specify how many elements we want it to initialize. This is different from **std::array** and the built-in array we saw earlier because **n** can be decided at runtime.

We need to call **delete[]** on the pointer returned by **new[]** when we do not need the objects anymore.

> **Note**
>
> For every call to **new[]**, there must be exactly one call to **delete[]** with the pointer returned by **new[]**.
>
> The **new** operator and **new[]** function calls, and **delete** and **delete[]** function calls, cannot be intermixed. Always pair the ones for an array or the ones for single elements!

Now that we have seen how to use dynamic memory, we can write the function to create our logger.

The function will call the new expression in its body to create an instance of the correct class, and it will then return a pointer to the base class so that the code calling it does not need to know about the type of logger created:

```
Logger* createLogger() {
  if (are_tests_running()) {
    TestLogger* logger = new TestLogger();
    return logger;
  } else {
    ReleaseLogger logger = new ReleaseLogger("Release logger");
    return logger;
  }
}
```

There are two things to note in this function:

- Even if we wrote the **new** expression twice, **new** will be called only once per function call.

  This shows us that it is not enough to make sure we type **new** and **delete** an equal number of times; we need to understand how our code is executed.

- There is no call to **delete**! This means that the code calling the **createLogger** function needs to make sure to call **delete**.

From these two points, we can can see why it is error prone to manage memory manually, and why it should be avoided whenever possible.

Let's look at an example of how to call the function correctly:

```
Logger* logger = createLogger();

myOperation(logger, argument1, argument2);

delete logger;
```

If `myOperation` does not call **delete** on the logger, this is a *correct* use of dynamic memory. Dynamic memory is a powerful tool, but doing it manually is risky, error prone, and easy to get wrong.

Fortunately, modern C++ provides some facilities to make all this much easier to do. It is possible to write entire programs without ever using **new** and **delete** directly.

We will see how in the next section.

Safe and Easy Dynamic Memory

In the previous section, we learned how dynamic memory could be useful when working with interfaces, especially when creating new instances of derived classes.

We also saw how working with dynamic memory can be hard – we need to make sure to call new and delete in pairs, and failing to do so always has negative effects on our program. Fortunately for us, since C++11, there are tools in the standard library to help us overcome such limitations – **smart pointers**.

Smart pointers are types that behave like pointers, which are called **raw pointers** in this context, but have additional functionality.

We are going to look at two smart pointers from the standard library: `std::unique_ptr` and `std::shared_ptr` (read as **unique pointer** and **shared pointer**). Both pointers are used to free the developer from the complexity of making sure to call **delete** appropriately.

They represent different ownership models. The owner of an object is the code that determines the lifetime of the object – the part of the code that decides when to create and when to destroy the object.

Usually, ownership is associated with the scope a function or method, since the lifetime of automatic variables is controlled by it:

```
void foo() {
    int number;
    do_action(number);
}
```

In this case, the scope of **foo()** owns the **number** object, and it will make sure it is destroyed when the scope exits.

Alternatively, classes might own objects when they are declared as value types between the data members of the class. In that case, the lifetime of the object will be the same as the lifetime of the class:

```
class A {
    int number;
};
```

number will be constructed when the **A** class is constructed and will be destroyed when the **A** class is destroyed. This is automatically done because the field **number** is embedded inside the class and the constructor and destructor of the class will automatically initialize **number**.

When managing objects in dynamic memory, ownership is not enforced by the compiler anymore, but it is helpful to apply the concept of ownership to the dynamic memory as well – the owner is who decides when to delete the object.

A function could be the owner of an object when the object is allocated with the new call inside the function, as in the following example:

```
void foo() {
    int* number = new number();
    do_action(number);
    delete number;
}
```

Or a class might own it, by calling **new** in the constructor and storing the pointer in its fields, and calling **delete** on it in the destructor:

```
class A {
    A() : number(new int(0)) {
    }
    ~A() {
        delete number;
    }
    int* number;
};
```

But the ownership of dynamic objects can also be passed around.

We looked at an example earlier with the **createLogger** function. The function creates an instance of **Logger** and then passes the ownership to the parent scope. Now, the parent scope is in charge of making sure the object is valid until it is accessed in the program and deleted afterward.

Smart pointers allow us to specify the ownership in the type of the pointer and make sure it is respected so that we do not have to keep track of it manually anymore.

> **Note**
>
> Always use smart pointers to represent the ownership of objects.
>
> In a code base, smart pointers should be the pointers that control the lifetime of objects, and raw pointers, or regular pointers, are used only to reference objects.

A Single Owner Using std::unique_ptr

unique_ptr is the pointer type that's used by default. The unique pointer points to an object that has a single owner; there is a single place in the program that decides when to delete the object.

An example is the logger from before: there is a single place in the program that determines when to delete the object. Since we want the logger to be available as long as the program is running, to always be able to log information, we will destroy the logger only at the end of the program.

The unique pointer guarantees the uniqueness of ownership: the unique pointer cannot be copied. This means that once we have created a unique pointer for an object, there can be only one.

Additionally, when the unique pointer is destroyed, it deletes the object it owns. This way, we have a concrete object that tells us the ownership of the created object, and we do not have to manually make sure that only one place is calling **delete** for the object.

A unique pointer is a template that can take one argument: the *type of the object*.

We could rewrite the previous example as follows:

```
std::unique_ptr<Logger> logger = createLogger();
```

While this code would compile, we would not be respecting the guideline we mentioned previously regarding always using smart pointers for ownership: **createLogger** returns a raw pointer, but it passes ownership to the parent scope.

We can update the signature of **createLogger** to return a smart pointer:

```
std::unique_ptr<Logger>createLogger();
```

Now, the signature expresses our intention, and we can update the implementation to make use of smart pointers.

As we mentioned earlier, with the use of smart pointers, code bases should not use **new** and **delete** anywhere. This is possible because the standard library, since C++14, offers a convenient function: **std::make_unique**. **make_unique** is a template function that takes the type of the object to create, and creates it in dynamic memory, passing its arguments to the object's constructor and returning a unique pointer to it:

```
std::unique_ptr<Logger>createLogger() {
  if (are_tests_running()) {
    std::unique_ptr<TestLogger> logger = std::make_unique<TestLogger>();
    return logger; // logger is implicitly moved
  } else {
    std::unique_ptr<ReleaseLogger> logger = std::make_
unique<ReleaseLogger>("Release logger");
    return logger; // logger is implicitly moved
  }
}
```

There are three important points regarding this function:

- There is no longer a new expression in the body; it has been replaced with `make_unique`. The `make_unique` function is simple to call because we can provide all the arguments we would pass to the constructor of the type and have it created automatically.

- We are creating a `unique_ptr` to a derived class, but we are returning a `unique_ptr` to a base class.

  Indeed, `unique_ptr` emulates the ability of raw pointers to convert pointers to derived classes to pointers to base classes. This makes using `unique_ptr` as simple as using **raw pointers**.

- We are using the move on the `unique_ptr`. As we said earlier, we cannot copy `unique_ptr`, but we are returning from a function, so we must use a value; otherwise, a reference would become invalid after the function returns, as we saw in *Chapter 2, Functions*.

  While it cannot be copied, `unique_ptr` can be moved. When we move `unique_ptr`, we are transferring the ownership of the object to which it points to the recipient of the value. In this case, we are returning value, so we are transferring the ownership to the caller of the function.

Let's now see how we can rewrite the class that owns the number we showed before:

```
class A {
  A(): number(std::make_unique<int>()) {}
  std::unique_ptr<int> number;
};
```

Thanks to the fact that `unique_ptr` deletes the object automatically when it is destroyed, we did not have to write the destructor for the class, making our code even easier.

If we need to pass a pointer to the object, without transferring ownership, we can use the `get()` method on the raw pointer. Remember that raw pointers should not be used for ownership, and code accepting the raw pointer should never call **delete** on it.

Thanks to these features, `unique_ptr` should be the default choice to keep track of the ownership of an object.

Shared Ownership Using std::shared_ptr

shared_ptr represents an object that has multiple owners: one out of several objects will delete the owned object.

An example could make a TCP connection, which is established by multiple threads to send data. Each thread uses the TCP connection to send data and then terminates.

We want to delete the TCP connection when the last thread has finished executing, but it is not always the same thread that terminates last; it could be any of the threads.

Alternatively, if we are modeling a graph of connected nodes, we might want to delete a node when every connection to it is removed from the graph. **unique_ptr** does not solve these cases, since there is not a single owner for the object.

shared_ptr can be used in such situations: **shared_ptr** can be copied many times, and the object pointed to by the pointer will remain alive until the last **shared_ptr** is destroyed. We guarantee that the object remains valid as long as there is at least one **shared_ptr** instance pointing to it.

Let's look at an example making use of it:

```
class Node {
  public:
    void addConnectedNode(std::shared_ptr<Node> node);
    void removeConnectedNode(std::shared_ptr<Node> node);


  private:
    std::vector<std::shared_ptr<Node>>d_connections;
};
```

Here, we can see that we are holding many **shared_ptr** instance to nodes. If we have a **shared_ptr** instance to a node, we want to be sure that the node exists, but when we remove the shared pointer, we do not care about the node anymore: it might be deleted, or it might be kept alive if there is another node connected to it.

Similar to the **unique_ptr** counterpart, when we want to create a new node, we can use the **std::make_shared** function, which takes the type of the object to construct as the template argument and the arguments to pass to the constructor of the object and returns **shared_ptr** to the object.

You might notice that there might be a problem in the example we showed: what happens if node **A** is connected to node **B** and node **B** is connected to node **A**?

Both nodes have a **shared_ptr** instance to the other, and even if no other node has a connection to them, they will remain alive because a **shared_ptr** instance to them exists. This is an example of circular dependency.

When using shared pointers, we must pay attention to these cases. The standard library offers a different kind of pointer to handle these situations: **std::weak_ptr** (read as **weak pointer**).

weak_ptr is a smart pointer that can be used in conjunction with **shared_ptr** to solve the circular dependencies that might happen in our programs.

Generally, **shared_ptr** is enough to model most cases where **unique_ptr** does not work, and together they cover the majority of the uses of dynamic memory in a code base.

Lastly, we are not helpless if we want to use dynamic memory for arrays of which we know the size only at runtime. **unique_ptr** can be used with array types, and **shared_ptr** can be used with array types starting from C++17:

```
std::unique_ptr<int[]>ints = std::make_unique<int[]>();

std::shared_ptr<float[]>floats = std::make_shared<float[]>();
```

Activity 26: Creating a Factory for UserProfileStorage

Our code needs to create new instances of the **UserProfileStorage** interface we wrote during *Activity 25: Retrieving User Information*:

1. Write a new **UserProfileStorageFactory** class. Now create a new **create** method which returns a **UserProfileStorage**:

2. In the **UserProfileStorageFactory** class, return **unique_ptr** so that it manages the lifetime of the interface:

```
class UserProfileStorageFactory {
public:
    std::unique_ptr<UserProfileStorage> create() const {
        // Create the storage and return it
    }
};
```

3. Now, in the **main** function, call the **UserProfileStorageFactory** class.

> **Note**
>
> The solution for this activity can be found at page 313.

Activity 27: Using a Database Connection for Multiple Operations

In our online store, after a user has paid for a purchase, we want to update their order list so that it is displayed on their profile. At the same time, we also need to schedule the processing of the order.

To do so, we need to update the records in our database.

We don't want to wait for one operation to perform the other, so we process the updates in parallel:

1. Let's create a **DatabaseConnection** class that can be used in parallel. We want to reuse this as much as possible, and we know we can use **std::async** to start a new parallel task.

2. Assuming that there are two functions, **updateOrderList(DatabaseConnection&)** and **scheduleOrderProcessing(DatabaseConnection&)**, write two functions, **updateWithConnection()** and **scheduleWithConnection()** which take a shared pointer to **DatabaseConnection** and call the respective function defined above:

    ```
    void updateWithConnection(std::shared_ptr<DatabaseConnection> connection)
    {
        updateOrderList(*connection);
    }
    void scheduleWithConnection(std::shared_ptr<DatabaseConnection>
    connection) {
        scheduleOrderProcessing(*connection);
    }
    ```

3. Use **shared_ptr** and keep a copy of **shared_ptr** in order to make sure that the connection remains valid.

4. Now let's write the **main** function, where we create a shared pointer to the connection and then we call **std::async** with the two functions we defined above, as illustrated:

```
int main()
{
    std::shared_ptr<DatabaseConnection> connection = std::make_
shared<DatabaseConnection>();
    std::async(std::launch::async, updateWithConnection, connection);
    std::async(std::launch::async, scheduleWithConnection, connection);
}
```

The output is as follows:

```
Updating order and scheduling order processing in parallel
Schedule order processing
Updating order list
```

Note

The solution for this activity can be found at page 314.

Summary

In this chapter, we saw how inheritance can be used to combine classes in C++. We saw what a base class is and what a derived class is, how to write a class that derives from another, and how to control the visibility modifier. We talked about how to initialize a base class in a derived one by calling the base class constructor.

We then explained polymorphism and the ability of C++ to dynamically bind a pointer or reference of a derived class to a pointer or reference of the base class. We explained what dispatch for functions is, how it works statically by default, and how we can make it dynamic with the use of the virtual keyword. Following that, we explored how to properly write virtual functions and how we can override them, making sure to mark such overrode functions with the **override** keyword.

Next, we showed how to define interfaces with abstract base classes and how to use pure virtual methods. We also provided guidelines on how to correctly define interfaces.

Lastly, we delved into dynamic memory and what problems it solves, but we also saw how easy it is to use it incorrectly.

We concluded the chapter by showing how modern C++ makes using dynamic memory painless by providing smart pointers that handle complex details for us: `unique_ptr` to manage objects with a single owner, and `shared_ptr` for objects owned by multiple objects.

All these tools can be effective at writing solid programs that can be effectively evolved and maintained, while retaining the performance C++ is famous for.

Appendix

About

This section is included to assist the students to perform the activities in the book.
It includes detailed steps that are to be performed by the students to achieve the objectives of
the activities.

Lesson 1: Getting Started

Activity 1: Find the Factors of 7 between 1 and 100 Using a while Loop

1. Import all the required header files before the **main** function:

   ```
   #include <iostream>
   ```

2. Inside the **main** function, create a variable **i** of type **unsigned**, and initialize its value as **1**:

   ```
   unsigned i = 1;
   ```

3. Now, use the **while** loop adding the logic where the value of **i** should be less than **100**:

   ```
   while ( i < 100){ }
   ```

4. In the scope of the **while** loop, use the if statement with the following logic:

   ```
   if (i%7 == 0) {
       std::cout << i << std::endl;
   }
   ```

5. Increase the value of the **i** variable to iterate through the **while** loop to validate the condition:

   ```
   i++;
   ```

   The output of the program is as follows:

   ```
   7
   14
   21
   28
   ...
   98
   ```

Activity 2: Define a Bi-Dimensional Array and Initialize Its Elements

1. After creating a C++ file, include the following header file at the start of the program:

   ```
   #include <iostream>
   ```

2. Now, in the **main** function, create a bi-directional array named **foo** of type integer, with three rows and three columns, as shown here:

```
int main()
{
   int foo[3][3];
```

3. Now, we will use the concept of a nested **for** loop to iterate through each index entry of the **foo** array:

```
for (int x= 0; x < 3; x++){
   for (int y = 0; y < 3; y++){


   }
}
```

4. In the second **for** loop, add the following statement:

```
foo[x][y] = x + y;
```

5. Finally, iterate over the array again to print its values:

```
for (int x = 0; x < 3; x++){
   for (int y = 0; y < 3; y++){
      std::cout << "foo[" << x << "][" << y << "]: " << foo[x][y] <<
std::endl;
   }
}
```

The output is as follows:

```
foo[0][0]: 0
foo[0][1]: 1
foo[0][2]: 2
foo[1][0]: 1
foo[1][1]: 2
foo[1][2]: 3
foo[2][0]: 2
foo[2][1]: 3
foo[2][2]: 4
```

Lesson 2: Functions

Activity 3: Calculating if a Person is Eligible to Vote or Not

1. Include the header file in the program to print the output as shown here:

   ```
   #include <iostream>
   ```

2. Now, create a function named **byreference_age_in_5_years** and the **if** loop with the following condition to print the message:

   ```
   void byreference_age_in_5_years(int& age) {
     if (age >= 18) {
       std::cout << "Congratulations! You are eligible to vote for your
   nation." << std::endl;
       return;
   ```

3. Add the **else** block to provide another condition if the age of the user is less than 18 years:

   ```
     } else{
       int reqAge = 18;
       int yearsToGo = reqAge-age;
       std::cout << "No worries, just "<< yearsToGo << " more years to go."
   << std::endl;
     }
   }
   ```

4. In the **main** function, create a variable of type integer and pass it as a reference in the **byreference_age_in_5_years** function as shown:

   ```
   int main() {
       int age;
       std::cout << "Please enter your age:";
       std::cin >> age;
       byreference_age_in_5_years(age);
   }
   ```

Activity 4: Apply the Understanding of Passing by Reference or Value in Functions

1. After adding all the required header files, create the first function of type integer as shown here:

    ```
    int sum(int a, int b)
    {
      return a + b
    }
    ```

    Take by value, return by value, since the types are small in memory and there is no reason to use references.

2. The second function should be written as follows:

    ```
    int& getMaxOf(std::array<int, 10>& array1, std::array<int, 10>& array2,
    int index) {
      if (array1[index] >= array2[index]) {
        return array1[index];
      } else {
        return array2[index];
      }
    }
    ```

Activity 5: Organizing Functions in Namespaces

1. Include the required header file and namespace to print the required output:

    ```
    #include <iostream>
    using namespace std;
    ```

2. Now, create a namespace named **LamborghiniCar** with the following **output** function:

    ```
    namespace LamborghiniCar
    {
      int output(){
        std::cout << "Congratulations! You deserve the Lamborghini." <<
    std::endl;
        return NULL;
      }
    }
    ```

3. Create another namespace named **PorscheCar** and add an **output** function as shown:

```
namespace PorscheCar
{
  int output(){
    std::cout << "Congratulations! You deserve the Porsche." << std::endl;
    return NULL;
  }
}
```

In the main function, create a variable named **magicNumber** of type integer to accept the input from the user:

```
int main()
{
  int magicNumber;
  std::cout << "Select a magic number (1 or 2) to win your dream car: ";
  std::cin >> magicNumber;
```

1. Add the following conditional **if**...**else-if**...**else** statement to complete the program:

```
if (magicNumber == 1){
  std::cout << LamborghiniCar::output() << std::endl;
} else if(magicNumber == 2){
  std::cout << PorscheCar::output() << std::endl;
}else{
  std::cout << "Please type the correct magic number." << std::endl;
}
}
```

Activity 6: Writing a Math Library for use in a 3D Game

1. Add the required header files at the start of the program (**mathlib.h** file is provided):

```
#include <mathlib.h>
#include <array>
#include <iostream>
```

2. Create a global **const** variable of type **float** as shown here:

```
const float ENEMY_VIEW_RADIUS_METERS = 5;
```

3. In the **main** function, create two arrays of type **float** and assign the following values:

```
int main() {
    std::array<float, 3> enemy1_location = {2, 2 ,0};
    std::array<float, 3> enemy2_location = {2, 4 ,0};
```

4. Now, create a variable named **enemy_distance** of type **float** and use the distance function to assign the value after calculating it:

```
float enemy_distance = johnny::mathlib::distance(enemy1_location,
enemy2_location);
    float distance_from_center = johnny::mathlib::distance(enemy1_
location);
```

5. Using the **circumference** function of **mathlib.h**, calculate and assign the enemy visual radius to **view_circumference_for_enemy** of type **float**:

```
using johnny::mathlib::circumference;
    float view_circumference_for_enemy = circumference(ENEMY_VIEW_RADIUS_
METERS);
```

6. Create a variable named **total_distance** of type **float** and assign the distance difference between the two enemies as shown in the following code:

```
float total_distance = johnny::mathlib::total_walking_distance({
        enemy1_location,
        {2, 3, 0}, // y += 1
        {2, 3, 3}, // z += 3
        {5, 3, 3}, // x += 3
        {8, 3, 3}, // x += 3
        {8, 3, 2}, // z -= 1
        {2, 3, 2}, // x -= 6
        {2, 3, 1}, // z -= 1
        {2, 3, 0}, // z -= 1
        enemy2_location
    });
```

7. Print the output using the following print statement:

```
std::cout << "The two enemies are " << enemy_distance << "m apart and
can see for a circumference of "
            << view_circumference_for_enemy << "m. To go to from one to
the other they need to walk "
            << total_distance << "m.";
}
```

Lesson 3: Classes

Activity 7: Information Hiding Through Getters and Setters

1. Define a class named **Coordinates** with its members under a **private** access specifier:

```
class Coordinates {
  private:
    float latitude;
    float longitude;
};
```

2. Add the four operations as specified above and make them publicly accessible by preceding their declaration with the **public** access specifier. The setters (**set_latitude** and **set_longitude**) should take an **int** as a parameter and return **void**, while the getters do not take any parameter and return a **float**:

```
class Coordinates {
  private:
    float latitude;
    float longitude;

  public:
    void set_latitude(float value){}
    void set_longitude(float value){}
    float get_latitude(){}
    float get_longitude(){}
};
```

3. The four methods should now be implemented. The setters assign the given value to the corresponding members they are supposed to set; the getters return the values that are stored.

```
class Coordinates {
  private:
    float latitude;
    float longitude;
```

```
  public:
    void set_latitude(float value){ latitude = value; }
    void set_longitude(float value){ longitude = value; }
    float get_latitude(){ return latitude; }
    float get_longitude(){ return longitude; }
};
```

An example is as follows:

```
#include <iostream>

int main() {
  Coordinates washington_dc;
  std::cout << "Object named washington_dc of type Coordinates created."
<< std::endl;

  washington_dc.set_latitude(38.8951);
  washington_dc.set_longitude(-77.0364);
  std::cout << "Object's latitude and longitude set." << std::endl;

  std::cout << "Washington DC has a latitude of "
  << washington_dc.get_latitude()
  << " and longitude of " << washington_dc.get_longitude() << std::endl;
}
```

Activity 8: Representing Positions in a 2D Map

1. The first step is to create a class named **Coordinates** containing the coordinates as data members. These are two floating-point values, **_latitude** and **_longitude**, which identify the coordinates on a geographic coordinate system. Additionally, these data members are initialized with a **private** access specifier:

```
class Coordinates {
  private:
    float _latitude;
    float _longitude;
};
```

2. Then, the class is extended with a **public** constructor which takes two arguments used to initialize the data members of the class:

```
class Coordinates {
  public:
    Coordinates(float latitude, float longitude)
    : _latitude(latitude), _longitude(longitude) {}

  private:
    int _latitude;
    int _longitude;
};
```

3. We can also add getters as seen previously to access the class members. An example is as follows:

```
#include <iostream>

int main() {
  Coordinates washington_dc(38.8951, -77.0364);
  std::cout << "Object named washington_dc of type Coordinates created."
  << std::endl;

  std::cout << "Washington DC has a latitude of "
  << washington_dc.get_latitude()
  << " and longitude of " << washington_dc.get_longitude()
  << std::endl;
}
```

Activity 9: Storing Multiple Coordinates of Different Positions in the Map

1. Using the RAII programming idiom, write a class that manages memory allocation and deletion of an array of **int**. The class has an array of integers as member data, which will be used to store the values.

   The constructor takes the size of the array as a parameter.

   The constructor also takes care of allocating memory, which is used to store the coordinates.

2. Finally, define a destructor and make sure to free the previously allocated array in its implementation.

3. We can add print statements to visualize what is happening:

```
class managed_array {
  public:
    explicit managed_array(size_t size) {
      array = new int[size];
      std::cout << "Array of size " << size << " created." << std::endl;
    }

    ~managed_array() {
      delete[] array;
      std::cout << "Array deleted." << std::endl;
    }

  private:
    int *array;
};
```

4. We can use our **managed_array** class as follows:

```
int main() {
    managed_array m(10);
}
```

The output will be as follows:

```
Array of size 10 created.
Array deleted.
```

Activity 10: The AppleTree Class, which Creates an Apple Instance

1. First, we need to create a class with a **private** constructor. In this way, the object cannot be constructed, because the constructor is not publicly accessible:

```
class Apple
{
  private:
    Apple() {}
    // do nothing
};
```

2. The **AppleTree** class is defined and contains a method called **createFruit** that is in charge of creating an **Apple** and returning it:

```
#include <iostream>

class AppleTree
{
  public:
    Apple createFruit(){
      Apple apple;
      std::cout << "apple created!" << std::endl;
      return apple;
    }
};
```

3. If we compile this code, we will get an error. At this point, the **Apple** constructor is **private**, so the **AppleTree** class cannot access it. We need to declare the **Apple-Tree** class as a **friend** of **Apple** to allow **AppleTree** to access the **private** methods of **Apple**:

```
class Apple
{
  friend class AppleTree;
  private:
    Apple() {}
    // do nothing
}
```

4. The **Apple** object can now be constructed using the following code:

```
int main() {
  AppleTree tree;
  Apple apple = tree.createFruit();
}
```

This prints the following:

```
apple created!
```

Activity 11: Ordering Point Objects

1. We need to add an overload for the **<** operator to the **Point** class that we have previously defined. This takes another object of type **Point** as an argument and returns a Boolean indicating whether the object is less than the one provided as the parameter, using the previous definition for how to compare the two points:

```
class Point
{
  public:
    bool operator< (const Point &other){
      return x < other.x || (x == other.x && y < other.y);
    }

  int x;
  int y;
};
```

2. At this point, we are able to compare the two **Point** objects:

```
#include <iostream>

int main() {
  Point p_1, p_2;

  p_1.x = 1;
  p_1.y = 2;

  p_2.x = 2;
  p_2.y = 1;

  std::cout << std::boolalpha << (p_1 < p_2) << std::endl;
}
```

3. Since in our example **p_1.x** is initialized to **1** and **p_2.x** to **2**, the result of the comparison will be **true**, which indicates that **p_1** comes earlier than **p_2** in the order.

Activity 12: Implementing Functors

1. Define a class constituted by a **private** data member of type **int** and add a
    constructor to initialize it:

    ```
    class AddX {
      public:
        AddX(int x) : x(x) {}

      private:
        int x;
    };
    ```

2. Extend it with the call operator **operator()** which takes an **int** as a parameter and
    returns an **int**. The implementation in the function body should return the addi-
    tion of the previously defined **x** value and the parameter of the function named **y**:

    ```
    class AddX {
      public:
        AddX(int x) : x(x) {}
        int operator() (int y) { return x + y; }

      private:
        int x;
    };
    ```

3. Instantiate an object of the class just defined and invoke the call operator:

    ```
    int main() {
      AddX add_five(5);
      std::cout << add_five(4) << std::endl;
    }
    ```

    The output will be as follows:

    ```
    9
    ```

Lesson 04: Generic Programming and Templates

Activity 13: Read Objects from a Connection

1. We start by including the headers of the files that provided the connection and the user account object:

```
#include <iostream>
#include <connection.h>
#include <useraccount.h>
```

2. We can then start to write the **writeObjectToConnection** function. Declare a template which takes two **typename** parameters: an **Object** and a **Connection**. Call the **static** method **serialize()** on the object to get the **std::array** representing the object, then call **writeNext()** on the connection to write the data to it:

```
template<typename Object, typename Connection>
void writeObjectToConnection(Connection& con, const Object& obj) {
    std::array<char, 100> data = Object::serialize(obj);
    con.writeNext(data);
}
```

3. We can then write **readObjectFromConnection**. Declare a template taking the same two parameters as before: an **Object** and a **Connection**. Inside, we call the connection **readNext()** to get the data stored inside the connection, then we call the **static** method on the object type **deserialize()** to get an instance of the object and return it:

```
template<typename Object, typename Connection>
Object readObjectFromConnection(Connection& con) {
    std::array<char, 100> data = con.readNext();
    return Object::deserialize(data);
}
```

4. Finally, in the **main** function, we can call the functions we created to serialize objects. Both with **TcpConnection**:

```
std::cout << "serialize first user account" << std::endl;
UserAccount firstAccount;
TcpConnection tcpConnection;
writeObjectToConnection(tcpConnection, firstAccount);
UserAccount transmittedFirstAccount =
readObjectFromConnection<UserAccount>(tcpConnection);
```

5. And with **UdpConnection**:

```
std::cout << "serialize second user account" << std::endl;
UserAccount secondAccount;
UdpConnection udpConnection;
writeObjectToConnection(udpConnection, secondAccount);
UserAccount transmittedSecondAccount =
readObjectFromConnection<UserAccount>(udpConnection);
```

The output of the program is as follows:

```
serialize first user account
the user account has been serialized
the data has been written
the data has been read
the user account has been deserialized

serialize second user account
the user account has been serialized
the data has been written
the data has been read
the user account has been deserialized
```

Activity 14: UserAccount to Support Multiple Currencies

1. We start by including the file defining the currencies:

```
#include <currency.h>
#include <iostream>
```

2. We then declare the template class **Account**. It should take a template parameter: **Currency**. We store the current balance of the account inside a data member of type **Currency**. We also provide a method in order to extract the current value of the balance:

```
template<typename Currency>
class Account {
  public:
    Account(Currency amount) : balance(amount) {}

    Currency getBalance() const {
        return balance;
```

```
    }

    private:
      Currency balance;
};
```

3. Next, we create the method **addToBalance**. It should be a template with one type parameter, the other currency. The method takes a value of **OtherCurrency** and converts it to the value of the currency of the current account with the **to()** function, specifying to which currency the value should be converted to. It then adds it to the balance:

```
template<typename OtherCurrency>
void addToBalance(OtherCurrency amount) {
    balance.d_value += to<Currency>(amount).d_value;
}
```

4. Finally, we can try to call our class in the **main** function with some data:

```
Account<GBP> gbpAccount(GBP(1000));
// Add different currencies
std::cout << "Balance: " << gbpAccount.getBalance().d_value << " (GBP)" <<
std::endl;
gbpAccount.addToBalance(EUR(100));
std::cout << "+100 (EUR)" << std::endl;
std::cout << "Balance: " << gbpAccount.getBalance().d_value << " (GBP)" <<
std::endl;
```

The output of the program is:

```
Balance: 1000 (GBP)
+100 (EUR)
Balance: 1089 (GBP)
```

Activity 15: Write a Matrix Class for Mathematical Operations in a Game

1. We start by defining a **Matrix** class which takes three template parameters: one type and the two dimensions of the **Matrix** class. The dimensions are of type **int**. Internally, we create a **std::array** with the size of the number of rows times the number of columns, in order to have enough space for all elements of the matrix. We add a constructor to initialize the array to *empty*, and a constructor to provide a list of values:

```
#include <array>

template<typename T, int R, int C>
class Matrix {
  // We store row_1, row_2, ..., row_C
  std::array<T, R*C> data;
  public:
    Matrix() : data({}) {}
    Matrix(std::array<T, R*C> initialValues) : data(initialValues) {}
};
```

2. We add a method **get()** to the class to return a reference to the element **T**. The method needs to take the row and column we want to access.

3. We make sure that the requested indexes are inside the bounds of the matrix, otherwise we call **std::abort()**. In the array, we first store all the elements of the first row, then all the elements of the second row, and so on. When we want to access the elements of the *nth* row, we need to skip all the elements of the previous rows, which are going to be the number of elements per row (so the number of columns) times the previous rows, resulting in the following method:

```
T& get(int row, int col) {
  if (row >= R || col >= C) {
    std::abort();
  }
  return data[row*C + col];
}
```

4. For convenience, we define a function to print the class as well. We print all the elements in the columns separated by spaces, with one column per line:

```
template<typename T, size_t R, size_t C>
std::ostream& operator<<(std::ostream& os, Matrix<T, R, C> matrix) {
    os << '\n';
    for(int r=0; r < R; r++) {
        for(int c=0; c < C; c++) {
            os << matrix.get(r, c) << ' ';
        }
        os << "\n";
    }
    return os;
}
```

5. In the **main** function, we can now use the functions we have defined:

```
Matrix<int, 3, 2> matrix({
    1, 2,
    3, 4,
    5, 6
});
std::cout << "Initial matrix:" << matrix << std::endl;
matrix.get(1, 1) = 7;
std::cout << "Modified matrix:" << matrix << std::endl;
```

The output is as follows:

```
Initial matrix:
1 2
3 4
5 6

Modified matrix:
1 2
3 7
5 6
```

Solution bonus step:

1. We can add a new method, **multiply**, which takes a **std::array** of type **T** with the length of **C** by **const** reference, since we are not modifying it.

    The function returns an array of the same type, but length **R**.

2. We follow the definition of matrix-vector multiplication to compute the result:

```cpp
std::array<T, R> multiply(const std::array<T, C>& vector){
    std::array<T, R> result = {};
    for(size_t r = 0; r < R; r++) {
      for(size_t c = 0; c < C; c++) {
        result[r] += get(r, c) * vector[c];
      }
    }
    return result;
}
```

3. We can now extend our **main** function to call the **multiply** function:

```cpp
std::array<int, 2> vector = {8, 9};
std::array<int, 3> result = matrix.multiply(vector);
std::cout << "Result of multiplication: [" << result[0] << ", "
  << result[1] << ", " << result[2] << "]" << std::endl;
```

    The output is as follows:

```
Result of multiplication: [26, 87, 94]
```

Activity 16: Make the Matrix Class Easier to Use

1. We start by importing **<functional>** in order to have access to **std::multiplies**:

```cpp
#include <functional>
```

2. We then change the order of the template parameters in the class **template**, so that the size parameters come first. We also add a new template parameter, **Multiply**, which is the type we will use for computing the multiplication between the elements in the **vector** by default, and we store an instance of it in the class:

```cpp
template<int R, int C, typename T = int, typename
Multiply=std::multiplies<T> >
class Matrix {
  std::array<T, R*C> data;
```

```
    Multiply multiplier;
    public:
      Matrix() : data({}), multiplier() {}
      Matrix(std::array<T, R*C> initialValues) : data(initialValues),
   multiplier() {}
    };
```

The **get()** function remains the same as the previous activity.

3. We now need to make sure that the **Multiply** method uses the **Multiply** type provided by the user to perform the multiplication.

4. To do so, we need to make sure to call **multiplier(operand1, operand2)** instead of **operand1 * operand2**, so that we use the instance we stored inside the class:

```
    std::array<T, R> multiply(const std::array<T, C>& vector) {
        std::array<T, R> result = {};
        for(int r = 0; r < R; r++) {
            for(int c = 0; c < C; c++) {
                result[r] += multiplier(get(r, c), vector[c]);
            }
        }
        return result;
    }
```

5. We can now add an example of how we can use the class:

```
    // Create a matrix of int, with the 'plus' operation by default
    Matrix<3, 2, int, std::plus<int>> matrixAdd({
        1, 2,
        3, 4,
        5, 6
    });

    std::array<int, 2> vector = {8, 9};
    // This will call std::plus when doing the multiplication
    std::array<int, 3> result = matrixAdd.multiply(vector);
    std::cout << "Result of multiplication(with +): [" << result[0] << ", "
            << result[1] << ", " << result[2] << "]" << std::endl;
```

The output is as follows:

```
    Result of multiplication(with +): [20, 24, 28]
```

Activity 17: Ensure Users are Logged in When Performing Actions on the Account

1. We first declare a template function which takes two type parameters: an **Action** and a **Parameter** type.

2. The function should take the user identification, the action and the parameter. The parameter should be accepted as a forwarding reference. As a first step, it should check if the user is logged in, by calling the **isLoggenIn()** function. If the user is logged in, it should call the **getUserCart()** function, then call the action passing the cart and forwarding the parameter:

```
template<typename Action, typename Parameter>
void execute_on_user_cart(UserIdentifier user, Action action, Parameter&&
parameter) {
    if(isLoggedIn(user)) {
        Cart cart = getUserCart(user);
        action(cart, std::forward<Parameter>(parameter));
    } else {
        std::cout << "The user is not logged in" << std::endl;
    }
}
```

3. We can test how **execute_on_user_cart** works by calling it in the **main** function:

```
Item toothbrush{1023};
Item toothpaste{1024};

UserIdentifier loggedInUser{0};
std::cout << "Adding items if the user is logged in" << std::endl;
execute_on_user_cart(loggedInUser, addItems,
std::vector<Item>({toothbrush, toothpaste}));

UserIdentifier loggedOutUser{1};
std::cout << "Removing item if the user is logged in" << std::endl;
execute_on_user_cart(loggedOutUser, removeItem, toothbrush);
```

The output is as follows:

```
Adding items if the user is logged in
Items added
Removing item if the user is logged in
The user is not logged in
```

Activity 18: Safely Perform Operations on User Cart with an Arbitrary Number of Parameters

1. We need to expand the previous activity to accept any number of parameters with any kind of ref-ness and pass it to the action provided. To do so, we need to create a **variadic** template.

2. Declare a **template** function that takes an action and a **variadic** number of parameters as template parameters. The function parameters should be the user action, the action to perform, and the expanded template parameter **pack**, making sure that the parameters are accepted as forwarding references.

3. Inside the function, we perform the same checks as before, but now we expand the parameters when we forward them to the action:

```
template<typename Action, typename... Parameters>
void execute_on_user_cart(UserIdentifier user, Action action,
Parameters&&... parameters) {
    if(isLoggedIn(user)) {
        Cart cart = getUserCart(user);
        action(cart, std::forward<Parameters>(parameters)...);
    } else {
        std::cout << "The user is not logged in" << std::endl;
    }
}
```

4. Let's test the new function in our **main** function:

```
Item toothbrush{1023};
Item apples{1024};

UserIdentifier loggedInUser{0};
std::cout << "Replace items if the user is logged in" << std::endl;
execute_on_user_cart(loggedInUser, replaceItem, toothbrush, apples);

UserIdentifier loggedOutUser{1};
std::cout << "Replace item if the user is logged in" << std::endl;
execute_on_user_cart(loggedOutUser, removeItem, toothbrush);
```

The output is as follows:

```
Replace items if the user is logged in
Replacing item
Item removed
Items added
Replace item if the user is logged in
The user is not logged in
```

Lesson 5: Standard Library Containers and Algorithms

Activity 19: Storing User Accounts

1. First, we include the header files for the **array** class and input/output operations with the required namespace:

    ```
    #include <array>
    ```

2. An array of ten elements of type **int** is declared:

    ```
    array<int,10> balances;
    ```

3. Initially, the values of the elements are undefined since it is an array of the fundamental data type **int**. The array is initialized using a **for** loop, where each element is initialized with its index. The operator **size()** is used to evaluate the size of the array and the subscript operator **[ ]** is used to access every position of the array:

    ```
    for (int i=0; i < balances.size(); ++i)
    {
      balances[i] = 0;
    }
    ```

4. We now want to update the value for the first and last user. We can use **front()** and **back()** to access the accounts of these users:

    ```
    balances.front() += 100;
    balances.back() += 100;
    ```

    We would like to store the account balance of an arbitrary number of users. We then want to add 100 users to the account list, with a balance of 500.

5. We can use **vector** to store an arbitrary number of users. It is defined in the **<vector>** header:

    ```
    #include <vector>
    ```

6. Then, we declare a vector of type **int**. Optionally, we reserve enough memory to store the 100 users' account by calling **reserve(100)** to avoid memory reallocation:

```
std::vector<int> balances;
balances.reserve(100);
```

7. Finally, we modify the **for** loop to add the balance for the users at the end of the accounts vector:

```
for (int i=0; i<100; ++i)
{
  balances.push_back(500);
}
```

Activity 20: Retrieving a User's Balance from their Given Username

1. Include the header file for the **map** class and the header for **string**:

```
#include <map>
#include <string>
```

2. Create a map with the key being **std::string** and the value **int**:

```
std::map<std::string, int> balances;
```

3. Insert the balances of the users inside **map** by using **insert** and **std::make_pair**. The first argument is the key, the second one is the value:

```
balances.insert(std::make_pair("Alice",50));
balances.insert(std::make_pair("Bob", 50));
balances.insert(std::make_pair("Charlie", 50));
```

4. Use the **find** function providing the name of the user to find the position of the account in the map. Compare it with **end()** to check whether a position was found:

```
auto donaldAccountPos = balances.find("Donald");
bool hasAccount = (donaldAccountPos != balances.end());
std::cout << "Donald has an account: " << hasAccount << std::endl;
```

5. Now, look for the account of **Alice**. We know **Alice** has an account, so there is no need to check whether we found a valid position. We can print the value of the account using **->second**:

```
auto alicePosition = balances.find("Alice");
std::cout << "Alice balance is: " << alicePosition->second << std::endl;
```

Activity 21: Processing User Registration in Order

1. First, we include the header file for the **stack** class:

   ```
   #include <stack>
   ```

2. Create a **stack** providing the type to **store**:

   ```
   std::stack<RegistrationForm> registrationForms;
   ```

3. We start by storing the form inside the **stack** when the user registers. In the body of the **storeRegistrationForm** function, push the element into the queue:

   ```
   stack.push(form);
   std::cout << "Pushed form for user " << form.userName << std::endl;
   ```

4. Now, inside **endOfDayRegistrationProcessing**, we get all the elements inside the **stack** and then process them. Use the **top()** method to access the top element in the **stack** and **pop()** to remove the top element. We stop getting and removing the first element when no element is left:

   ```
   while(not stack.empty()) {
     processRegistration(stack.top());
     stack.pop();
   }
   ```

5. Finally, we call our functions with some test data:

   ```
   int main(){
     std::stack<RegistrationForm> registrationForms;
     storeRegistrationForm(registrationForms, RegistrationForm{"Alice"});
     storeRegistrationForm(registrationForms, RegistrationForm{"Bob"});
     storeRegistrationForm(registrationForms, RegistrationForm{"Charlie"});
     endOfDayRegistrationProcessing(registrationForms);
   }
   ```

Activity 22: Airport System Management

1. We start by creating the class for **Airplane**. Make sure to first include the header for **variant**:

   ```
   #include <variant>
   ```

2. Then, create the class with a constructor that sets the current state of the airplane to **AtGate**:

```
class Airplane {
  std::variant<AtGate, Taxi, Flying> state;
  public:
    Airplane(int gate) : state(AtGate{gate}) {
      std::cout << "At gate " << gate << std::endl;
    }
};
```

3. Now, implement the **startTaxi()** method. First, check the current state of the airplane with **std::holds_alternative<>()**, and if the airplane is not in the correct state, write an error message and return.

4. If the airplane is in the correct state, change the state to taxi by assigning it to the **variant**:

```
void startTaxi(int lane, int numPassengers) {
    if (not std::holds_alternative<AtGate>(state)) {
        std::cout << "Not at gate: the plane cannot start taxi to lane "
<< lane << std::endl;
        return;
    }
    std::cout << "Taxing to lane " << lane << std::endl;
    state = Taxi{lane, numPassengers};
}
```

5. We repeat the same process for the **takeOff()** method:

```
void takeOff(float speed) {
    if (not std::holds_alternative<Taxi>(state)) {
        std::cout << "Not at lane: the plane cannot take off with speed "
<< speed << std::endl;
        return;
    }
    std::cout << "Taking off at speed " << speed << std::endl;
    state = Flying{speed};
}
```

6. We can now start looking at the **currentStatus()** method. Since we want to perform an operation for each of the states in the **variant**, we can use a visitor.

7. Outside the **Airplane** class, create a class that has a method **operator()** for each of the types in the airplane state. Inside the method, print the information of the state. Remember to make the methods public:

```
class AirplaneStateVisitor {
  public:
    void operator()(const AtGate& atGate) {
        std::cout << "AtGate: " << atGate.gate << std::endl;
    }

    void operator()(const Taxi& taxi) {
      std::cout << "Taxi: lane " << taxi.lane << " with " << taxi.
numPassengers << " passengers" << std::endl;
    }

    void operator()(const Flying& flying) {
      std::cout << "Flaying: speed " << flying.speed << std::endl;
    }
};
```

8. Now, create the **currentStatus()** method and call the visitor on the state using **std::visit**:

```
void currentStatus() {
    AirplaneStateVisitor visitor;
    std::visit(visitor, state);
}
```

9. We can now try to call the functions of **Airplane** from the **main** function:

```
int main()
{
    Airplane airplane(52);
    airplane.currentStatus();
    airplane.startTaxi(12, 250);
    airplane.currentStatus();
    airplane.startTaxi(13, 250);
    airplane.currentStatus();
    airplane.takeOff(800);
    airplane.currentStatus();
    airplane.takeOff(900);
}
```

Lesson 6: Object-Oriented Programming

Activity 23: Creating Game Characters

1. Create a **Character** class that has a **public** method **moveTo** that prints **Moved to position**:

```cpp
class Character {
  public:
    void moveTo(Position newPosition) {
      position = newPosition;
      std::cout << "Moved to position " << newPosition.positionIdentifier
<< std::endl;
    }
  private:
    Position position;
};
```

2. Create a **struct** named **Position**:

```cpp
struct Position {
  // Fields to describe the position go here
  std::string positionIdentifier;
};
```

3. Create two classes **Hero** and **Enemy** that are derived from the class **Character**:

```cpp
// Hero inherits publicly from Character: it has
// all the public member of the Character class.
class Hero : public Character {

};

// Enemy inherits publicly from Character, like Hero
class Enemy : public Character {

};
```

4. Create a class **Spell** with the constructor that prints the name of the person casting the spell:

```cpp
class Spell {
public:
    Spell(std::string name) : d_name(name) {}

    std::string name() const {
```

```
        return d_name;
    }
private:
    std::string d_name;
};
```

5. The class **Hero** should have a public method to cast a spell. Use the value from the **Spell** class:

```
public:
    void cast(Spell spell) {
        // Cast the spell
        std::cout << "Casting spell " << spell.name() << std::endl;
    }
```

6. The class **Enemy** should have a public method to swing a sword which prints **Swinging sword**:

```
public:
    void swingSword() {
        // Swing the sword
        std::cout << "Swinging sword" << std::endl;
    }
```

7. Implement the **main** method that calls these methods in various classes:

```
int main()
{
    Position position{"Enemy castle"};
    Hero hero;
    Enemy enemy;

    // We call moveTo on Hero, which calls the method inherited
    // from the Character class
    hero.moveTo(position);
    enemy.moveTo(position);

    // We can still use the Hero and Enemy methods
    hero.cast(Spell("fireball"));
    enemy.swingSword();
}
```

Activity 24: Calculating Employee Salaries

1. We can create a class **Employee** with two virtual methods, **getBaseSalary** and **getBonus**, since we want to change those methods based on the type of employee:

```
class Employee {
  public:
    virtual int getBaseSalary() const { return 100; }
    virtual int getBonus(const Deparment& dep) const {
      if (dep.hasReachedTarget()) {
      }
      return 0;
    }
```

2. We also define a method, **getTotalComp**, which does not need to be virtual, but will call the two virtual methods:

```
    int getTotalComp(const Deparment& dep) {


    }
};
```

3. We then derive a **Manager** class from it, overriding the method for computing the bonus. We might also want to override **getBaseSalary** if we want to give a different base salary to managers:

```
class Manager : public Employee {
  public:
    virtual int getBaseSalary() const override { return 150; }
    virtual int getBonus(const Deparment& dep) const override {
      if (dep.hasReachedTarget()) {
        int additionalDeparmentEarnings = dep.effectiveEarning() - dep.
espectedEarning();
        return 0.2 * getBaseSalary() + 0.01 * additionalDeparmentEarnings;
      }
      return 0;
    }
};
```

4. Create a class **Department** as shown:

```
class Department {
  public:
    bool hasReachedTarget() const {return true;}
    int espectedEarning() const {return 1000;}
    int effectiveEarning() const {return 1100;}
};
```

5. Now, in the **main** function, call the **Department**, **Employee**, and **Manager** classes as shown:

```
int main()
{
  Department dep;
  Employee employee;
  Manager manager;
  std::cout << "Employee: " << employee.getTotalComp(dep) << ". Manager: "
<< manager.getTotalComp(dep) << std::endl;
}
```

Activity 25: Retrieving User Information

1. We have to write the code that can be independent of where the data is coming from. So, we create an interface **UserProfileStorage** for retrieving the **Customer-Profile** from a **UserId**:

```
struct UserProfile {};
struct UserId {};

class UserProfileStorage {
  public:
    virtual UserProfile getUserProfile(const UserId& id) const = 0;

    virtual ~UserProfileStorage() = default;

  protected:
    UserProfileStorage() = default;
    UserProfileStorage(const UserProfileStorage&) = default;
    UserProfileStorage& operator=(const UserProfileStorage&) = default;
};
```

2. Now, write the **UserProfileCache** class that inherits from **UserProfileStorage**:

```
class UserProfileCache : public UserProfileStorage {
  public:
    UserProfile getUserProfile(const UserId& id) const override {
      std::cout << "Getting the user profile from the cache" << std::endl;
      return UserProfile(); }
};
void exampleOfUsage(const UserProfileStorage& storage) {
    UserId user;
    std::cout << "About to retrieve the user profile from the storage"
<<std::endl;
    UserProfile userProfile = storage.getUserProfile(user);
}
```

3. In the **main** function, call the **UserProfileCache** class and **exampleOfUsage** function as shown:

```
int main()
{
  UserProfileCache cache;
  exampleOfUsage (cache);
}
```

Activity 26: Creating a Factory for UserProfileStorage

1. Write the following code that needs the **UserProfileStorage** class, as shown. To allow that, we provide a factory class, which has a method **create** that provides an instance of **UserProfileStorage**. Write this class making sure that the user does not have to manage the memory for the interface manually:

```
#include <iostream>
#include <memory>
#include <userprofile_activity18.h>

class UserProfileStorageFactory {
public:
    std::unique_ptr<UserProfileStorage> create() const {
        return std::make_unique<UserProfileCache>();
    }
};
```

2. We want the **UserProfileStorageFactory** class to return a **unique_ptr** so that it manages the lifetime of the interface:

    ```
    void getUserProfile(const UserProfileStorageFactory& storageFactory) {
      std::unique_ptr<UserProfileStorage> storage = storageFactory.create();
      UserId user;
      storage->getUserProfile(user);
      // The storage is automatically destroyed
    }
    ```

3. Now, in the **main** function, call the **UserProfileStorageFactory** class as shown:

    ```
    int main()
    {
      UserProfileStorageFactory factory;
      getUserProfile(factory);
    ```

Activity 27: Using a Database Connection for Multiple Operations

1. First, create a **DatabaseConnection** class that can be used in parallel. We want to reuse it as much as possible, and we know we can use **std::async** to start a new parallel task:

    ```
    #include <future>

    struct DatabaseConnection {};
    ```

2. Assuming there are two functions **updateOrderList(DatabaseConnection&)** and **scheduleOrderProcessing(DatabaseConnection&)**, write a function that creates a **DatabaseConnection** and gives it to the two parallel tasks. (Note that we don't know which task finishes first):

    ```
    void updateOrderList(DatabaseConnection&) {}
    void scheduleOrderProcessing(DatabaseConnection&) {}
    ```

3. You must understand when and how to create a **shared_ptr**. You can also use the following code to write the **shared_ptr** correctly.

    ```
    /* We need to get a copy of the shared_ptr so it stays alive until this
    function finishes */
    void updateWithConnection(std::shared_ptr<DatabaseConnection> connection)
    {
        updateOrderList(*connection);
    }
    ```

    There are several users of the connection, and we do not know which one is the owner, since the connection needs to stay alive as long as anyone is using it.

4. To model this, we use a **shared_ptr**. Remember that we need a copy of the **shared_ptr** to exist in order for the connection to remain valid:

```
/* We need to get a copy of the shared_ptr so it stays alive until this
function finishes. */
void scheduleWithConnection(std::shared_ptr<DatabaseConnection>
connection) {
    scheduleOrderProcessing(*connection);
}
```

5. Create the **main** function as follows:

```
int main()
{
    std::shared_ptr<DatabaseConnection> connection = std::make_
shared<DatabaseConnection>();
    std::async(std::launch::async, updateWithConnection, connection);
    std::async(std::launch::async, scheduleWithConnection, connection);
}
```

Index

About

All major keywords used in this book are captured alphabetically in this section. Each one is accompanied by the page number of where they appear.

A

ability: 2, 45, 79, 81, 92, 101, 145, 160, 179, 218, 250-251, 274, 278

access: 16, 37-38, 40, 50-53, 57, 61, 76-78, 83-84, 86-89, 92, 94, 96, 99, 108, 111-114, 116, 130, 138, 145, 148, 151, 155-156, 162, 166, 169, 172-173, 175, 178-179, 182, 184, 186, 188, 190-191, 195, 199-201, 209, 211, 215, 217-218, 225-226, 237, 241-242, 247, 268, 288-290, 292, 298, 300, 304, 306

account: 137-138, 142-144, 152-154, 168, 176, 191, 196-197, 234-236, 295-297, 302, 304-305

action: 7, 96, 163, 165-172, 174-175, 230, 271, 302-303

actions: 40, 168-170, 174, 225, 261-262, 302

activity: 36, 40, 63, 72, 78, 80, 98-99, 108-109, 111, 116-117, 127-130, 151, 153-154, 156-157, 162-163, 168, 170, 174-175, 191, 196-197, 201-202, 214, 249-250, 258, 260, 264-265, 276-278, 282, 284-286, 288-291, 293-296, 298, 300-306, 309, 311-314

actual: 4, 15-16, 186, 226

addition: 40, 93, 95, 101, 126, 129, 210, 294

additional: 21, 72, 79, 154-155, 166, 170, 199, 202, 204, 209, 216, 218, 245, 261-262, 270

address: 15-16, 21, 96, 119, 121, 210

advantage: 73, 101, 155, 166, 190

advantages: 40, 44, 84, 130, 144, 168, 254

algorithm: 45, 67, 134, 182, 224-225, 228, 230-235

aliases: 150, 173, 175, 177, 179

allocate: 37, 111, 159

allocated: 106, 111, 271, 290

allocation: 111, 185, 290

almost: 44, 174, 207

amount: 45, 137-138, 155, 159, 296-297

anymore: 32, 167, 178, 187, 217, 267, 269, 271-272, 275

anywhere: 22, 65, 87-88, 90, 246, 273

applies: 16, 190, 262

approach: 85, 149, 240

arbitrary: 58, 143, 168, 170-171, 174, 182, 191, 240, 303-304

argument: 58-61, 63-64, 71-72, 75, 97, 103, 106, 117, 121, 127, 139-140, 153, 158, 160-163, 173-174, 179, 193, 197, 210, 226, 270, 273, 275, 293, 305

arguments: 9, 43, 46, 57-60, 65, 67, 70, 72-73, 75-76, 79, 81, 108, 128, 136, 139-140, 142, 158-161, 163, 170-174,

179, 206, 210, 224-225, 268, 273-275, 290

arises: 33, 124, 268

arithmetic: 1, 40, 218

arrays: 1, 30, 36, 38-40, 72, 184, 186, 268, 276, 287

assign: 40, 62, 67, 70, 84, 91, 99, 121, 123, 203, 209, 215, 247, 252, 264, 287-288

assigned: 70, 126, 214, 252

assignment: 13, 16, 69-70, 83, 117, 119-121, 123-124, 245, 253, 263-264

associate: 90, 195, 236

associated: 11, 17, 53, 86, 90, 93, 98, 111, 194-196, 207, 271

assume: 4, 89, 121, 201

automatic: 53, 56, 59, 67, 70, 106, 266-267, 271

B

balance: 137, 153-154, 176, 191, 196-197, 224, 234-236, 296-297, 304-305

balances: 176, 197, 223, 234-236, 304-305

because: 5, 15, 44, 51, 53, 60, 67, 72-73, 76-77, 79-80, 100-101, 113, 116, 124, 136-137, 144, 150, 161, 167-168, 177, 193, 196-198, 210, 219, 221, 224, 243, 250-251, 253, 257, 261, 264, 268, 271, 273-274, 276, 291

before: 4-5, 13, 32, 36, 48, 53-55, 68-69, 76, 87, 94, 102-104, 127,

www.ingramcontent.com/pod-product-compliance
Lightning Source LLC
Chambersburg PA
CBHW080617060326
40690CB00021B/4728